SELF AND IDENTITY
THROUGH THE LIFE COURSE
IN CROSS-CULTURAL PERSPECTIVE

Advances in Life Course Research (formerly Current Perspective on Aging and the Life Cycle)

Timothy J. Owens, Series Editor

Volume 1: *Work Retirement and Social Policy*
edited by Zena Smith Blau, 1985

Volume 2: *Family Relations in Life Course Perspective*
edited by David I. Kertzer, 1986

Volume 3: *Personal History Through the Life Course*
edited by R. S. Olusegun Wallace, 1993

Volume 4: *Delinquency and Disrepute in the Life Course*
edited by Zena Smith Blau and John Hagen, 1995

SELF AND IDENTITY
THROUGH THE LIFE COURSE
IN CROSS-CULTURAL PERSPECTIVE

Edited by   TIMOTHY J. OWENS
Department of Sociology
Indiana University, Indianapolis

JAI PRESS INC.
Stamford, Connecticut

CONTENTS

LIST OF CONTRIBUTORS

Pamela Aronson

Department of Sociology
Indiana University, Bloomington

Michelle Stem Cook

Department of Sociology
Johns Hopkins University

Susan E. Cross

Department of Psychology
Iowa State University

Suzanne R. Goodney

Department of Sociology
Indiana University, Bloomington

Alexandra R. Goulding

Minnesota Indian Women's
    Resource Center

Shaheen Halim

Department of Sociology
Texas A&M University

Howard B. Kaplan

Department of Sociology
Texas A&M University

K. Jill Kiecolt

Department of Sociology
Virginia Polytechnic Institute and
    State University

Robert K. Leik

Department of Sociology
University of Minnesota

J. Beth Mabry

Ethel Percy Andrus Geronlotogy
    Center
University of Southern California

Susan Perschbacher Melia

Department of Sociology
Assumption College

John Modell   Department of Sociology
                              Brown University

Timothy J. Owens   Department of Sociology
                              Indiana University, Indianapolis

Melvin Pollner   Department of Sociology
                              University of California, Los Angeles

Dana Rosenfeld   Department of Sociology
                              University of California, Los Angeles

PREFACE

This volume represents a new name and a new focus for its predecessor, *Current Perspectives on Aging and the Life Cycle* (volumes 1-4). We begin our new series, now titled *Advances in Life Course Research*, with volume 5. Its statement of purpose is *the publication of theoretical analyses, reviews, policy analyses and positions, and theory-based empirical papers on issues involving all aspects of the human life course*. It adopts a broad conception of the life course, and invites and welcomes contributions from all disciplines and fields of study interested in understanding, describing, and predicting the antecedents of and consequences for the course that human lives take from birth to death, within and across time and cultures (construed in its broadest sense), regardless of methodology, theoretical orientation, or disciplinary affiliation.

In order to give the volumes in the series coherence and impact, each will revolve around a particular theme. For example, volume 5 is subtitled *Self and Identity through the Life Course in Cross-Cultural Perspective*; volume 6 (due in August 2000) is subtitled *Children at the Millennium: Where Have We Come From, Where Are We Going?*; and volume 7 (due in August 2001) is subtitled *New Frontiers in Socialization*. Other themes for other volumes are being developed and will be announced when appropriate.

Contributions to each volume are a combination of author-initiated and invited papers. Regardless of origin, submissions are peer reviewed. Announcements for upcoming volumes appear here and in a variety of professional newsletters, mailings, and Web sites, including the one maintained by the series editor.

While the series is intended to be an outlet for papers longer, more theoretically oriented, and more integrative than typical journal articles, we also welcome shorter empirical pieces, papers employing conventional and unconventional theoretical and substantive frames, and integrative reviews of research programs. True to a life course perspective that acknowledges the potential for lifelong change and development, we hope that this series opens a dialogue between and among "senior" and "junior" members of the academic and policy communities. Consequently, we strongly urge contributions from younger and older scholars so an authentic, two-way dialogue is established: one that is unafraid to tackle and criticize or defend and expand conventional or "normal science" views of the life course, push our thinking into new areas, and open new lines of life course inquiry.

CONTENTS OF VOLUME 5

Each of the 10 chapters in this volume makes a theoretical or substantive contribution to life course research, with an emphasis this time on issues surrounding self, identity, and culture. Since we define culture in the broadest possible terms, the cultural focus in this volume is quite eclectic, including race, ethnic, national, occupational, gender, sexual, age-graded, and historical cultures and subcultures. For example, the chapter by Cook looks at the lives of Jewish émigrés from the former Soviet Union, Pollner and Rosenfeld examine the meaning of being an elderly gay or lesbian in the post-Stonewall era, and Leik and Goulding examine the unique problems and challenges that many faculty of color face in American institutions of higher learning. The use of self and identity, the most uniform theme running through the volume, nevertheless represents different conceptualizations and theoretical traditions. For example, Kaplan and Halim, Kiecolt and Mabry, and Owens and Goodney employ, in part, global self-esteem, while Modell focuses on two aspects of academic self-concept (math and science ability).

Two chapters are especially concerned with self and identity formation and change. In one, Aronson examines the emergence of feminist identities among politically active women in the 1950s and 1960s as compared to those active in the 1970s and 1980s. In the other, Kiecolt and Mabry address the issue of intentional change in the self among a sample of college students. Three additional chapters are more concerned with identity maintenance: Cook's study of Jews from the former Soviet Union, Perschbacher Melia's study of elderly Catholic nuns, Leik and Goulding's study of junior faculty who are also identified as racial minorities (especially African American).

The chapters by Cross and Modell take a definite international and comparative focus, with Cross examining some of the social and cultural elements in the construction of the self in Japan and the United States. Modell, on the other hand, compares and contrasts expressions of self-concept (especially academic) among English and American school children. Finally, two chapters, one by Kaplan and Halim, the other by Owens and Goodney, are centered on the role that deviance and its emotional fallout play in the self-concept and the life course.

ACKNOWLEDGMENTS

I wish to thank my dean, Herman J. Saatkamp, and my chair, David A. Ford, for providing the time and resources necessary for launching and editing the series; without their support I would never have taken on the job, even though it's a labor of love. Heather M. Wolny provided service throughout the launching of the series and production of the volume. My colleagues Patricia Wittberg, Colin Williams, Carol Brooks Gardner, and Linda Haas graciously devoted time and effort to reviewing and improving some of the manuscripts. The other reviewers, who requested anonymity, are also heartily thanked. Finally, I thank the contributors themselves for choosing the series as an outlet for their work.

Timothy J. Owens
Series Editor

AGGRESSION AND SELF-DEROGATION

MODERATING INFLUENCES OF GENDER, RACE/ETHNICITY, AND STAGE IN THE LIFE COURSE

Howard B. Kaplan and Shaheen Halim

ABSTRACT

Informed by a general theory of deviant behavior, it was hypothesized that (1) the effect of aggression on later self-derogation will vary with stage in the life course, and (2) the effect will be moderated by gender and race/ethnicity. Structural equation models are estimated for approximately 4,000 subjects tested in the seventh grade, in the third decade of life, and again in the fourth decade of life. The models were estimated separately for males and females, and for white-Anglo, African-American, and Mexican-American participants. Multigroup tests of invariance were performed to assess differences in parameters among groups while within group invariance tests allowed assessment of stability of the parameters over time. As expected, for females only, aggression in early adolescence anticipated decreases in self-derogation in young adulthood; and, aggression increased self-derogation

Advances in Life Course Research, Volume 5, pages 1-32.

1

between the third and fourth decades of life. For white-Anglo and African-American subjects aggression in early adulthood was related to increased self-derogation in later adulthood, but for Mexican-American subjects, early adult aggression decreased self-derogation by later adulthood. The results are interpretable in terms of self-enhancing implications of aggression for disempowered groups, and in terms of subcultural differences in acceptability of aggressive adaptations to stress at different stages in the life course.

Members of a population are differentiated according to the social positions they occupy and the social identities they internalize that are correlated with those social positions. Regardless of their social identities, they share expectations and normative judgments regarding how individuals occupying complementary social identities will and should behave. Both males and females agree to some extent as to how males should behave and both males and females agree to some extent as to how females should behave. Similarly, white Anglos, African Americans, and Mexican Americans raised in the same society agree in many respects regarding how members of each of these groups will and should behave. That is, they share a common culture. Nevertheless, individuals who share a social identity also come to share only among themselves expectations regarding how they will and should act toward each other and how they will and should relate to others who do not share their identity. That is, they share a subculture. In part, these subcultural expectations are a function of the increased interaction among individuals who share a social identity; and, in part, people develop consensual subcultural expectations as to how to respond because they are all objects of similar responses from others who are reacting to their social identity. Thus, considering social identities differentiated according to gender, males and females develop identity-specific modes of responding due to higher rates of interaction with like-gender partners than with opposite gender partners, and due to the fact that males and females are treated differently by virtue of their respective social identities. Similarly, due to differential rates of interaction and/or differential evocation of responses to their respective social identities, white Anglos, African Americans, and Mexican Americans develop identity-specific modes of response.

Members of a society also share expectations as to how people will and should behave at different stages in the life course. Youths, adolescents, and young adults all share expectations to some degree as to how people in each of those categories will and should behave. That is, they share a common culture regarding what normative expectations are applicable to people at different stages in the life course. In addition, because of increased rates of interaction among people who share a particular social identity and because people at a particular stage in a life course are treated differently than others at different stages of the life course, people who share a social identity based on a stage in the life course will develop subcultural expectations that are shared among themselves but are not shared with others who are at different stages in the life course. Hence, we may speak of a youth (sub)culture or an adolescent (sub)culture.

Among the problems faced by all individuals in all social identities is how to cope with self-devaluing experiences and concomitant self-derogation. While individuals who share some social identities are more vulnerable to the experience of self-devaluing circumstances, among those who share any given social identity a good deal of variability will be noticed in exposure to such circumstances and, therefore, in the need to cope with these circumstances in ways that will assuage distressful derogatory self-attitudes. Further, the ways in which people who share a social identity will attempt to adapt to the experience of self-derogation will be more or less effective in reducing self-derogation. The coping pattern may be ineffective in reducing self-derogation in large part because the pattern itself is devalued, or because it does not directly deal with the source of the self-derogation.

In the present analyses we examine the effects of particular modes of coping, aggressive responses, on later levels of self-derogation. We also examine the moderating influences of social identities based on differentiation according to gender, race/ethnicity, and stage in the life course. Our hypothesized models are informed by a general theory of deviant behavior, the literature dealing with the moderating influence of social identities on the correlates of self-derogation, and the more specific literature that has relevance for understanding the implications of social identities for the relationship between aggression and self-derogation.

THEORETICAL ORIENTATION

These analyses are informed by a general theory of deviant behavior (Kaplan 1975, 1980, 1982, 1984, 1986, 1995, 1996). The theoretical model guiding the present analyses is based upon the postulate of the self-esteem motive, whereby, universally and characteristically, a person is said to behave so as to maximize the experience of positive self-feelings, and minimize the experience of negative self-feelings. Self-feelings refer the person's more or less intense positive and negative affective experiences upon perceiving and evaluating his or her own attributes and behavior. In general, where individuals are unable to forestall or cope with a history of failure and rejection in their membership groups they will develop highly distressful negative self-feelings; and where people have a history of success and social acceptance they will tend to develop positive self-feelings. Since negative self-feelings (self-derogation) in fact are the result of social failure and rejection, the person will come to associate in his or her own mind the adverse social experiences with the painful self-rejecting feelings; and, since positive self-feelings in fact are the result of social success and acceptance, the person will recognize the relationship between positive self-feelings and the group experiences. The person's recognition of the group as a cause of self-derogation will lead to a loss of motivation to conform to the group norms and to a search for alternative deviant patterns that will lead to more positive self-feelings. Deviant patterns are expected to forestall or reduce the experience of negative self-feelings by facilitating avoidance of experiences of failure and rejection in the conventional group, by substituting new (deviant) standards of behavior according to which the person might judge himself to be worthy of acceptance by self and others, and, most germane to the present analyses, by behaving aggressively toward representations of the conventional expectations according to which the person is judged to be a failure and worthy of rejection.

However, the observation of the effect of self-derogatory experiences upon aggression, and the self-enhancing effects of aggression, will depend upon the presence of certain conditions. For example, self-derogation will lead to aggression against the group only where alternative conventional routes to success and acceptance are lacking and where aggression is not expected to have self-devaluing consequences. Similarly, the likelihood that aggression will improve one's self-attitudes will depend upon such conditions as the source of the negative self-attitudes being associated with the object of the aggression, and the absence of self-devaluing consequences of the aggressive acts.

Whether or not these conditions will hold in turn will depend upon the individual's social identities, cultural expectations that define appropriate behavior for individuals having those identities, and identity-related experiences. Among the more salient social identities are those based upon differentiation according to gender, race/ethnicity, and stage in the life course. We would expect that, for example, males and females might suffer self-derogatory attitudes for different reasons. Therefore, aggressive acts might have different implications for reducing the self-derogatory feelings. Further, we might expect that proscriptive attitudes toward aggression and the self-devaluing implications of aggression would vary according to whether the person was male or female. Similarly, we might expect that the source of negative self-feelings might vary according to the person's racial/ethnic identity and so aggression might be differentially self-enhancing depending upon the meaning of aggression in the various groups. In some groups aggression might be more valued than in others. Therefore, aggression might have differentially self-enhancing effects in the various groups. Regarding social identities based on stage in the life course, aggression may be personally and socially less acceptable at particular times of life. At an earlier stage in the life course the coping pattern may be effective in reducing feelings of distress because it obviates the source of the distress. At another stage in the life course, however, the coping pattern may be counter productive because of the adverse consequences evoked by a pattern that is consensually disvalued for people at that stage in the life course.

SOCIAL IDENTITIES AND SELF-DEROGATION

The literature is replete with references to the influence of social identities on coping strategies in response to self-derogation and on the relationship of such strategies and other correlates to level of and changes in self-attitudes. This is particularly the case regarding identities based on differentiation according to gender, race/ethnicity, and stage in the life-course.

It has long been noted that *gender* profoundly influences the person's self-concept, self-evaluation, and self-feelings. Dooley and Prause (1997, pp. 178-179) observe that:

> a key developmental task of adolescence is establishing an identity, and an important part of an adolescent's sense of self is his or her gender identity (Hendry 1987). Thus young people may base their global levels of self-esteem on the successful display of culturally prescribed gender-specific behaviours (Josephs, Markus, and Tafarodi 1992). Specifically, boys may tend to base their self-esteem somewhat more on "agentic" traits such as autonomy, assertiveness, rationality, and technical competence that can lead to objectively observable competitive success, whereas girls may tend to base their self-esteem somewhat more on "communal" traits such as connectedness, warmth, caring, and interpersonal adequacy (Harter 1990; Stein, Newcomb, and Bentler 1992). Other gender-related traits such as depressive vulnerability may also play a role in the way males and females differ in their reactions to stressful events such as leaving school and entering the job market (Leadbeater, Blatt, and Quinlan 1995).

In some studies, females are more likely to report engaging in social relationships and creating change whether in actual or cognitive terms, while males more frequently used stress reduction activities or diversions (Copeland and Hess 1995). Regarding outcomes of self-esteem, the relationship between lower self-esteem in high school and employment status several years later was stronger for males than females and for whites than blacks (Dooley and Prause 1997). The literature also suggests that outcomes for the same coping patterns may be different for each gender. For example, for males, coping patterns most closely associated with the feminine gender role, that is, turning to religion and to friends, predicted poor adult adaptation. In contrast, for females these behaviors that are congruent with the gender role anticipated good adult adaptation (Feldman, Fisher, Ransom, and Dimiceli 1995).

Depending upon one's gender, the same past experiences will have different implications for contemporary feelings of self-derogation. Thus, Kaplan and Pokorny (1972) reported differential associations between adult self-derogation and retrospective reports of twelve childhood experiences. For female subjects only, respondents were significantly more likely to display high self-derogation scores at the time of testing if they reported childhood experiences of receiving less attention from their parents than their siblings received, having mothers who were less educated than their fathers, their families never going to church, their family considering religion to be not at all or not very important, and receiving

poorer grades than most other children they knew, than under the mutually exclusive conditions. These results were interpreted in terms of the relatively greater
female dependence upon familial evaluation, circumstances detracting from the
positive evaluation of like-sex objects of identification, and failure to fulfill
requirements of the traditional female role. For male subjects only, respondents
were significantly more likely to manifest high self-derogation scores if they
reported that as children they were very much afraid of being laughed at by other
children and were very much afraid of being punished by their parents, than under
mutually exclusive conditions. These results were interpreted in terms of failure
to display characteristics associated with the masculine role, mainly, the display
of dominant assertive behavior and independence of parental standards.

   In international as well as national samples significant differences between the
genders have been noted regarding self-esteem, self-values, and negative
self-feelings. Thus, in a sample of adolescents from Switzerland, girls tended to
have lower self-esteem than boys. Girls evaluated themselves against personal
criteria and ideals while boys focused upon achievements. Girls tended to have
higher levels of depressive mood and anxiety than boys (Bolognini, Plancherel,
Bettschart, and Halfon 1996). The origins, dimensions, and responses to low
self-esteem also vary according to *race/ethnicity* (Martinez and Dukes 1991; Olah
1995; Wade, Thompson, Tashakkori, and Valente 1989). For example, Ross
(1994) reported that for blacks, both personal and group measures of self-esteem
were related to delinquency while for white Anglos personal identity better predicted delinquency; and, Mexican-American subjects were more likely to use
social activities and seeking spiritual support as coping mechanisms when
compared to white Anglos (Copeland and Hess 1995).

   Stage in the life course simultaneously reflects stage of psychological and physical development, the normative prescription and proscriptions associated with
particular ages, and time in history in which developmental stages are embedded
and which reflect the occurrence of events that have differential impact on individuals conditional upon their age when events occur (Elder, George, and Shanahan 1996). Both past experiences and contemporary circumstances are related to
self-derogation depending upon stage in the life course. Thus, a different pattern
of childhood experiences was significantly associated with high self-derogation
scores for different age groupings. Subjects below the age of thirty tended to have
high self-derogation scores if they reported that during childhood they were very
much afraid of being punished by their parents, they received poorer grades than
most of the children they knew, and they were not as good looking as most of the
children they knew. Subjects aged thirty to thirty-nine tended to have high
self-derogation scores if they reported that during childhood they were somewhat
or very much afraid of being laughed at by other children. Subjects aged forty to
forty-nine tended to manifest high self-derogation if they reported that as children
their health was better than most of the children they knew (Kaplan and Pokorny
1970). Similarly, for each age group, a different combination of contemporary

variables was observed to be associated with high self-derogation scores. Among the subjects below the age of thirty, high self-derogation scores tended to be associated with reports that the subject's spouse had no college education, and the subject had lived in his current residence less than two years. Among subjects aged thirty to thirty-nine, high self-derogation scores were associated with subject reports that the subject had less than three children living at home, and that the subject was a member of less than three organizations. For subjects aged forty to forty-nine, high self-derogation scores tended to be associated with reports that religion was more important to either the subject or the spouse (as opposed to being equally important to both) and that the subject did not do as well in life as his or her siblings. Regarding this last relationship, perhaps it is during this decade that the subject feels he has sufficient evidence of how far he will go in life to make such relative judgments. It is also during these years that he is expected to approach his peak of achievement. Therefore, it is at this time of life that judgments of relative performance are most likely to be related to level of self-evaluation and associated self-feelings (Kaplan 1971).

Given, such identity-related influences on the sources of self-derogation and the nature of the coping responses and their sequelae it is to be expected that various social identities would influence the effectiveness of specific coping patterns such as aggression in reducing self-esteem both because of their relevance for the sources of self-esteem and their acceptability as normative coping patterns. Certainly the literature suggests that this is the case.

SOCIAL IDENTITIES, AGGRESSION, AND SELF-DEROGATION

While the literature suggests that a reciprocal relationship exists between aggression and self-derogation (Kaplan 1975, 1980, 1986; Kaplan and Peck 1992), it also indicates that the nature of this relationship is contingent upon the person's social identities based on differentiation according to gender, race/ethnicity, and stage in the life course. The conditional nature of the relationship is based upon differences in the relevance of aggression for (1) forestalling or reducing the distress associated with salient self-devaluing circumstances, and (2) defining the normative acceptability of aggression, for people with these identities. If, for example, self-derogation was associated with a perceived lack of empowerment experienced in particular by adolescent females and Mexican Americans, then aggressive responses that obviated this perception would decrease self-derogatory attitudes. Or, if aggression was considered inappropriate by individuals with certain identities (women, adults) then resorting to aggression would invite condemnation from self and others, and so increase self-derogation. Much of the literature on identity and aggression is compatible with this reasoning.

Conventional wisdom would have it that boys in our society are socialized to express anger and aggression to a greater extent than females, for whom such expressions are less acceptable (Lerner 1985). Two types of evidence support this generalization: the differential prevalence of physical aggression by males and females; and, the self- and other-disapproval of aggression by females.

Consistent with the expectation that antisocial coping mechanisms would be more deplored for women than for men, men were observed to be more likely to use antisocial and aggressive coping strategies while women tended to be more prosocial in their coping (Hobfoll, Dunahoo, Ben-Porath, and Monnier 1994). Males are generally more likely to instigate physical violence than females (Harris 1992). In an at-risk sample (Job Corps residency) adolescent boys reported more aggressive acts against friends and strangers than did girls (Langhinrichsen-Rohling and Neidig 1995).

In one study, 50 percent of boys under age sixteen reported owning a gun compared with 5 percent of the girls (Cairns and Cairns 1994). Harris and Knight-Bohnhoff (1996a) observed among both college students and persons working on a military base that men displayed higher scores on a physical aggression scale than women. Numerous other reports in this and other cultures concur that physical aggression is less prevalent among females than among males (Fitzpatrick 1997; Lindeman, Harakka, and Keltigangas-Jarvinen 1997; Owens and MacMullin 1995; Rys and Bear 1997).

To the extent that lesser prevalence implies greater disapproval of aggression by females we would expect to find in the literature indications of negative sanctions by self and others for female aggression whether in this culture or cross-culturally.

The theoretically plausible hypothesis that women experience greater guilt about, and anticipate adverse reactions from others for aggression because of stereotypical beliefs about the appropriateness or inappropriateness of aggression for females in fact has received a good deal of attention in the literature (Eatough, Gregson, and Shevlin 1997). Eagly and Steffen (1986) reported that females were more likely to expect to experience guilt following aggression, and to believe that dangerous consequences might ensue from aggressing. In a sample of male and female high school sophomores in the Slovak Republic, gender-related differences in responses to hypothetical behavior by a victimizer that resulted in intentional and unintentional injury were observed. Females tended to more harshly assess the victimizer than males. Kogut, Langley, and O'Neal (1992, p. 356) cite a series of studies by Broverman, Vogel, Broverman, Clarkson, and Rosenkrantz (1972) in which men and women strongly agree about which traits characterize and are prescribed attributes for each gender.

Some of these traits which can also serve as affective labels that are commonly ascribed to females, include submissive, passive, not at all aggressive, and very uncomfortable about being aggressive. The opposites of these qualities are stereotypic males. Furthermore, labels generally assigned to males were rated as socially undesirable for females and uncharacteristic of the "ideal women."

Girls early on are socialized to hide their anger, particularly in the presence of adults (Underwood, Coie, and Herbsman 1992) and are more likely to have experienced negative interpersonal effects for behaving aggressively (Harris 1992). These processes are nicely summarized by White and Kowalski (1994, p. 493) who observe that

> aggressive women are labeled more deviant and pathological than are comparably aggressive men.... The possibility that women's aggression is justified is reduced, and the legitimacy of their behavior is discounted. Women thus develop feelings of anxiety and guilt about expressing their anger and frustration in aggressive ways. Given that deviance is commonly defined as behavior that departs from cultural norms and that violence is not socially condoned, it is hardly surprising that "aggressive" women have been labeled more deviant than "aggressive" men (Anderson 1993).

At the same time that women are inhibited from expressing aggression, and therefore tend to experience exacerbation of self-rejecting experiences when expressing their aggressive impulses, the nature of their socialization is such that they experience an increased need to express their aggressive impulses. In general, research has demonstrated that males tend to manifest higher rates of physical aggression than females (Loeber and Hay 1997). This is not to say, however, that females are not aggressive. Rather they may use more verbal and indirect aggression as opposed to physical aggression. They may manifest relational aggression such as gossip, ostracism, and disruption of the relational bonds between others (Crick and Grotpeter 1995). Indeed, it is possible that females may use physical aggression but do it in ways that is not observed by others, or may be less willing to admit to engaging in physical aggression (Pepler and Craig 1995). In any case, females have aggressive impulses and feel somewhat inhibited from expressing their impulses. Males and females tend to view aggression differently. For women the function of aggression is expressive, that is, a way of dealing with one's feelings when out of control, while men view aggression as instrumental to the achievement of goals or to exercising control (Campbell, Muncer, and Gorman 1993). Yet women tend to cope with general stressful situations through self-blame more frequently than men (Korabik and Van Kampen 1995). The requirement that women inhibit the expression of aggression is evidence both of the general devaluation of these behaviors by females and of the need to express oneself that goes unfulfilled.

To the extent that certain social identities were more vulnerable to a sense of being inhibited from expressing their aggressive needs, the individuals sharing that identity would be more likely to experience self-enhancing effects of engaging in that pattern. If females, for example, were more likely to feel unable to express their aggressive impulses than males, then aggressive responses would be more likely to have self-enhancing outcomes for females than for males. If, by virtue of gender-specific socialization women are constrained from expressing aggression, they will be less able than males to attack the source of their self-devaluing experience. Hence, when these inhibitions are overcome they should have a greater opportunity to decrease their self-derogatory feelings. At the same time, the ability to exercise control over one's own outcomes should provide a source of pride and so enhance self-feelings.

In an apparent contradiction, then, the literature suggests that women are more likely to suffer increased self-derogation by expressing aggression, but at the same time are more likely to experience decreased self-derogation by virtue of acting out aggressive impulses that were theretofore inhibited. This apparent contradiction may be resolved if the proscription against aggression is more applicable during the adult years, and the intensified need for self-assertion (due to excessive familial and societal controls placed on the female particularly during adolescence) and the accompanying self-enhancement resulting from acting on aggressive impulses occur predominately during adolescence. *Based on these considerations we would hypothesize that for female subjects uniquely aggression would be self-enhancing (that is, would reduce self-derogation) during the period between early adolescence and young adulthood, but would exacerbate self-derogation for the period between young adulthood and the fourth decade of life when the expression of aggressive impulse would be deplored.*

Regarding the moderating influence of *race/ethnicity*, in the literature the potentially self-enhancing consequences of aggressive behavior appears to be most closely associated with Mexican-American cultures. In these cultures, the motivation for, and the self-enhancing function of aggressive behavior is viewed by many as intricately tied to the concept of machismo. The concept of machismo, associated with some Mexican-American cultures, appears to be a complex of virility-related values that are expressed in the exercise of control over females by men, sexual promiscuity, the fathering of numerous children, fearlessness, and pugnacity (Cubitt 1988; Hines and Fry, 1994). Ingoldsby (1991) notes that a principle characteristic in machismo is aggressiveness. Citing Giraldo (1972) Ingoldsby observes that a macho must meet abuse from others (whether physical or verbal) with weapons or fists. Mexican-American males are expected to act aggressively whenever their honor is at stake.

It is widely believed that machismo is a mechanism employed to counteract feelings of inferiority (Ingoldsby 1991, p. 59):

It appears that machismo may be due to feelings of inferiority, which men try to hide by acting superior. This is accomplished by avoiding feminine traits and emphasizing strong masculine ones. Ramos (1951) and Stycos (1965) both concur that an inferiority complex is the basis of machismo.

The adaptive functions of aggressive coping strategies has been noted in a variety of contexts including deviant subgroups in Mexican society. Thus, the aggressive aspects of a cultural ideal of "machismo" have been observed to provide the male Mexican heroin addict with an effective means of adaptation to a risky social environment. Through acting out the machismo ideal in quotidian social transactions, the male Mexican heroin addict achieves prestige and a way to defend himself against threats in his environment (Quintero and Estrada 1998). Consistent with these speculations, using data from male arrestees in Dallas, Houston, and San Antonio Texas, Mexican Americans were observed to be most likely arrested for aggressive crimes (Valdez, Yin, and Kaplan 1997).

On the basis of these observations we anticipate that *Mexican-American subjects would be more likely to experience self-enhancement (reduced self-derogation) as a result of engaging in aggressive behavior*. Presumably the aggressive responses evidence approximation of salient machismo-related self-evaluative standards. This justification would appear to relate to Mexican-American males in particular. However, we might also hypothesize a self-enhancing effect of aggressive behavior for Mexican-American women as well on the grounds that they represent an overcontrolled population and therefore would most appreciate the sense of empowerment that derives from self-assertion. As Hines and Fry (1994, pp. 216-217) observe:

> As elsewhere in Latin America, in Argentina there is an ideology of behavior for women called *marianismo*, the submissive female role. In this ideology, a woman is "gentle, kind, long-suffering, loving and submits to the demands of men, whether they be husbands, fathers, sons, or brothers" (Cubitt, 1988, p. 104).

Such repressive activities might well exacerbate a need for assertiveness that is satisfied when circumstances lead to the (rare) expression of aggression.

On the basis of observations in the literature it would seem that whether aggression has self-enhancing or self-devaluing consequences also is contingent in part on the *stage of the life course* in which the aggression is displayed. Manifestations of aggression change between childhood and early adulthood depending on the gender of the subjects (Loeber and Hay 1997). Over the course of adolescence, girls become less violent while boys continue to engage in aggression and related behaviors (Cairns and Cairns 1994). Support for the observation that with increasing age aggression is less likely to have a self-enhancing effect on and, indeed, is more likely to increase self-derogation is provided by reports that age distinguishes between aggressive and nonaggressive youths (Fitzpatrick 1997). Finally, Harris and Knight-Bohnhoff (1996a) report that age is negatively related to tolerance for aggression, and also report an association between increasing age and lower aggressiveness for both genders in samples of college students and persons working on a military base (Harris and Knight-Bohnhoff 1996b).

Based on these considerations, we hypothesize that *aggression will be associated with increases in self-derogation for later stages in the life cycle except where there is reason to believe that aggression reflects approximation of culturally endorsed evaluative standards or represents relief from culturally repressive standards.*

MODELS

In the present analyses, we examine the effectiveness of aggressive coping responses to self-derogation on the reduction of these negative self-feelings. Based on the foregoing considerations we anticipate that the effectiveness of aggressive responses on the reduction of self-derogating feelings will depend on social identities differentiated according to gender, race/ethnicity, and stage in the life course. These social identities will be related to different sources of self-derogation. Therefore, the self-enhancing potential of aggressive responses will be more or less great depending upon the ability of these particular coping responses to obviate the putative source of the aggression. We also expect that social identities will be related to the acceptability of aggressive responses as coping mechanisms. The acceptability of aggressive responses as coping patterns (will be positively related to the effectiveness of these responses in reducing self-derogation).

We estimate models that take the form pictured in Figure 1. The models reflect: (1) effects of self-derogation on aggression at three points in time (self-derogation is modeled as causally prior to aggression at each point in time although the measures of the two constructs are taken at the same point in time); (2) the effect of aggression at Time 1 on self-derogation at Time 2, and the effects of aggression at Time 2 on self-derogation at Time 3 (net of their common association with earlier self-derogation); and, (3) the stability effects of self-derogation and aggression at earlier points in time on these same constructs measured at later points in time. The models are estimated separately for males and females, and for white-Anglo, African-American, and Mexican-American subjects separately.

For present purposes we are most interested in the lagged effects of aggression on self-derogation. We expect that, particularly at earlier stages in the life course, females will experience a reduction in self-derogation after aggression on the grounds that experiences of being overcontrolled will render instances of aggressive self-assertion as evidencing self-efficacy. However, at later stages in the life course, aggression will be evaluated negatively by self and others, and so will eventuate in increases in self-derogation. We further expect that Mexican Americans over the life course will experience a remarkable decrease in self-derogation following aggression on the grounds that cultural premises support aggressive responses to insults.

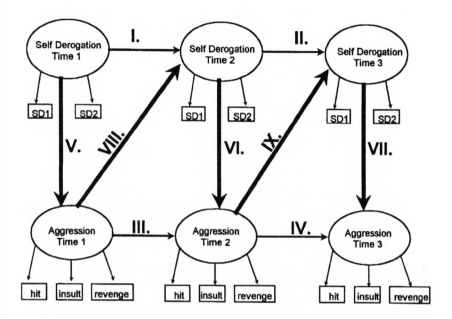

Figure 1. Conceptual Diagram of Structural Equation Model

METHOD

Data Collection and Sample Characteristics

The subjects consisted of approximately 4,000 subjects tested at three points in time. The first testing occurred by self-administered questionnaires when the subjects were in the seventh grade (between 11 and 14 years of age, Time 1). The second testing was conducted by household interviews when the subjects were in their twenties (early adulthood, Time 2). The third testing, via household interviews, occurred when the subjects were in the fourth decade of life (between 35 and 39 years of age, Time 3). The gender composition was 45 percent males and 55 percent females. Regarding race/ethnicity, 54 percent were white Anglo, 26 percent were African American, and 10 percent were Mexican American.

Measures

The measures used in this study reflect self-derogation and aggression at three different stages in the life course: adolescence, young adulthood, and mid-to-late thirties. Self-derogation is measured by seven dichotomous items, administered in each of the three time periods. The items are reproduced below.

Self-derogation (a = .6205)

I wish I could have more respect for myself.

I feel I don't have much to be proud of.

All in all, I am inclined to feel that I am a failure.

At times, I think I am no good at all.

I certainly feel useless at times.

On the whole, I am satisfied with myself (REVERSED).

I take a positive attitude toward myself (REVERSED).

These seven items are used as a single summed scale in paired and independent samples *t*-tests. For identification purposes regarding latent variables in structural equation modeling, this scale is divided into two subsets (items 1-5 and items 6-7) (Bollen 1989).

Aggression is measured by three dichotomous items asked in each of the three periods of this study. The items, reproduced below, are used as separate indicators of latent variables in structural equation modeling, and as a summed scale in paired samples and independent samples *t*-tests.

Aggression (a = .6106)

If someone insulted me, I would probably hit him.

If someone insulted me, I would probably insult him back.

If someone insulted me, I would probably think about ways I could get even.

ANALYSIS

Four sets of analyses were performed on the variables: paired samples *t*-tests, independent samples *t*-tests structural equation modeling, and within-group structural invariance tests. Each analysis was performed separately for males and females, and for white Anglos, African Americans, and Mexican Americans in order to examine subgroup differences. Within group analyses were performed to examine differences at various stages in the life course.

Paired and Independent Samples *T*-tests

A *t*-test allows comparisons of sample means to determine if they, and hence their corresponding populations, differ significantly with respect to a variable. Paired samples *t*-tests allow for the comparison of means of a variable measured at different points in time for a single group. Independent samples *t*-tests allow comparison of the mean of a variable for two different groups or samples.

We first conducted paired samples *t*-tests in order to examine whether the means of the self-derogation and aggression scales differ significantly at various stages in the life course. Self-derogation at Time 1 was compared with self-derogation at Time 2 and Time 3, and self-derogation at Time 2 was compared with self-derogation at Time 3. Likewise, aggression at Time 1 was compared with aggression at Time 2 and Time 3, and aggression at Time 2 was compared with aggression at Time 3

We then conducted independent samples *t*-tests to see if there were differences between subgroup means in self-derogation and aggression measured at three points in the life course. We compared the means of both self-derogation and aggression between males and females, and between white Anglos and African Americans, white Anglos and Mexican Americans, and African Americans and Mexican Americans at three points in time.

Structural Equation Modeling

LISREL 8.14 was used to estimate the Structural Equation models. These parameter estimates were obtained using maximum likelihood procedures. Starting values of .5 were used to begin the iterative estimation procedure, and the first indicator of each set of observed variables defining a latent construct was used to set the scale metric for the latent variable (Joreskog and Sorbom 1996). The full latent variable model consists of the relationships between observed variables and the latent variable representing their common underlying concept (measurement model) and the relationships among the latent variables (structural model) (Bollen 1989). The structural models specify: within-wave effects of self-derogation on aggression at each of three points in time, the stability effects for self-derogation and aggression, respectively, between adjacent points in time, and the lagged effects of aggression on self-derogation between adjacent points in time.

One measure of model fit in a structural equation model is the model X^2, which measures discrepancy between the observed (sample) covariance matrix, and an expected covariance matrix which would best fit the data, given the model specified by the researcher (Bollen 1989; Hoyle 1995; Joreskog and Sorbom 1996). By this criteria, a large and significant X^2 would indicate a poor fitting model. However, it is widely recognized , that the model X^2 is highly influenced by sample size, with large samples making even minute discrepancies between the observed and expected covariance matrix statistically significant (Bollen and Long 1992; Hu and Bentler 1995). Thus, in addition to the model X^2, we have provided several measures of model fit which are robust with respect to sample size, and number of parameters estimated. In Table 5, we have reported the goodness of fit index, adjusted goodness of fit index, normed fit index, non-normed fit index, root mean squared error of approximation, and the root mean square residual along with the model X^2.

The goodness of fit index is a sample-based measure of fit which compares the fit of the specified model to the fit of a null model (no parameters specified) while the normed fit index measures fit of the observed covariance matrix to the expected covariance matrix under assumptions of noncentrality. The adjusted goodness of fit index and non-normed fit index corrects for the number of parameters in the model. Values of .90 or above are considered reasonably good fits for these four measures (Hu and Bentler 1995). Unlike the previous four indices, the RMSEA is a population-based index, measuring how well a model fits a theoretical population covariance matrix based on discrepancies between distributions of random variables (Browne and Cudeck 1992). The RMR measures the average of the predicted residuals resulting for a model (Joreskog and Sorbom 1996). Values of .05 or below are considered acceptable for these two fit indices. Despite the questionable validity of the model X^2 in assessing overall model fit, it is useful in testing hypotheses regarding nested models, and invariance of measurement and structural parameters both within group and across groups (Hu and Bentler 1995).

Within-Group Analysis of Invariant Causal Structure over Time

After each subgroup model was estimated, we conducted within-group invariance tests of structural parameters at different stages in the life course. This was done in order to test whether self-derogation and aggression were stable over the life course, to test the equality on within wave effects of self-derogation on aggression and lagged effects of aggression of self-derogation at various stages in the life course. This was accomplished by imposing equality constraints on the structural parameters, and determining if the X^2 of the test model (model with constraint) is significantly higher than the baseline null model (model without constraints). The difference in the X^2 (ΔX^2) is calculated upon setting a parameter equal to another parameter. A significant difference in the X^2 indicates that the addition of the equality constraint significantly worsens the fit of the model, and hence that the two parameters being equated are in actuality unequal (Byrne 1998; Byrne, Muthen, and Shavelson 1989). Such tests were performed on each of the five subgroups, equating structural parameters I and II , III and IV, V and VI, VI and VII, V and VII, and VIII and IX (see Figure 1).

RESULTS

We first examine the means and standard deviations of the study variables across time for the full sample and for subgroups, and between subgroups differentiated by gender and race/ethnicity at each point in time. We then examine the structural equation models for the full sample and the subgroups.

Table 1. Descriptive Statistics for Summed Scales Across Groups

		Full (n = 3,992)	Male (n = 1,790)	Female (n = 2,200)	White Anglo (n = 2,484)	African American (n = 996)	Mexican American (n = 384)
Self-Derogation T1	Mean	2.347	2.272	2.408	2.276	2.337	2.732
	Std. Dev.	1.739	1.701	1.767	1.793	1.615	1.652
Self-Derogation T2	Mean	1.134	1.034	1.195	1.125	1.005	1.341
	Std. Dev.	1.497	1.432	1.546	1.519	1.346	1.670
Self-Derogation T3	Mean	.9678	.8590	1.032	.9769	.9137	.8962
	Std. Dev.	1.508	1.383	1.585	1.548	1.361	1.523
Aggression T1	Mean	1.122	1.378	.9086	1.056	1.228	1.229
	Std. Dev.	1.052	1.068	.9919	1.029	1.079	1.083
Aggression T2	Mean	.5485	.6575	.4368	.5168	.5603	.6119
	Std. Dev.	.7956	.8343	.7241	.7715	.8085	.8033
Aggression T3	Mean	.4217	.5211	.3181	.3790	.4779	.4299
	Std. Dev.	.7015	.7565	.6190	.6568	.7540	.7289

17

18   HOWARD B. KAPLAN and SHAHEEN HALIM

Study Variables

The means and standard deviations of the study variables are summarized in Table 1. As noted above, the measurements of self-derogation and aggression were taken at three points in time. The first point was when the subjects were in the seventh grade (between 11 and 14 years of age, Time 1). The second point was when the subjects were in their twenties (early adulthood, Time 2). The third point was when the subjects were in the fourth decade of life (between thirty-five and thirty-nine years of age, Time 3).

For the full sample and for all subgroups scores on self-derogation decrease over the life course as do scores on the index of aggression. This is consistent with the literature that suggests that over time individuals are able to cope better with feelings of self-derogation. The literature also suggests that with maturity individuals are less likely to employ aggressive patterns of coping. As reference to Table 2 will indicate, for the full sample and for all subgroups differentiated on the basis of gender and race/ethnicity, the decreases in self-derogation and deviance over time were statistically significant with only one exception. The decrease in self-derogation between Time 2 and Time 3 for African Americans was not significant.

Table 2.   Correlations and Within-group Paired Sample *T*-tests of
Summed Scale Means over Time

	Full (n = 3,992)	Male (n = 1,790)	Female (n = 2,200)	White Anglo (n = 2,484)	African American (n = 996)	Mexican American (n = 384)
Self-Derogation T1	.222	.199	.236	.210	.219	.313
vs. Self-Derogation T2	38.147	26.557	27.423	27.433	22.319	14.234
Self-Derogation T2	.401	.387	.407	.400	.381	.460
vs. Self-Derogation T3	5.954	4.171	4.265	4.086	1.818[n.s]	4.616
Self-Derogation T1	.163	.173	.153	.172	.117	.244
vs. Self-Derogation T3	41.352	29.626	29.118	29.771	22.369	17.905
Aggression T1	.184	.193	.124	.198	.107	.253
vs. Aggression T2	31.426	25.632	19.209	23.494	16.725	10.595
Aggression T2	.381	.403	.329	.425	.342	.251
vs. Aggression T3	10.437	6.794	7.974	9.427	2.929	4.381
Aggression T1	.182	.140	.170	.189	.177	.130
vs. Aggression T3	40.145	30.673	26.467	31.073	19.973	13.638

Notes: First value = correlation coefficient. Second value = Paired difference *T*-test.
Unless otherwise indicated, all values are significant at *p* < .01.
[n.s] indicates non-significance.

Table 3. Independent Samples *T*-tests Comparing Means of Summed Scale Variables across Groups (Equal Variances not Assumed)

	Male vs. Female	White vs. African American	White vs. Mexican American	African American vs. Mexican American
Self-Derogation T1	−2.586**	−1.023	−5.213**	−4.218**
Self-Derogation T2	−3.631**	2.460*	−2.542*	−3.776**
Self-Derogation T3	−3.894**	1.266	1.012	.207
Aggression T1	15.061**	−4.590**	−3.067**	−.010
Aggression T2	9.416**	−1.57	−2.314*	−1.145
Aggression T3	9.756**	−3.904**	−1.370	1.161

Notes: * $p < .05$.
\ \ \ \ \ \ ** $p < .01$.

The results comparing self-derogation and aggression scores for the gender and race/ethnicity differentiated subgroups are summarized in Table 3. Again, consistent with much of the literature, at each point in time females had significantly higher self-derogation scores and significantly lower aggression scores. These results are compatible with our expectations that women are more inhibited in expressing aggression but at the same time have a stronger need (reflected in greater self-derogation) to assert themselves. Consistent with our expectations, the Mexican-American subjects had significantly higher self-derogation scores at both Time 1 and Time 2 than either the African-American or white-Anglo subjects. But at Time 3 no significant differences were observed among the groups, perhaps adumbrating the hypothesized self-enhancing effect of aggressive coping styles among Mexican-American subjects between Time 2 and Time 3. Although we did not anticipate this finding, we also observed that at Time 2 white Anglos were significantly more self-derogatory than African-American subjects.

Structural Equation Models

The measurement models are summarized in Table 4. All of the maximum likelihood estimates of the measurement variables' loadings on the hypothetical latent constructs are statistically significant.

The maximum likelihood estimates of structural parameters for the full sample model and for the subgroups differentiated according to gender and race/ethnicity are summarized in Table 5. The parenthetical Roman numerals in the left-hand column refer to the structural parameters represented in Figure 1.

The estimated model for the full sample, as anticipated, showed significant positive effects of self-derogation on aggression at each point in time. Stability effects for self-derogation and aggression between Time 1 and Time 2, and between Time 2 and Time 3 were positive and significant. The lagged effect of

Table 4.   Factor Loadings (Standardized) of
Measurement Variables on Latent Constructs

		Full $(n = 3,992)$	Male $(n = 1,790)$	Female $(n = 2,200)$	White Anglo $(n = 2,484)$	African American $(n = 996)$	Mexican American $(n = 384)$
Self-Derogation	T1						
	SD1	.75	.78	.75	.79	.64	.53
	SD2	.40	.37	.41	.49	.20	.33
Self-Derogation	T2						
	SD1	.85	.84	.88	.86	.89	.81
	SD2	.58	.56	.59	.61	.47	.64
Self-Derogation	T3						
	SD1	.89	.84	.92	.92	.83	.83
	SD2	.65	.62	.66	.67	.52	.75
Aggression	T1						
	hit	.46	.44	.44	.43	.52	.44
	insult	.59	.52	.63	.57	.61	.62
	revenge	.75	.76	.71	.79	.67	.75
Aggression	T2						
	hit	.37	.37	.36	.35	.40	.45
	insult	.60	.60	.58	.61	.62	.50
	revenge	.57	.57	.61	.59	.57	.53
Aggression	T3						
	hit	.29	.30	.27	.26	.39	.30
	insult	.60	.60	.57	.60	.61	.60
	revenge	.57	.59	.55	.57	.55	.53

Note: All factor loadings were significant at $p < .01$.

aggression at Time 1 on self-derogation at Time 2 was negative and significant. The effect of aggression at Time 2 on self-derogation at Time 3 was positive and significant. The question arises, however, as to whether these effects were moderated by the gender and race/ethnicity of the subjects.

For both males and females, the within-wave effects of self-derogation on aggression at each point in time were positive and significant. Similarly, for both males and females, the stability effects of both self-derogation and aggression between Time 1 and Time 2, and between Time 2 and Time 3, were positive and significant. However, the lagged effects noted for the full sample were apparently accounted for by the female subjects. For the female subjects aggression had a significant and inverse effect on self-derogation between adolescence and young adulthood, and a significant positive effect of aggression on self-derogation between young adulthood and the fourth decade of life. While the effects noted for males were in the same directions, these effects were not significant. Thus, as

Table 5. Maximum Likelihood Estimates of Structural Parameters among Latent Constructs

Path		Full (n = 3,992)	Male (n = 1,790)	Female (n = 2,200)	White Anglo (n = 2484)	African American (n = 996)	Mexican American (n = 384)
SD1 to SD2	(I)	.34**a	.27**	.38**	.30**	.48*	1.04*
		(.36)b	(.31)	(.39)	(.33)	(.44)	(.76)
		.04c	.01	.05	.04	.20	.43
		[8.58]d	[4.93]	[6.93]	[7.66]	[2.39]	[2.43]
SD2 to SD3	(II)	.50**	.49**	.49**	.50**	.43**	.66**
		(.50)	(.52)	(.47)	(.49)	(.47)	(.71)
		.03	.04	.03	.03	.06	.09
		[19.02]	[11.94]	[14.02]	[15.60]	[7.43]	[7.18]
Agg1 to Agg2	(III)	.15**	.14**	.11**	.14**	.10**	.20**
		(.30)	(.27)	(.22)	(.30)	(.21)	(.31)
		.01	.02	.02	.02	.03	.07
		[9.76]	[6.05]	[5.67]	[7.80]	[3.80]	[3.07]
Agg2 to Agg3	(IV)	.31**	.33**	.27**	.25**	.42**	.18**
		(.69)	(.71)	(.60)	(.77)	(.59)	(.42)
		.03	.04	.04	.03	.07	.06
		[10.74]	[7.37]	[7.22]	[8.16]	[6.03]	[2.82]
SD1 to Agg1	(V)	.06**	.06**	.05**	.04**	.04**	.13**
		(.32)	(.31)	(.37)	(.29)	(.37)	(.52)
		.01	.01	.01	.01	.01	.05
		[8.28]	[4.93]	[6.85]	[6.91]	[6.91]	[2.73]
SD2 to Agg2	(VI)	.02**	.01**	.02**	.01**	.02**	.04**
		(.16)	(.13)	(.23)	(.14)	(.13)	(.36)
		.00	.00	.00	.00	.01	.01
		[6.45]	[3.35]	[6.24]	[4.65]	[2.68]	[3.60]
SD3 to Agg3	(VII)	.01**	.01**	.01**	.00**	.02**	.01
		(.20)	(.23)	(.23)	(.20)	(.26)	(.12)
		.00	.00	.00	.00	.01	.01
		[7.26]	[5.34]	[5.67]	[5.70]	[4.33]	[1.45]
Agg1 to SD2	(VIII)	−.34*	−.06	−.53*	−.47**	−.38	−1.08
		(−.06)	(−.01)	(−.08)	(−.08)	(−.09)	(−.21)
		.13	.18	.25	.18	.34	.97
		[−2.50]	[−.33]	[−2.14]	[−2.62]	[−1.12]	[−1.11]
Agg2 to SD3	(IX)	.50*	.33	.87*	.71*	.91*	−1.55*
		(.05)	(.04)	(.06)	(.05)	(.12)	(−.21)
		.23	.29	.42	.35	.37	.70
		[2.15]	[1.16]	[2.06]	[2.05]	[2.44]	[−2.23]
Model X^2_{df}		590.56$_{81}$	339.55$_{81}$	316.53$_{81}$	486.08$_{81}$	171.03$_{81}$	134.90$_{81}$
RMSEA		.040	.042	.036	.045	.033	.042
RMR		.0097	.012	.0089	.012	.0096	.017
GFI		.98	.98	.98	.97	.98	.95
AGFI		.97	.96	.97	.96	.97	.93
NFI		.93	.91	.94	.92	.91	.86
NNFI		.92	.90	.94	.91	.93	.92

Notes: *p<.05. **p<.01.
aunstandardized coefficient
b(standardized coefficient)
cstandard error
d[T- value]

expected, gender moderated the nature of the relationship between aggression and self-derogation.

When the model was estimated separately for white-Anglo, African-American, and Mexican-American subjects, we observed that for all three groups at each point in time self-derogation had a significant positive effect on aggression with the exception that for the Mexican-American subjects at Time 3 the effect of self-derogation on aggression although positive was not significant. The stability effects for self-derogation and aggression were positive and significant for both time intervals in all three race/ethnic categories. The lagged effects of aggression on later self-derogation between Time 1 and Time 2 were negative for all three groups but (perhaps due to power differentials) was only statistically significant for the white-Anglo grouping. The lagged effect of aggression on later self-derogation between Time 2 and Time 3 was positive and significant for the white-Anglo and the African-American subjects. For the Mexican-American subjects, however, as expected the effect of aggression on later self-derogation was inverse and significant. Thus, as hypothesized Mexican-American identity moderated the lagged effect of aggression on self-derogation.

The examination of the within-group invariance tests of structural parameters at different stages of the life course revealed that stage of the life course indeed does moderate structural effects. These results are summarized in Table 6.

Table 6.   Within-group Comparisons of Structural Parameters Across Time

		Full $(n = 3,992)$	Male $(n = 1,790)$	Female $(n = 2,200)$	White Anglo $(n = 2,484)$	African American $(n = 996)$	Mexican American $(n = 384)$
Original X^2_{df} (unconstrained model)		590.56_{81}	339.55_{81}	316.53_{81}	486.08_{81}	171.03_{81}	134.90_{81}
Paths constrained for comparison							
I. & II.	X^2_{df}	600.20_{82}	347.83_{82}	318.69_{82}	500.27_{82}	171.07_{82}	136.05_{82}
	ΔX^2_{df}	9.64_1^{**}	8.28_1^{**}	2.16_1	14.19_1^{**}	$.04_1$	1.15_1
III. & IV.	X^2_{df}	616.09_{82}	352.71_{82}	332.64_{82}	493.98_{82}	194.45_{82}	134.93_{82}
	ΔX^2_{df}	25.53_1^{**}	13.16_1^{**}	16.11_1^{**}	7.90_1^{**}	23.42_1^{**}	$.03_1$
V. & VI.	X^2_{df}	636.76_{82}	355.62_{82}	343.74_{82}	518.32_{82}	177.04_{82}	140.97_{82}
	ΔX^2_{df}	46.20_1^{**}	16.07_1^{**}	27.21_1^{**}	32.24_1^{**}	6.01_1^{*}	6.07_1^{*}
VI. & VII.	X^2_{df}	596.81_{82}	339.64_{82}	326.41_{82}	492.04_{82}	172.05_{82}	143.60_{82}
	ΔX^2_{df}	6.25_1^{*}	$.09_1$	9.88_1^{**}	5.96_1^{*}	1.02_1	8.70_1^{**}
V. & VII.	X^2_{df}	662.41_{82}	358.51_{82}	368.46_{82}	547.70_{82}	176.01_{82}	152.21_{82}
	ΔX^2_{df}	71.85_1^{**}	18.96_1^{**}	49.77_1^{**}	61.62_1^{**}	4.98_1^{*}	17.31_1^{**}
VIII. & IX.	X^2_{df}	599.97_{82}	340.85_{82}	324.64_{82}	494.91_{82}	178.17_{82}	135.03_{82}
	ΔX^2_{df}	9.41_1^{**}	1.30_1	8.11_1^{**}	8.83_1^{**}	7.14_1^{**}	$.13_1$

Notes: $^*p<.05.$ $^{**}p<.01.$

For the full sample, the stability of self-derogation between Time 2 and Time 3 was significantly greater than that observed between Time 1 and Time 2. Similarly, the stability of aggression between Time 2 and Time 3 was significantly greater than that between Time 1 and Time 2. The effect of self-derogation on aggression at Time 1 was significantly greater than the effect observed at Time 2 or Time 3. The lagged effect of aggression at Time 1 on self-derogation at Time 2 was significantly different from the lagged effect observed between Time 2 and Time 3. The former effect was inverse while the latter effect was positive.

These observations were further moderated, as expected by the subculturally defined identities based on differentiation according to gender and race/ethnicity. The increase in stability of self-derogation scores between Time 2 and Time 3 over that observed between Time 1 and Time 2 was statistically significant for the males but not for the females. However, the increase in stability of aggression between Time 2 and Time 3 over that observed between Time 1 and Time 2 was significant for both males and females. For both males and females the effect of self-derogation at Time 1 on aggression at Time 1 was significantly greater than that observed for Time 2 and Time 3.

No significant difference was observed in the lagged effects of aggression on later self-derogation between Time 1 and Time 2 compared to that observed between Time 2 and Time 3 for males. For females, however, the inverse effect of aggression on self-derogation between Time 1 and Time 2 was significantly different from the positive effect of aggression on self-derogation observed between Time 2 and Time 3. For present purposes, this represents the most salient observation among those related to differences in gender-based effects over time.

Regarding the groupings differentiated according to race/ethnicity, the stability effects of self-derogation between Time 2 and Time 3 were significantly greater than those observed between Time 1 and Time 2 for the white-Anglo subjects but not for the African-American or Mexican-American subjects. The increase in stability of aggression between Time 2 and Time 3 over that observed between Time 1 and Time 2 was statistically significant for the white-Anglo and African-American subjects but not for the Mexican-American subjects. The positive effect of self-derogation on aggression at Time 1 was significantly greater than the effect observed at Time 2 and Time 3 for all three race/ethnic categories. The difference in the effects of aggression on self-derogation observed between Time 1 and Time 2 and those observed between Time 2 and Time 3 were significant for both white-Anglo and African-American subjects but not for Mexican-American subjects. For the former groupings the effect changed from self-enhancing to self-derogating effects, while for the latter group the effect remained in the self-enhancing direction between the two points in Time.

DISCUSSION

Social identities based on differentiations according to gender and race/ethnicity or other socially salient characteristics in combination with identities based on the stage in the life course both derive from common experiences (including the reactions of significant others) and result in the sharing of normative expectations regarding the appropriateness of reactions to those experiences. Among the experiences associated with particular social identities are those that are interpreted as self-devaluing in nature and so generate distressful self-derogating feelings. In response to self-derogation individuals, regardless of social identities, will engage in self-enhancing/self-protective strategies in order to reduce or forestall self-derogation. However, the effectiveness of these strategies in reducing self-derogation will depend upon (1) the extent to which the strategy relates to the source of the self-derogation, and (2) the evaluation of the strategy as more or less appropriate. Both of these phenomena are related to the social identities that characterize the person.

In the present analyses we examine the effectiveness of the disposition to engage in aggressive strategies on coping with (that is, reducing) self-derogation. We expect that for social identities, in which a salient source of self-derogation is the perceived barrier against self-assertiveness, empowerment, or taking action on one's own behalf, the adoption of aggressive dispositions will be self-enhancing. If the source of self-derogation for females and Mexican Americans is perceived to be the social disempowerment of these identities, then the adoption of aggressive stances by persons characterized by these identities will result in the reduction of self-derogation. If the perceived disempowerment is experienced more greatly at earlier stages in the life course then the reduction in self-derogation consequent upon the adoption of aggressive behaviors will be associated with earlier stages in the life course.

Similarly, we expect that for social identities in which the adoption of aggressive dispositions is deplored, the adoption of such strategies will increase rather than decrease self-derogation. If females, particularly during adulthood, view aggression as inappropriate and are negatively sanctioned for their disposition to aggressively respond to self-devaluing circumstances, then they will experience exacerbation of their self-derogation following adoption of aggressive coping dispositions.

These expectations were tested using data from a panel tested at three points during the life course (early adolescence, young adulthood, and the latter half of the fourth decade of life). The basic model specified effects of self-derogation on aggression at each point in time, stability effects of self-derogation and aggression between adjacent stages of the life course, and lagged effects of aggression at earlier points in time on self-derogation at later points in time.

This model was estimated for males and females separately, and for white-Anglo, African-American, and Mexican-American subjects separately. We expected that gender and race/ethnicity would moderate the model in accordance with the expectations specified above. Although we presented and briefly discussed subgroup differences for all parameters, for present purposes we are most concerned with the moderating influence of gender and race/ethnicity on the lagged effects of aggression on later self-derogation (net of the association of those constructs with earlier self-derogation). We focus on these effects in our discussion.

In general the estimation of the structural equation models were congruent with our expectations. We consider in turn gender-specific and race/ethnicity-specific effects of aggression on later self-derogation over the life course.

Gender-Specific Effects

We observed that between adolescence and young adulthood aggressive dispositions were significantly and inversely related to later self-derogation for the female subjects alone. Further, between young adulthood and the fourth decade of life aggressive dispositions were significantly and positively related to later self-derogation, for the female subjects alone. The effects for the male subjects were in the same direction but did not approach statistical significance.

The question arises as to why self-enhancing outcomes for females should be experienced uniquely between early adolescence and young adulthood (and why males did not experience an equivalent decrease in self-derogation over this period). It may be argued, that during this period the struggle for emancipation from parents, as a reflection of the need for autonomy, is most intense. It may be further argued that traditional gender-based role prescriptions exercise greater constraints on females who are seeking independence than on males. Therefore, the assertions of independence as reflected in aggressive behaviors would be more self-enhancing for females than for males (Demo 1992). For females, aggressive stances reflect a less accustomed and more gratifying exercise in control over the environment.

The dynamics involved in the motivation of women to engage in aggression, and the experience of self-enhancement (reduced self-derogation) as a consequence of the aggression, we interpret at an individual level as paralleling the movement that facilitated the empowerment of women.

> History is replete with examples of the power women garnered from recognizing their victimization. Empowerment comes from the knowledge gained by naming. Once victimization of women was named for what it was (i.e., rape, battering), women could band together to protest it. Women can emerge from being victims with a sense of entitlement and efficacy. Many protest movements gained their energy from collective anger (White and Kowalski 1994, p. 503).

Particularly during their young years, women when they are least powerful and most vulnerable would gain greater satisfaction from being able to act on their own behalf, that is, aggressively. Against the background of traditional expectations of passive adaptations to life stress, the proliferation of gender movements (Pelak, Taylor, and Whittier 1999) over the past three decades has resulted in part in some degree of collective disinhibition of self-assertive strategies. The social support for such self-assertive tactics has permitted those who engaged in more aggressive adaptations to feel a sense of accomplishment, self-efficacy, and self-assurance that had hitherto not been experienced by women individually or collectively considered.

Support for the interpretation that those more disempowered (females) were more likely to experience self-enhancing outcomes of aggression was provided by other analyses (not reported here). Although we did not have sufficient cases to estimate the model properly for males and females separately within each race/ethnic grouping, we did observe that the overall self-enhancing effect of aggression for females between Time 1 and Time 2 was accounted for primarily by the Mexican-American females who for reasons noted above could be considered the most disempowered of the three groups. We observed that, although the self-enhancing trend was observed for white-Anglo and African-American females as well, the inverse effect of Time 1 aggression on Time 2 self-derogation was statistically significant only for Mexican-American females.

The need for self-validation that appears to be assuaged by aggressive coping patterns between adolescence and young adulthood may well be experienced between the third and fourth decades of life as well. However, the proscriptions against aggressive responses on the part of females by those who have accepted the role obligations associated with later periods of adulthood more than counterbalance the need for self-assertion. The need to fulfill the roles associated with marriage and motherhood may well inhibit the need to assert oneself.

Female-specific self-enhancing effect of aggression between early adolescence and young adulthood, then, is interpreted here as the use of aggression to overcome feelings of powerlessness in one's environment. The resultant feelings of self-efficacy improve self-attitudes. The presumed need to aggress as a way of overcoming feelings of impotency is consistent with a number of observations in the literature where overcontrolled or inhibited individuals tend to act out. Loeber and Hay (1997) cite a number of such observations. Overcontrolled individuals adopt aggressive patterns when anger arousal is sufficiently intense to overcome constraints (personal and social) against acting out (Blackburn 1993; Megargee 1966). Of particular interest, Pulkkinen (1982) reported that highly submissive girls were at risk for antisocial behavior.

The absence of a significant self-enhancing effect of aggression on self-derogation for males between adolescence and young adulthood may be accounted for by the fact that a sense of disempowerment did not characterize males and, therefore, aggressive responses did not satisfy a need. For females, however, a sense of disempowerment would be belied by the self-perception of engaging in aggressive responses and so would have a self-enhancing effect. The source of their self-derogation (disempowerment) was obviated by the aggressive responses resulting in decreased self-derogation. However, this self-enhancing affect was observed only between adolescence and young adulthood. Between young adulthood and the fourth decade of life engaging in aggressive responses by females presumably violated internalized proscriptions against the use of aggressive responses during one's mature years. This internalized proscription appeared to be gender identity-related insofar as the positive effect of aggression on self-derogation was significant for females but not for males.

These gender-related findings may be specific to particular times in our history. Perhaps it is only during the time of consciousness raising among females and perseveration on the need for empowerment that aggressive responses to self-derogation would be self-enhancing. The general principle would still hold, however. A coping pattern will be self-enhancing to the extent that it obviates the source of the self-derogation.

Race/Ethnicity—Specific Effects

Our race/ethnicity-based expectations centered primarily on the self-enhancing effects of aggressive disposition for our Mexican-American subjects in large measure because of machismo-relevant issues. If machismo-related aggressive responses may properly be viewed as self-protective devices adopted to assuage the negative self-feelings associated with experiences of powerlessness and self-attributed inferiority in their life experiences, then we would expect our Mexican-American subjects to enjoy a greater reduction in self-derogation following adoption of aggressive responses on the grounds that Mexican Americans tended to be less educated and to have lower self-esteem than African-American or white-Anglo subjects (Neff, Prihoda, and Hoppe 1991). In fact, this is what we observed between the third and fourth decades of life. For Mexican-American subjects aggressive behaviors resulted in a decrease in self-derogation, while for white-Anglo and African-American subjects aggression was associated with an increase in self-derogation over the same period of time. It may be regarded as consistent with our findings that Mexican-American arrestees were more likely to be arrested for aggressive crimes than either African-American or white-Anglo arrestees (Valdez, Yin, and Kaplan 1997). We may speculate that the experience of self-enhancing outcomes of aggression by Mexican-Americans may increase the disposition to engage in such behavior.

However, if the machismo interpretation were the primary dynamic operating we would expect that the self-enhancing effect observed for Mexican-American subjects between Time 2 and Time 3 would be accounted for primarily by the males in this grouping. In fact, our further analyses (not reported here) did indicate that the self-enhancing effect was significant only for the males. Nevertheless, a similar (nonsignificant) trend was observed for the females as well suggesting that disempowered groups (such as Mexican-American females) in particular are most likely to benefit in the form of reduced self-derogation from aggressive dispositions. We have already noted that the inverse (self-enhancing) effect of aggression during adolescence on self-derogation during young adulthood was significant only for the Mexican-American females. These findings taken together suggest that for the period between early adolescence and young adulthood a female-specific sense of disempowerment was the dominant dynamic, while for the period between the second and fourth decades of life a machismo-like process was operative (although the disempowerment reaction appears to be present to some extent as well). During this same period, however, for white-Anglo and African-American subjects, the prosription against aggressive dispositions appears to be operative and/or a sense of disempowerment and cultural support for aggressive self-protective mechanism appears to be lacking, resulting in an increase in self-derogation for those who adopt aggressive responses to self-derogation.

In general, then, our results are quite consistent with the generalization that self-protective mechanisms in response to self-derogation will result in reduced or increased self-derogation depending on (1) the ability of the mechanism (here, aggressive disposition) to obviate salient sources of self-derogation and (2) subcultural endorsement of the mechanism. Insofar as subculturally defined social identities influence these phenomena these identities will be expected to moderate the lagged effects of the self-protective mechanism on self-derogation. We have assumed that gender and race/ethnicity in interaction with stage of the life course influence (1) the sources (e.g., disempowerment) of self-derogation and the relevance of a specific self-protective mechanism (aggression) for obviating the source and (2) the personal and social approbation of the mechanism. Our results, while compatible with these expectations, do not demonstrate the theoretical linkages and conditions that we have assumed. Therefore, we urge caution in accepting our conclusions. Although the findings are compatible with the theoretical substrate, we lack sufficient power in our data set to test models that specify others theoretically indicated moderators and mediators in these relationships. To the extent that the conditions that are presumed to hold in fact hold and that the variables that are presumed to mediate the relationships in fact mediate the relationships, the guiding theoretical framework will be increasingly credible.

We have investigated only a few of a person's subculturally defined social identities and addressed only one of a range of self-protective mechanisms. The estimation of models incorporating the interactive contexts of these identities, identity-specific sources of self-devaluation, the identity-specific relevance of a range of mechanisms for addressing sources of self-devaluation, and the self-enhancing/self-derogating consequences of these mechanisms for people characterized by various combinations of socially defined identities should be high on the agenda of researchers interested in the moderating influence of social identities on the relationship between self-devaluing experiences and adaptations to life stress on the one hand, and between particular coping strategies and the enhancement of self-attitudes on the other hand. In this paper we have provided a tentative theoretical and analytical template for engaging in such research.

ACKNOWLEDGMENTS

This work was supported by a research grant (RO1 DA 02497) and Career Scientist Award (KO5 DA 00136) to the first author from the National Institute on Drug Abuse.

REFERENCES

Anderson, M.L. 1993. *Thinking about Women: Sociological Perspectives on Sex and Gender*. New York: Macmillan.

Blackburn, R. 1993. *The Psychology of Criminal Conduct*. Chichester, UK: Wiley.

Bollen, K.A. 1989. *Structural Equations with Latent Variables*. New York: John Wiley and Sons.

Bollen, K.A., and J.S. Long. 1992. "Tests for Structural Equation Models: Introduction." *Sociological Methods and Research* 21(2): 123-131.

Bolognini, M., B. Plancherel, W. Bettschart, and O. Halfon. 1996. "Self-Esteem and Mental Health in Early Adolescence: Development and Gender Differences." *Journal of Adolescence* 19(3): 233-245.

Browne, M.W., and R. Cudeck. 1992. "Alternative Ways of Assessing Model Fit." *Sociological Methods and Research* 21 (2): 230-258.

Broverman, I.K., S.R. Vogel, D.M. Broverman, F.E. Clarkson, and P. Rosenkrantz. 1972. "Sex-Role Stereotypes: A Current Appraisal." *Journal of Social Issues* 28: 59-78.

Byrne, B.M. 1998. "Testing for Invariant Factorial Structure of a Theoretical Construct (First-Order CFA Model)." In *Structural Equation Modeling with LISREL, PRELIS, and SIMPLIS: Basic Concepts, Applications, and Programming*. Mahwah, NJ: Lawrence Erlbaum Associates, Inc.

Byrne, B.M., B. Muthen, and R.J. Shavelson. 1989. "Testing for the Equivalence of Factor Covariance and Mean Structures: The Issue of Partial Measurement Invariance." *Psychological Bulletin* 105(3): 456-466.

Cairns, R.B., and B.D. Cairns. 1994. *Lifelines and Risks: Pathways of Youth in Our Time*. Cambridge, England: University of Cambridge Press.

Campbell, A., S., Muncer, and B. Gorman. 1993. "Sex and Social Representations of Aggression: A Communal—Agentic Analysis." *Aggressive Behavior* 19: 125-135.

Copeland, E.P., and R.S. Hess. 1995. "Differences in Young Adolescents' Coping Strategies Based on Gender and Ethnicity." *Journal of Early Adolescence* 15(2): 203-219.

Crick, N.R., and J.K. Grotpeter. 1995. "Relational Aggression, Gender, and Social-Psychological Adjustment." *Child Development* 66: 710-722.

Cubitt, T. 1988. *Latin American Society*. New York: Wiley and Sons.

Demo, D.H. 1992. "The Self-Concept Over Time: Research Issues and Directions." *Annual Review of Sociology* 18: 303-326.

Dooley, D., and J. Prause. 1997. "Effect of Students' Self-Esteem on Later Employment Status: Interactions of Self-Esteem with Gender and Race." *Applied Psychology: An International Review* 46(2): 175-198.

Eagly, A.H., and V.J. Steffen. 1986. "Gender and Aggressive Behavior: A Meta-Analytic Review of the Social Psychological Literature." *Psychological Bulletin* 100: 309-330.

Eatough, V., M. Gregson, and M. Shevlin. 1997. "Comments on SP0409: A. Campbell, M. Sapochnik and S. Muncer's Sex Differences in Aggression: Does Social Representation Mediate Form of Aggression? BJSP, 1997, 36, 161-171." *British Journal of Social Psychology* 36(3): 383-384.

Elder, G.H., L.K. George, and M.J. Shanahan. 1996. "Pcyhosocial Stress Over the Life Course." Pp. 247-292 in *Psychosocial Stress: Perspectives on Structure, Theory, Life-Course, and Methods*, edited by H.B. Kaplan. San Diego, CA: Academic Press.

Feldman, S.S., L. Fisher, D.C. Ransom, and S. Dimiceli. 1995. "Is 'What is Good for the Goose Good for the Gander?' Sex Differences in Relations Between Adolescent Coping and Adult Adaptation." *Journal of Research on Adolescence* 5(3): 333-359.

Fitzpatrick, K.M. 1997. "Aggression and Environmental Risk Among Low-Income African-American Youth." *Journal of Adolescent Health* 21(3): 172-178.

Giraldo, O. 1972. "El Machismo Como Fenomeno Psiocultural." *Revista Latino Americana de Psicologia* 4(3): 295-309.

Harris, M.B. 1992. "Sex and Ethnic Differences in Past Aggressive Behaviors." *Journal of Family Violence* 7(2): 85-102.

Harris, M.B., and K, Knight-Bohnhoff. 1996a. "Gender and Aggression I: Perceptions of Aggression." *Sex Roles* 35(1/2): 1-25.

_____. 1996b. "Gender and Aggression II: Personal Aggressiveness." *Sex Roles* 35(1/2): 27-42.

Harter, S. 1990. "Self and Identity Development." Pp. 352-387 in *At the Threshold: The Developing Adolescent*, edited by S. Feldman and G.R. Elliot. Cambridge, MA: Harvard University Press.

Hendry, L. 1987. "Young People: From School to Employment." Pp. 195-218 in *Unemployment: Personal and Social Consequences*, edited by S. Fineman. London: Tavistock.

Hines, N.J., and D.P. Fry. 1994. "Indirect Modes of Aggression Among Women of Buenos Aires, Argentina." *Sex Roles* 30(3/4):213-236.

Hobfoll, S.E., C.L. Dunahoo, Y. Ben-Porath, and J. Monnier. 1994. "Gender and Coping: The Dual-Axis Model of Coping." *American Journal of Community Psychology* 22(1): 49-82.

Hoyle, R.H. (Ed.). 1995. *Structural Equation Modeling: Concepts, Issues and Applications.* Thousand Oaks, CA: Sage Publications.

Hu, L., and P.M. Bentler. 1995. "Evaluating Model Fit". In *Structural Equation Modeling: Concepts, Issues and Applications*, edited by R.H. Hoyle. Thousand Oaks, CA: Sage Publications.

Ingoldsby, B.B. 1991. "The Latin American Family: Familism Vs. Machismo." *Journal of Comparative Family Studies* 22(1): 57-62.

Joreskog, K., and D. Sorbom. 1996. *LISREL 8: User's Reference Guide.* Chicago: Scientific Software International.

Josephs, R., H. Markus, and R. Tafarodi. 1992. "Gender and Self-Esteem." *Journal of Personality and Social Psychology* 63: 391-402.

Kaplan, H.B. 1971. "Age-Related Correlates of Self-Derogation: Contemporary Life Space Characteristics." *Aging and Human Development* 2: 305-313.

_____. 1975. *Self-Attitudes and Deviant Behavior.* Santa Monica, CA: Goodyear.

_____. 1980. *Deviant Behavior in Defense of Self.* New York: Academic Press.

_____. 1982. "Self-Attitudes and Deviant Behavior: New Directions for Theory and Research." *Youth and Society* 14: 185-211.

_____. 1984. *Patterns of Juvenile Delinquency.* Beverly Hills, CA: Sage Publications.

_____. 1986. *Social Psychology of Self-Referent Behavior.* New York: Plenum Press.

_____. 1995. "Drugs, Crime, and Other Deviant Adaptation." Pp. 3-46 in *Drugs, Crime, and other Deviant Adaptations Longitudinal Studies*, edited by H.B. Kaplan. New York: Plenum Press.

_____. 1996. "Psychosocial Stress from the Perspective of Self Theory." Pp. 175-244 in *Psychosocial Stress: Perspectives on Structure, Theory, Life-Course, and Methods*, edited by H.B. Kaplan. San Diego, CA: Academic Press.

Kaplan, H.B., and B.M. Peck. 1992. "Self-Rejection, Coping Style and Mode of Deviant Response." *Social Science Quarterly* 73: 903-919.

Kaplan, H.B., and A.D. Pokorny. 1970. "Age-Related Correlates of Self-Derogation: Report of Childhood Experiences." *British Journal of Psychiatry* 117: 533-534.

_____. 1972. "Sex-Related Correlates of Adult Self-Derogation: Reports of Childhood Experiences." *Developmental Psychology*, 6(3): 536.

Kogut, D., T. Langley, and E.C. O'Neal. 1992. "Gender Role Masculinity and Angry Aggression in Women." *Sex Roles* 26(9/10): 355-68.

Korabik, K., and J. Van Kampen. 1995. "Gender, Social Support, and Coping with Work Stressors among Managers." *Journal of Social Behavior and Personality* 10(6): 135-148.

Langhinrichsen-Rohling, J., and P. Neidig. 1995. "Violent Backgrounds of Economically Disadvantaged Youth: Risk Factors for Perpetrating Violence." *Journal of Family Violence* 10(4): 379-397.

Leadbeater, B.J., S.J. Blatt, and D.M. Quinlan. 1995. "Gender-Linked Vulnerabilities to Depressive Symptoms, Stress, Nad Problem Behaviors in Adolescents." *Journal of Research on Adolescence* 5: 1-29.

Lerner, H.G. 1985. *The Dance of Anger*. New York: Harper and Row.

Lindeman, M., T. Harakka, and L. Keltikangas-Jarvinen. 1997. "Age and Gender Differences in Adolescents' Reactions to Conflict Situations: Aggression, Prosociality, and Withdrawal." *Journal of Youth and Adolescence* 26(3): 339-351.

Loeber, R., and D. Hay. 1997. "Key Issues in the Development of Aggression and Violence from Childhood to Early Adulthood." *Annual Review of Psychology* 48: 371-410.

Martinez, R., and R. Dukes. 1991. "Ethnic and Gender Differences in Self-Esteem." *Youth and Society* 22: 318-338.

Megargee E.I. 1966. "Undercontrolled and Overcontrolled Personality Types in Extreme Antisoical Aggression." *Psychological Monograph* 80: Whole No. 611.

Neff, J.A., T.J. Prihoda, and S.K. Hoppe. 1991. "'Machismo,' Self-Esteem, Education and High Maximum Drinking Among Anglo, Black and Mexican-American Male Drinkers." *Journal of Studies on Alcohol* 52(5): 458-463.

Olah, A. 1995. "Coping Strategies Among Adolescents: A Cross-Cultural Study." *Journal of Adolescence* 18(4): 491-512.

Owens, L.D., and C.E. MacMullin. 1995. "Gender Differences in Aggression in Children and Adolescents in South Australian Schools." *International Journal of Adolescence and Youth* 6(1): 21-35.

Pelak, C.F., V. Taylor, and N. Whittier. 1999. "Gender Movements." Pp. 147-175 in *Handbook of Sociology of Gender*, edited by J.S. Chafetz. New York: Kluwer Academic/Plenum Publishers.

Pepler, D.J., and W.M. Craig. 1995. "A Peek Behind the Fence: Naturalistic Observations of Aggressive Children with Remote Audiovisual Recording." *Developmental Psychology* 31: 548-553.

Pulkkinen, L. 1982. "Self-Control and Continuity from Childhood to Late Adolescence." Pp. 63-105 in *Life-Span Development and Behavior*, edited by P.B. Baltes and O.G. Brim. New York: Academic.

Quintero, G., and A.L. Estrada. 1998. "'Machismo,' Drugs and Street Survival in a U.S.-Mexico Border Community." *Free Inquiry in Creative Sociology* 26(1): 3-10.

Ramos, S. 1951. *The Male Profile and Culture in Mexico*. Buenos Aires, Argentina.

Ross, L.E. 1994. "The Impact of Race-Esteem and Self-Esteem on Delinquency." *Sociological Focus* 27(2): 111-129.

Rys, G.S., and G.G. Bear. 1997. "Relational Aggression and Peer Relations: Gender and Developmental Issues." *Merrill-Palmer Quarterly* 43(1): 87-106.

Stein, J., M. Newcomb, and P. Bentler. 1992. "The Effect of Agency and Communality on Self-Esteem: Gender Differences in Longitudinal Data." *Sex Roles* 26: 465-483.

Stycos, J.M. 1965. "Female Employment and Fertility in Lima, Peru." *Milband Fund Quarterly* 43: 42-54.

Underwood, M.K., J.D. Coie, and C.R. Herbsman. 1992. "Display Rules for Anger and Aggression in School-Age Children." *Child Development* 63: 366-380.

Valdez, A., Z. Yin, and C.D. Kaplan. 1997. "A Comparison of Alcohol, Drugs, and Aggressive Crime Among Mexican-American, Black and White Male Arrestees in Texas." *American Journal of Drug and Alcohol Abuse* 23(2): 249-265.

Wade, T., V. Thompson, A. Tashakkori, and E. Valente. 1989. "A Longitudinal Analysis of Sex by Race Differences in Predictors of Adolescent Self-Esteem." *Personality and Individual Differences* 10: 717-729.

White, J.W., and R.M. Kowalski. 1994. "Deconstructing the Myth of the Nonaggressive Woman." *Psychology of Women Quarterly* 18: 487-508.

SELF, IDENTITY, AND
THE MORAL EMOTIONS
ACROSS THE LIFE COURSE

Timothy J. Owens and Suzanne Goodney

ABSTRACT

This paper explores how guilt and shame interrelate with the self and self-esteem. Using a bidimensional conceptualization of global self-esteem—that is, self-esteem not linked to specific contexts or activities—we propose that guilt is substantially associated with the positive dimension of self-esteem (self-worth) but not the negative dimension (self-deprecation). Conversely, we argue that shame is strongly associated with self-deprecation, but has no appreciable relation to self-worth. We further assert that research with the "moral emotions" of guilt and shame has been frustrated by measures too heavily linked to particular cultures and life course eras. Building on Tangney's Test of Self-Conscious Affect scale (TOSCA), we propose a new Guilt and Shame Scale (GASS) that substantially reduces the class, ethnic, and cultural biases imbedded in the TOSCA scale. Implications of our theoretical and empirical expectations on prosocial behavior and emotional well-being are explored.

Advances in Life Course Research, Volume 5, pages 33-53.
ISBN: 0-7623-0033-7

Before the 1970s, if sociologists discussed emotion at all, it was invariably secondary to their main theoretical or empirical concerns (MacKinnon 1994). This stance is undoubtedly rooted to some extent in the post-World War II ascendancy of functionalist views in sociology and the dominance of rational actor ideologies. Beginning in the late 1970s, however, the theoretical paradigm shifted in favor of a more comprehensive and purposeful examination of the role of emotion in sociological discourse, precipitated in great measure by Kemper's (1978) influential work on emotion and interaction. Indeed, Kemper opened his book by observing:

> There are many theories of emotion, but none is sociological. This is astonishing, because in most cases the actions of others toward us, or our actions toward them, have instigated joy, sadness, anger, or despair. Thus an effort to explain emotions as a product of social interaction is long overdue (Kemper 1978, p. 1).

This comment presaged a spate of important books and articles which began to do just that; among them, Denzin (1984), Heise (1979), Hochschild (1979, 1983), Scheff (1979), and Shott (1979). Scarcely a decade later, the American Sociological Association approved a new section devoted to "the study of . . . emotions in social life, emotionality in research, and the integration of emotions into all appropriate areas of sociological research" (American Sociological Association Section on the Sociology of Emotions "Purpose Statement" 1988).

Our paper and its modest proposal builds on the earlier sociological work on emotions, integrates ideas from identity and self-esteem theory, and attempts to break new groud in the search for a broad conceptualization of the self and emotions nexus which is responsive to culture and the human life course. In particular, we attempt to connect the concept of the moral emotions of guilt and shame with self-esteem theory and, in so doing, generate a longer-term effort to integrate emotion and self-esteem theory into the literatures on social control, prosocial behavior, and mental health. In the present paper, we will assert that guilt and shame have a unique relation to self-esteem and that an understanding of that relationship is fundamentally advanced by taking identity, culture, and the life course into account. We examine guilt and shame, the so-called moral emotions, for two reasons.[1] First, they are interesting theoretically because of: (1) their hypothesized relationship to the formation and maintenance of the self; and (2) the important role they play in social behavior, especially that which might be called prosocial, or behavior oriented toward supporting, upholding, or otherwise reflecting the norms and standards of conduct society considers decent and proper. The impetus for these expectations stems from preliminary data reported elsewhere (Owens 1993) suggesting that guilt and shame are differentially related to aspects of global self-esteem: namely, the subdimensions of general self-worth and general self-denigration. Examining the interplay, then, promises to shed significant light on the behavior of both self-esteem and these moral emotions, our second motivation. Before discussing that contention further, however, we begin with an overview of our theoretical frames and key concepts.

OVERVIEW

Self-Esteem Theory

Self-esteem may be defined as a "positive or negative attitude toward a particular object, namely, the self" (Rosenberg 1965, p. 30). Persons with high self-esteem possess respect for themselves and enjoy feelings of worthiness, pride, and satisfaction, all while acknowledging they certainly have faults and shortcomings. It is thus crucial to note that high self-esteem is not equivalent to overweening pride, arrogance, or narcissism. On the other hand, persons with low self-esteem characteristically lack self-respect, tend to acknowledge only their faults and weaknesses, and thus come to define themselves as seriously flawed and unworthy (Rosenberg and Owens forthcoming).

Self-esteem is both a social product and a social force (Rosenberg 1981). As a social product, the social origins of the self-concept in general and self-esteem in particular are investigated. Such inquiries tend to be of particular interest to sociologists. Following a symbolic interactionist framework, it can be taken axiomatically that the self arises—socially—through the innumerable encounters we have with self and others, including specific groups, institutions, and society itself. Self-esteem theory helps explain how this occurs. Codifying a century of research on the self, Rosenberg (1979) outlined four principles of self-esteem formation: (1) The principle of *reflected appraisals* is central to the symbolic interactionist's insistence that (a) the self is a social product derived from the attitudes and behaviors others exhibit toward one's self, and that (b) individuals eventually come to see themselves as they believe others do (Cooley 1902; Mead 1934). (2) Through *social comparisons*, people judge and evaluate themselves vis-à-vis particular individuals, groups, and social categories. Social comparisons are rooted in two mechanisms: criteria-based and normative-based comparisons. Through criteria-based comparisons, people judge themselves in relation to others as superior or inferior, better or worse, or morally equal or inferior. Via normative-based comparisons, people perceive themselves to be deviant or conforming with respect to others, or the same as or different than others. (3) The concept of *self-attribution* holds that individuals draw conclusions about their qualities and characteristics (e.g., "I am...compassionate/popular/ugly/athletic, etc.) by observing their own actions and the outcomes of those actions. (4) The principle of *psychological centrality* holds that the self is an interrelated system of hierarchically organized components wherein some identities and attributes are rendered more important to the self than others. According to psychological centrality, the self essentially helps protect self-esteem by pushing potentially damaging self-attributes and identities to the periphery of the self system while holding enhancing attributes closer to the center.

Being aware of and sensitive to these theoretical underpinnings of self-esteem is fundamental to posing reasonable hypotheses, accurately interpreting empirical data on the self, and making sound conclusions and extensions. And, as we shall argue in reference to the interplay between the moral emotions and self-esteem, these underpinnings also highlight the necessity of taking identity, culture, and the life course into account. We turn now to our operationalization and conceptualization of self-esteem.

A Self-Esteem Construct

Self-esteem scales abound and we will make no attempt to comment on them as a body. Instead, our articulation of self-esteem comes from the well-known Rosenberg Self-Esteem Scale (Rosenberg 1979). It is particularly appropriate because of its wide use across many social and behavioral science fields, its brevity, its well-documented psychometric properties, and its known association with other relevant variables. Most of all, this scale is useful here because it allows for a general measure of self-worth that is not tied to any particular role, identity, social context, or even life course era.[2] Using this general conception and measurement of self-esteem is in no way meant to imply that role-related or identity-related conceptions of self-esteem should be overlooked or deemed irrelevant. In fact, Rosenberg (1979; Rosenberg, Schooler, Schoenbach, and Rosenberg 1995), extending the theoretical work of James (1890), has argued forcefully for recognizing that global self-esteem is shaped by the esteem an individual ascribes to her[3] various self-attributes (e.g., identities, roles, and personal qualities), which are in turn shaped by the psychological centrality of these attributes within the individual's self system. Our employment of a general measure of self-esteem is arguably merited in addition by our desire to establish a foundation for assessing the relationship of guilt and shame to self-esteem which might be applicable to a variety of cultures and life course eras. We address this issue in more detail later.

The Rosenberg Self-Esteem Scale is a 10-item Likert-type scale evenly divided between statements connoting a positive attitude toward the self or a negative one, indicating feelings of self-worth and self-denigration, respectively. Response options typically include strongly agree, agree, disagree, or strongly disagree. Prior confirmatory factor analyses of this self-esteem construct have shown it to be adequately structured, factorially invariant[4] across contiguous age groups, and bidimensional with respect to its self-worth and self-denigration subdimensions. The ideas put forth in this paper rely on a bidimensional view of general self-esteem (Owens 1993, 1994; Owens and King forthcoming; Owens, Mortimer, and Finch 1996; Wright, Gronfein, and Owens 2000).

A Bidimensional View of Self-Esteem

A bidimensional view of *general* self-esteem, and of Rosenberg's construct in particular, acknowledges that self-esteem can be legitimately conceptualized and empirically divided along generally positive and generally negative subdimensions, as reflected on the two self-esteem subscales (Owens 1993). The positive component of self-esteem, referred to as self-worth, includes not only the degree to which one is self-assured of one's capacities but also the degree to which one believes in his or her moral worth or virtue (see Gecas 1982; Owens 1993). Examples of items representing self-worth are: "I feel that I am a person of worth, at least the equal of others; I feel that I have a number of good qualities; and I take a positive attitude toward myself." Self-deprecation, on the other hand, is the self-critical and negative part of self-esteem—the degree to which individuals disparage themselves and characterize themselves as fundamentally inadequate, disreputable, inferior, or otherwise seriously flawed. Examples of items representing self-denigration are: "All in all, I am inclined to feel that I am a failure; I feel I do not have much to be proud of; at times I think I am no good at all." The result is a conceptualization of self-esteem divided empirically along generally positive and generally negative subdimensions, as reflected on the two self-esteem subscales. This distinction also recognizes that one can be "simultaneously confident of one's capacities and critical of oneself" (Kohn 1977, p. 82).

In a previous examination of the theoretical importance of bidimensional general self-esteem, Owens (1993) employed self-esteem theory to link: (1) theories of self-verification and positivity strivings (Swann, Seroussi, and Giesler 1992) to self-deprecation, and (2) self-efficacy theory and the motivation to be effective in one's life to the positive dimension of self-esteem (see also Gecas 1982; Gecas and Schwalbe 1983; Greenwald 1980). That paper demonstrated that self-deprecation occurs in people who are at variance with themselves and others and who report experiencing heightened psychological and emotional distress. Further, self-worth was linked to prosocial attitudes and behaviors and to psychological and social well-being.

Applying self-deprecation and self-worth—a bidimensional view of self-esteem—to guilt and shame is a logical and potentially fruitful next step in a better understanding of the moral emotions under consideration. Indeed, as MacKinnon (1994, 1998) correctly argues, while self-image is the cognitive dimension of the self-concept, self-esteem is one's affective response to it. Self-worth evokes positive emotions (e.g., happiness, pride), while self-deprecation elicits negative emotions (e.g., depression, anxiety). Consequently, the study of self-esteem implicitly engages one in the study of emotions (MacKinnon 1998). And it is within one's identities and social roles that these processes play out; hence, it is eminently reasonable for an individual to feel pride through the fulfillment of one salient role and utterly inadequate in another. The upshot is a person—through this complex hierarchy of identities, roles, and experiences—

who simultaneously feels varying degrees of self-denigration and self-worth conterminously and in parallel.

IDENTITY THEORY

The identity theory employed here stems from a structural symbolic interactionist framework (Stryker 1980).[5] Like symbolic interactionism generally, the structural identity framework emphasizes the importance of the socially produced, reflexive self (Mead 1934). More specifically, since self emerges from social interaction, it reflects the qualities and the structure of the society where the interaction occurs. Consequently, if one wants to investigate the self in a given society, one must be prepared to ultimately grapple with the nature and structure of the society within which that self emerges.

Stryker, for instance, tackles the problem by incorporating social structure into his theoretical framework by using the concept of identity commitment. Instead of focusing on subjective commitments (e.g., declarations of presumed importance), he argues the merits of ascribing identities to the number or affective importance of *social ties* that link individuals to particular identities: "A man is committed to the role of 'husband' to the degree that the number of persons and the importance to him of those persons requires his being in the position of husband playing that role" (Stryker and Serpe 1982, p. 207). Identity is also a cognitive schema capable of screening information from the individual's external world. As a result, an identity and its associated salience serves a delimiting function by simplifying input from the outside world, which makes behavioral and affective choices more scrutable. We will expand upon identity salience and commitment shortly.

Present-day sociology recognizes that since most contemporary societies are highly complex and differentiated, so too are the selves which flow from and interact with them. Yet, unlike earlier personality (e.g., Allport 1961; Lecky 1945) and sociological theorists (e.g., Mead 1934; Parsons 1951) who tended toward a more unitary conception of the self, contemporary identity theorists envision a self which possesses multiple modalities—composed of, for instance, the cognitive ("I am"), the cathectic ("I feel"), and the conative ("I want") (see Stryker 1980). Furthermore, theory and research on the "cognitive modality of self" has established that there are "as many identities as the individual holds distinct roles in networks of social relationships" (Ervin and Stryker forthcoming).

As Figure 1 illustrates, identity theory originally sought to explain role-related behavior via a three-part causal chain.

Role-related behaviors, which are predicted by identity commitment and identity salience, involve choices among identities, such as a writer choosing to spend the evening reworking a manuscript rather than attending her child's soccer game. But it also involves identity contingencies and imperatives, such as the same writer

Identity Commitment → Identity Salience → Role-Related Behavior

Figure 1. Simple Causal Relations among Commitment, Salience, and Role Behavior

getting a telephone call from her daughter (invoking the mother role) pleading for her work at the snack bar during half-time (invoking her volunteer role).

Identity commitment may be broadly defined as the *strength* of one's ties to an organized network of social relations in terms of a particular identity and that identity's associated roles (Stryker 1980). Stryker and Serpe (1994) have recently distinguished interactional commitments from affective commitments, which, though related, may nevertheless operate independently. Interactional commitments are defined by the extensiveness[6] of a social network to which one relates by virtue of a given identity. Affective commitments, which are especially relevant to this discussion, refer to the *emotional significance* of others in one's given social networks.

The concept of identity salience, on the other hand, assumes that a person's identities are organized into a hierarchy defined by the *probability* that they might be invoked in or across social situations (Stryker 1980). The higher one's identity salience in relation to other identities held by an individual, the more likely the person is to invoke that identity, as when a person's ethnic identity is more often invoked over his occupational identity.[7] Furthermore, an elaboration of identity theory has shown that identity salience and psychological centrality, used here to connote one's subjective sense of an identity's importance, are related but largely independent (Stryker and Serpe 1994). While both have implications for role-related choices, identity salience explicitly recognizes the importance of an individual's structural embeddedness on the probability that a given identity will be invoked, regardless of the person's intention for or against the invocation.[8] Finally, while Stryker relies on traditional symbolic interactionist principles to defend the basic directional impact that each of these three variables has, he also recognizes that role-related behaviors can influence identity, which, in turn, impact commitments (Ervin and Stryker forthcoming). The modified causal relationships are illustrated in Figure 2.

SHAME AND GUILT

The Concept of Shame

We begin with shame because it is one of our most deeply felt emotions, arguably even a master emotion (Lewis 1992; Scheff 1988). Shame is central to human existence; scarcely a person who has lived, past or present, within and

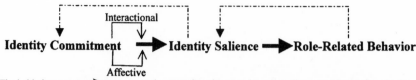

The bolded arrows (➤) represent the prevailing directionality originally posited by Stryker, the thinner arrows (➤) signify the elaborated bifurcation of interactional commitments, while the dashed arrows (---➤) illustrate the theory's current acknowledgement of the of secondary feedback loops.

Figure 2.   Elaborated Causal Relations among Commitment, Salience, and Role Behavior

across cultures, from child to octogenarian, has not at one time or another felt the flash or smolder of shame. As a repudiation of the self, shame encompasses the whole of us; "it generates a wish to hide, to disappear, or even to die" (Lewis 1992, p. 2). It has been linked to a number of emotional states such as depression, rage, and anxiety as well as to such behaviors as aggression, violence, withdrawal, and suicide (Kemper 1978; Lewis 1992; Scheff and Retzinger 1992). Shame, or the threat of it, influences many aspects of human lives, from the middle-aged Indian struggling to avoid bringing shame upon himself or his family by failing to care for his elderly parents to the somnolent high school sophomore upbraided by his first period teacher to the mentally alert, though frail, elderly matriarch who must increasingly rely on others for her intimate day-to-day care. Recognizing shame in others and ourselves can be rather easy, though inexact, since it is frequently accompanied by visible signs (Nathanson 1992). This is generally true because shame has the ability to substantially afflict a person's mental processes and body (e.g., muscle tone and blood flow to the head and neck) (Nathanson 1992). Still, succinctly defining this emotional state is much more difficult. Broadly speaking, we define it here as:

> the feeling derived by reflecting on one's thoughts or behaviors and concluding that one has done or thought something sufficiently wrong, careless or disgraceful that he or she may likely be fundamentally *bad* or *disreputable*.

Here, the final cognitive attribution and conclusion is key. One is bad, disreputable, and quite possibly disgusting in the eyes of self and, the shamed individual presumes, other people, especially if they are salient to his identity. The attribution is squarely focussed on the nature and quality of the individual; the conclusion the individual draws—or believes others have or will draw—is that he is bad; a potentially unfit human being; unwanted, unloved, and quite possibly despised.[9] And while specific adjectives used to label the ugly self vary within and across cultures and the life course, the shamed person's self has been exposed and stripped naked with little or no opportunity for concealment or evasion (see Lewis 1992; Lynd 1958; Piers and Singer 1953). Once this flawed self has been laid bare, there is, in terms of the self definitions and emerging identity of the shamed, little recourse but to shrink from view, minimize one's self, and try to wait for the resulting feelings to subside. It is conceivable that the shamed individual, particularly if from a "shame culture" such as Japan (Benedict 1946), may even wish to annihilate the self through suicide. More broadly, and without the specific cultural referent, this is Goffman's (1963) discreditable stigma realized.

In the sense used here, shame is primarily derived from some misdeed or negative behavior that has been detected, or that one assumes will be detected, by another, by God or Allah, by one's family or community. It is important to recognize that while the violation of deep-seated taboos may constitute nearly universal sources of shame when exposed (e.g., incest, patricide), the shame-inducing events people typically encounter are socially and culturally defined and thus highly diverse. Furthermore, as a socially-defined construct, behaviors deemed shameful in one culture, context, or point in the life course are not necessarily shameful in others. This observation begs a question. If shame is culturally defined, must social scientists who desire to study it restrict themselves to constructs particular to a given culture and appropriate to specific life course eras? The answer to this can be both yes and no depending on one's ultimate goal. In the almost complete absence of any well-established guilt and shame research instruments, such considerations must, for now, remain speculative. If one's aim is to examine shame as a social force (e.g., causing destructive behavior toward self or others, withdrawal, or depression) then one need not necessarily use a culturally specific conceptualization or measure of shame. Detecting it's general presence or propensity may be sufficient. The guilt and shame scale we propose later in the paper takes this approach. However, if one wants to examine shame as a social product, one must attend to the social, cultural, institutional, and historical influences which give rise to beliefs about shame in particular cultures and life course eras.[10] Here, too, attention might also be profitably directed toward the modal role-behaviors associated with particular identities within a given culture or life course era.[11] It is amidst examination of these normative expectations that we can begin to examine the concept of guilt as it relates to self processes.

The Concept of Guilt

Unlike shame, guilt generally does not penetrate the self as deeply, painfully, or fundamentally. It nevertheless remains a powerful and impressible emotion (Lewis 1992; Nathanson 1992). Guilt may be distinguished from shame not only by a matter of the degree of potential pain and discomfort it can generate, but, more importantly, by its emphasis on the violation of a group's norms or rules. It assigns fault by focussing on one's *actions or behaviors*, but without taking the further step of specifically trying to damn the self or suggest that it is fundamentally flawed. Guilt may be further viewed as the result of a social transgression accompanied by *fear* of retribution, temporal or "divine." Although guilt has drawn less attention in the social sciences than shame,[12] it is sociologically ripe and begs serious attention. In the language of symbolic interactionism, guilt can be thought to emanate from the generalized other (Mead 1934), or society's "internal representative" in the self. It arises from the recognition that one has violated internalized values and norms (Lynd 1958), which presupposes a relatively developed self. No such assumption seems to necessarily apply to shame; indeed, researchers have reported observing shame in infants (see Nathanson 1992).

A manifestation of the presupposition of a developed self is reflected in the "little adult assumption" grown-ups sometimes apply to children (Phelan 1995). The controlling belief here is that children would cease their annoying and errant behavior if they could be made to understand their behavior in terms of its *consequences* for others, as adults typically do. This is essentially an appeal to the child's capacity to experience guilt over the violation of particular rules and norms. A problem occurs when the child's developmental imperatives are not taken into account, which in turn demands that the child negotiate mental processes of which she may not yet be entirely capable. In short, invoking the "little adult assumption" by attempting to conjure feelings of guilt in a young child is frequently ineffectual. However, it can serve an anticipatory socialization function by rehearsing for later feelings of guilt.

The foregoing discussion leads to our general definition of guilt, which employs aspects of the previous definition of shame but with the adjustment of adding the concept of behavioral attribution. Guilt may be broadly defined as:

> the feeling derived by evaluating one's thoughts or behaviors and concluding that those *thoughts or behaviors* are inappropriate or wrong because they violate rules or norms of conduct typically valued by the individual and his or her group or society.

In terms of social control, then, guilt is more internally based, while shame is more externally based, or predicated upon disapproval coming from outside the person (Lynd 1958). To use a Christian analogy, guilt is equivalent to hating the sin, shame to hating the sinner.

Toward a More Bias Free Measure of Shame and Guilt

In this section we introduce a new measure of shame and guilt that seeks to overcome some of the cultural and life course biases in other measures, most notably Tangney's (Tangney, Wagner, and Gramzow 1989). No measure of these emotions can avoid some form of bias, for, as we have argued, though guilt and shame may be nearly universal emotions, the cues triggering them can be culturally specific. And while Tangney's Test of Self-Conscious Affect (TOSCA) is a good start, several of its cues and responses have marked biases toward college educated middle and upper-middle class adult European Americans. For instance, several of its branch and stem questions revolve around work and completing work projects. While the former presumes a certain life course experience, the latter tends to presume professional or managerial work-roles, an assumption to which many blue-collar and manual workers would have difficulty relating. In addition, several words and phrases connote a middle class vocabulary (e.g., "inconsiderate," "witty") or sensibility (e.g., "volunteer to help with the local Special Olympics," "out with friends one evening").

Our guilt and shame scale (GASS) (see the Appendix) builds on some of Tangney's (1995, 1996) innovations but attempts to broaden its applicability to more life course eras (e.g., pre-work teenhood), social classes, and ethnic groups. We have selected our branch and stem questions with language and cues as neutral and general as possible while still connoting scenarios of guilt-proneness and shame-proneness that are general enough for most Americans (at least) to relate, even if they have not actually experienced them. When speaking of "proneness" we are essentially gauging the degree to which people know or recognize guilt and shame, not necessarily the degree to which they might be in a state of guilt or shame at the time of the interview. After pretesting a number of questions with a sample of college students from a wide-range of socioeconomic, ethnic, age, work, and regional backgrounds, we identified 10 branch questions each with two stems illustrative of guilt or shame. Initial analysis of comments and suggestions made by the subjects give us confidence that the measures have face validity. However, at the time of this printing, data on the scale's validity and reliability among a general population has not been analyzed, including the estimation of a measurement model. The latter is an essential next step in the development of our new scale and for understanding the extent to which guilt and shame covary.

The GASS scale's 10 items revolve around behaviors or actions that might be classified as acts commission, omission, and carelessness, with the former being the most prevalent. All questions, however, deal with breaches of folkways and mores. The scenarios involve common occurrences that most people in the United States from adolescence onward are likely to have experienced or at least relate to. The shame responses connote generalized self-reproach or an impulse to hide, thus following the inward punishment paradigm illustrated earlier. The guilt responses, on the other hand, connote generalized efforts toward restoration or conciliation, thus being outwardly directed though inwardly felt.

The Self-Esteem/Moral Emotions Nexus

We turn now to a theory linking self-esteem to the moral emotions of guilt and shame. Our argument hinges on the two-dimensional view of general self-esteem discussed earlier. The impetus for this inquiry stems from preliminary empirical evidence (Owens 1993) suggesting that, as self-deprecation increases, expressed feelings of shame (as measured by a single item on the ten-

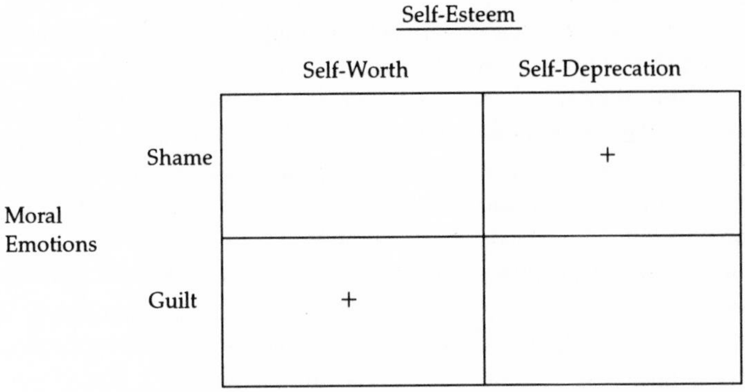

Self-Esteem

	Self-Worth	Self-Deprecation
Shame		+
Guilt	+	

Moral Emotions (row label for Shame/Guilt)

Figure 3.   Theoretial Relationship of Self-Esteem Dimensions and
Moral Emotions

dency to blame oneself when things go wrong) also increases ($r = .17$, $p < .05$). The relation of shame to self-worth, however, is not significant. Conversely, as self-worth increases, expressed feelings of guilt (as measured by a single item on feeling punished by one's conscience after having done something wrong) also increase ($r = .14$, $p < .05$).[13] That is, people with high self-worth expressed more feelings of guilt than those with low self-worth. The relationship of guilt to self-deprecation was not significant. Figure 3 illustrates these hypothesized relationships. The plus sign (+) indicates the expectation of an empirical relationship between self-esteem and the moral emotions while a blank cell denotes the presumption of no empirical relationship.

If the relationships depicted in Figure 3 hold up to further testing, they are potentially very interesting on methodological, theoretical, and substantive grounds. Methodologically, these findings suggest further evidence that global self-esteem may be composed of distinct parts, which though linked, nevertheless behave independently. Theoretically and substantively, the hypothesized relations suggest that guilt, albeit in reasonable doses, since we are not addressing morbid guilt or abnormal psychology, can have a positive impact on the self while shame tends to have a negative one. Why? Again, guilt is a powerful emotion predicated on the recognition that one has violated accepted norms, that one has failed to meet one's own expectations for one's self or one's group. Pangs of conscience or guilt directly link with one's *positive* sense of self. And following a long tradition in arguing the prepotency of the self-esteem motive (Maslow 1970; Kaplan 1975), guilt affects the self-concept by threatening one's *positive* feelings toward the self. Such feeling may direct people's attention *outward* toward the wronged other, thus steering the transgressor's future social participation in a more constructive and rewarding manner and evoking healthy prosocial behavior which carries with it the possibility of a reconciliation with self or others. Guilt thus carries with it the possibility of its own corrective, or some means by which amends or reparations can be made. The net result is the distinct possibility of an enhancement and empowerment of the self leading to the restoration of self-worth.

Shame, on the other hand, appears to have a very different effect on the self. Unlike guilt, once triggered, shame turns profoundly inward. It is associated with self-deprecation because it embodies a sharp and painful reproach of the person and the self, which places the self in a varying state of condemnation and disgrace, which highlights the person's unworthiness, weakness, and other *negative* features. Shame may be sparked from the outside (as Benedict 1946 would argue), but its impact is decidedly internal. Shame, then, awakens the negative dimension of the self, or one's feelings of self-deprecation (see Goffman's [1963] concept of discreditable stigma). Also, shame, unlike guilt, adds to a person's memory of *personal* failings and forces the individual to consider who she was before shame ensued and to what sense of self and identity she will return when the shame subsides (Nathanson 1992, p. 211). Finally, shame is a "crisis emotion" (Scheff 1994, p. 40), which may be expressed inwardly by means of self-punishment and, occasionally, suicide or outwardly via interpersonal violence and aggression (Gilligan 1996), as in the shame-rage spiral which has been argued to lead to some expressions of domestic violence (Scheff and Retzinger 1992).[14]

Under the rubric of the self/shame nexus, "shame is the affect most likely to direct attention to the *nature of the self*. Shame produces a painful self-awareness at every stage in human development simply because of the ability of this affect script to interfere with every pleasant way in which we know ourselves" (Nathanson 1992, p. 211, emphasis added). A bidimensional approach to general self-esteem helps to bring into sharper relief the nuances and subtleties of this emotion's impact on the self. Unlike guilt, and still consistent with the self-esteem motive, shame's power over the self-concept works by driving up painful negative feelings toward the self. Shame, for example, can make the ordinarily high self-esteem person feel terrible about himself and bring to the fore, even if only temporarily, the discomfort, confusion, avoidance, and depression associated with low self-esteem people (see Rosenberg and Owens forthcoming).

Incorporating aspects of identity theory discussed earlier can further our understanding of the self-esteem/moral emotions nexus. One of the merits of drawing on theories of self-esteem and identity in the examination of the moral emotions is their potential for elucidating situational, "spontaneous," emotional responses,[15] while bringing important aspects of the self to the forefront. For instance, think back to a time when you became unexpectedly angry or upset about something, with intensity seemingly disproportional to the stimulus. Perhaps you were just arriving at work when a co-worker asked, "Where were you yesterday?" in reference to you missing a routine faculty meeting the previous afternoon. That question, that single stimulus, may have caused you flashes of alternating anger and shame through the rest of the day. You may have even felt a little guilty at the implied suggestion that you shirked a duty. Why? It was not the first faculty meeting you missed, and it certainly will not be the last. The sociologically interesting point lies in examining the possible roles played by identity salience and commitment, as well as reflected appraisals, self-attribution, and psychological centrality, in your reaction and its aftermath.

In terms of identity salience (the probability of an identity being enacted within or across social situations), the question, in the situation in which it arose, would have immediately catapulted your "faculty identity" to the fore and called your commitment to it into question. If the "faculty identity" is a salient one (the reader will please recall that identity also encompasses a cognitive schema), then one's attention would likely have been focussed upon the circumstances and associated role-based behaviors surrounding the missed meeting. Perhaps your "parent identity" had been invoked because your child got sick at school and you needed to pick her up, causing you to miss the meeting. If so, perhaps you would be angry with your colleague for intimating that your actions were other than the dutiful fulfillment of an important social role. Perhaps instead you had decided to go to a nursery and buy mulch for your roses, thus invoking your "gardener identity." It seemed like a good idea at the time and, you may have presumed, your absence at the faculty meeting probably wouldn't be commented on. Now, however, you might be feeling guilt or shame because of your actions and the fact that they were pointed out to you. The theoretically important point is that both emotions were mediated by your self-concept and identity via your identity salience hierarchy and identity commitment.

CONCLUSIONS AND IMPLICATIONS

In this paper, we argue that guilt and shame play an essential role in the maintenance of society by regulating not only deviant behavior, but behavior that a culture generally deems counter to expected standards of decent conduct. Without these emotions, and the cultural codes of conduct they embody and reinforce, social control would be especially problematic. However, the measurement of guilt and shame has not been very satisfactory. A primary reason for this lapse is the inherent difficulty in designing a construct that is not overly tied to a particular culture (or subculture) or life course era. We propose a brief guilt and shame scale that assesses the degree to which individuals "know" or are "prone" to experiencing these emotions, without undue reliance on culturally specific cues which people from different social class and ethnic backgrounds, for instance, would have difficulty relating. Much work remains in both the validation and refinement of our measure, and in the further explication of the self-esteem/moral emotions nexus. Still, we see merit in pursuing such an integration, but argue that future research must also seriously consider the role of identity, culture, and life course in the quest.

APPENDIX
GUILT AND SHAME SCALE (GASS)

Read each statement and tell us how <u>likely or unlikely</u> you would respond to the two options provided. If it has never happened to you, make your best guess of how you would probably act. It is important to answer both options.

	Very Likely	Somewhat Likely	Somewhat Unlikely	Very Unlikely
1. You make plans to meet a friend at a specific time and place but then don't show up.				
a) *You worry that your friend must really think you're a jerk.	1	2	3	4
b) You try to apologize to your friend as soon as you can.	1	2	3	4
2. While in a store, you accidentally break something cheap—but nobody saw you do it.				
a) You tell a clerk what happened.	1	2	3	4
b) *You try to leave the store as quickly as possible, avoiding eye contact with other people.	1	2	3	4
3. You make a mistake and later find out someone you know got blamed for it.				
a) *You say nothing and largely avoid the person who was blamed.	1	2	3	4
b) You try to correct the situation.	1	2	3	4
4. You make a commitment to stop a bad habit but quickly fall back into your old ways.				
a) You try to make up for it by putting extra effort into stopping.	1	2	3	4
b) *You feel disgusted with your lack of will power and self-control.	1	2	3	4

	Very Likely	Somewhat Likely	Somewhat Unlikely	Very Unlikely
5. While walking down the street you throw a piece of paper in a wastebasket but it misses.				
a) *You scurry away hoping no one saw you.	1	2	3	4
b) You don't want to be a litterbug so you go back and put it in.	1	2	3	4
6. A friend tells you a personal secret and you promise not to repeat it. A few days later you find out your friend knows you actually told someone else.				
a) *You avoid your friend for a while.	1	2	3	4
b) You try to apologize to your friend as soon as possible.	1	2	3	4
7. You know a person with a problem and give them some advice. It makes things a lot worse for them.				
a) *You pray your friend never mentions the bad advice.	1	2	3	4
b) You apologize to the person as soon as can.	1	2	3	4
8. You tell someone you know a lie about yourself.				
a) *Later you worry a lot that they might find out and think you're a liar.	1	2	3	4
b) Later you think to yourself that you really shouldn't have done that because lying isn't right.	1	2	3	4

	Very Likely	Somewhat Likely	Somewhat Unlikely	Very Unlikely
9. You mistreat a pet.				
a) Later, you make a special effort to be nice to the animal.	1	2	3	4
b) *You think: "I'm a really awful person. What sort of person is mean to an animal?"	1	2	3	4
10. You tell an off-color joke and someone says, "That's disgusting."				
a) You say that you didn't mean any harm, that you were only joking.	1	2	3	4
b) *You wish you could just disappear.	1	2	3	4

Key: * designates shame.

ACKNOWLEDGMENTS

The first author gratefully acknowledges the support of a National Research Service Award from the National Institute of Mental Health (PHST 32 MH 14588) during the preparation of the manuscript. An earlier version of the paper was presented at the conference on "Identity through the Life Course in Cross-Cultural Perspective," The Life Course Center, University of Minnesota, May 7-8, 1998. We thank the participants and discussant for helpful comments. All deficiencies, of course, are the sole responsibility of the authors.

NOTES

1. While others might qualify as "moral emotions" (e.g., moral outrage, indignation), the nature of guilt and shame, as we will argue later, are particularly implicated in socially approved and disapproved behavior.

2. The Rosenberg Self-Esteem Scale is typically not used among grade-school-aged children.

3. We interchange male and female pronouns throughout the paper in the service of concision.

4. Factorial (or structural) invariance exists when a construct measured over time retains the same dimensions and pattern of relations among the observed indicators used to measure it.

5. See Thoits and Virshup 1997 for an extended comparison of various approaches to identity research.

6.   Network extensiveness refers to such things as the number of people befriended within a given network, as well as the time, energy, and resources one devotes to activities within a network (see Stryker, Owens, and White 2000).

7.   Imagine, for example, a person who is being interviewed by a dating referral service and is asked: "Tell us about yourself so that we know you." This person might reply, "I am Puerto Rican, college educated, a professional, athletic, and an ex-Catholic." In this instance five salient identities have been expressed, though the person certainly possesses others which have not arisen in this situation. If so interested, the interviewer could easily create a salience hierarchy for this customer with respect to the five identities mentioned. One way to do so would be to ask the customer to imagine that he is introducing himself to another person amidst a particular social setting (e.g., a volunteer committee, a jury-pool waiting room, or a neighborhood block party). The person would then be asked to rank which of the five identities they would most likely mention first, second, and so on in each of the specified settings. The salience hierarchy would consist of the orderings of these identities from most to least frequently invoked across settings.

8.   An extreme, though apt, example of this phenomenon is illustrated by the couple that shuttered their two young daughters inside their suburban Chicago home and forbade them to use the lights or open the curtains while the parents traveled to Acapulco for a Christmas holiday. Upon deplaning in Chicago after returning from their trip, and completely unaware they were under suspicion, the *parent* identity which they seemed to have been attempting to temporarily escape was suddenly and dramatically made salient when the police arrested them at the gate in Chicago amidst a mob of reporters, camerapersons, and angry bystanders.

9.   Such conclusions are readily apparent when one looks at a typical childhood shaming experience, as when one's parent says, "Look at what *you have done*. Shame on you; you're a *bad boy!*"

10.   If one seeks to address shame (and guilt) more as a social force which impacts self and society, one should certainly be aware that cultural and life course differences exist, but that does not necessarily preclude the development of measures appropriate within or across several cultures or phases of the life course. Still, at this point, an all-purpose, universal, instrument is probably unattainable. Cultural variation across *all* human societies is simply too great. Language differences also present formidable obstacles to cognitive and emotional meanings across wide linguistic groups (Wierzbicka 1992). However, if we can assume that shame (and guilt), if not completely ubiquitous, is at least represented in a vast number of cultures and societies, then a promising and theoretically compelling step would be to develop measures general enough to apply to an array of cultures and subcultures, as well as being relevant to women and men and people with different racial, ethnic, and social class backgrounds.

11.   Identity here refers broadly to what it means to be who one is (Gecas and Burke 1995).

12.   An exception might be that of legal guilt, which is beyond the scope of this paper.

13.   It must be recognized that these modest associations are based on zero-order correlations stemming from rather inexact, single, measures suggestive of shame and guilt. Furthermore, the sample used consisted of white adolescent boys attending American public high schools. The developing theory does not depend on these correlations, and much empirical work awaits more satisfactory measures of these complex concepts.

14.   Gilligan's (1996) work offers compelling evidence that shame acts as an engine for violence. He contends that, for males especially, a pervasive feeling of acute, deep shame is often masked by "machismo" and that the "snap" into aggression effectively functions as a means of self-maintenance for an individual who largely lacks guilt, or, in symbolic interactionist terms, an internalized sense of the generalized other. Such individuals are more prone toward reacting to an "attack" on their selves violently because they have a decreased awareness of the generalized other, or the social commonalities they share with diverse others, which effectively serves as a buffer system for the self. A person not overwhelmed by shame and its resulting negative self-view is not so likely to internalize blame or critical comments. An individual who is punished regularly and harshly, for example, does not develop this internal barometer. Straus's (1994) work on the disciplining of children in American fam-

ilies underlines this thesis and questions Gottfredson and Hirschi's (1990) identification of ineffective parenting, defined as parents not recognizing and punishing deviant behavior, as the major catalyst of low self-control in future adults. A punitive approach to socialization may in fact draw too much on shame thereby weighting the self-esteem with a negative, defensive anchor.

15. This is quite different from the socialized emotional responses governed by, for example, feeling rules (Hochschild 1979, 1983). Any resultant aggressive behavior is, then, arguably less a function of low self-control that of self-defensive postures elicited in interaction.

REFERENCES

Allport, G.W. 1961. *Pattern and Growth in Personality*. New York: Holt, Rinehart and Winston.

American Sociological Association Section on the Sociology of Emotions. 1998. Available at http://www.asanet.org//Sections/emotions.htm.

Benedict, R. 1946. *The Chrysanthemum and the Sword: Patterns of Japanese Culture*. Boston: Houghton Mifflin.

Cooley, C.H. 1902. *Human Nature and the Social Order*. New York: Charles Scribner's Sons.

Denzin, N. 1984. *On Understanding Emotion*. San Francisco: Jossey-Bass.

Ervin, L., and S. Stryker. Forthcoming. "Theorizing the Relationship Between Self-Esteem and Identity." In *Extending Self-Esteem Theory and Research: Sociological and Psychological Currents*, edited by T.J. Owens, S. Stryker, and N. Goodman. New York: Cambridge University.

Gecas, V. 1982. "The Self-Concept." *Annual Review of Sociology* 8: 1-33.

Gecas, V., and P.J. Burke. 1995. "Self and Identity." Pp. 41-67 in *Sociological Perspectives on Social Psychology*, edited by K.S. Cook, G.A. Fine, and J.S. House. Boston: Allyn and Bacon.

Gecas, V., and M.L. Schwalbe. 1983. "Beyond the Looking-Glass Self: Social Structure and Efficacy-Based Self-Esteem." *Social Psychology Quarterly* 46:77-88.

Gilligan, J. 1996. *Violence: Reflections on a National Epidemic*. New York: Vintage Books.

Greenwald, A.G. 1980. "The Totalitarian Ego: Fabrication and Revision of Personal History." *American Psychologist* 7: 603-618.

Goffman, E. 1963. *Stigma: Notes on the Management of Spoiled Identity*. New York: Touchstone.

Gottfredson, M.R., and T. Hirschi. 1990. *A General Theory of Crime*. Stanford, CA: Stanford University Press.

Heise, D.R. 1979. *Understanding Events: Affect and the Construction of Social Action*. New York: Cambridge University Press.

Hochschild, A.R. 1979. "Emotion Work, Feeling Rules, and Social Structure." *American Journal of Sociology* 85: 551-575.

———. 1983. *The Managed Heart: Commercialization of Human Feeling*. Los Angeles: University of California Press.

James, W. 1890. *The Principles of Psychology*. New York: Henry Holt.

Kaplan, H.B. 1975. "The Self-Esteem Motive and Change in Self-Attitudes." *Journal of Nervous and Mental Disease* 161: 265-275.

Kemper, T.D. 1978. *A Social Interactional Theory of Emotions*. New York: Wiley.

Kohn, M.L. 1977. *Class and Conformity: A Study in Values,* 2nd ed. Chicago: University of Chicago Press.

Lecky, P. 1945. *Self-Consistency: A Theory of Personality*. New York: Island Press.

Lewis, M. 1992. *Shame: The Exposed Self*. New York: Free Press.

Lynd, H.M. 1958. *On Shame and the Search for Identity*. New York: Harcourt, Brace and Company.

MacKinnon, N. 1994. *Symbolic Interaction As Affect Control*. Albany, NY: State University of New York Press.

Maslow, A.H. 1970. *Motivation and Personality,* 2nd ed. New York: Harper and Row.

Mead, G.H. 1934. *Self and Society*. Chicago: University of Chicago Press.

Nathanson, D.L. 1992. *Shame and Pride: Affect, Sex, and the Birth of the Self*. New York: W. W. Norton.

Owens, T.J. 1993. "Accentuate the Positive-and the Negative: Rethinking the Use of Self-Esteem, Self- Deprecation, and Self-Confidence." *Social Psychology Quarterly* 56: 288-299.

_____. 1994. "Two Dimensions of Self-Esteem: Reciprocal Effects of Positive Self-Worth and Self-Deprecation on Adolescent Problems." *American Sociological Review* 59: 391-407.

Owens, T.J., and A. King. Forthcoming. "Considering Race, Ethnicity and Gender in the Measurement of Self-Esteem." *Extending Self-Esteem Theory and Research: Sociological and Psychological Currents*, edited by T.J. Owens, S. Stryker, and N. Goodman. New York: Cambridge University.

Owens, T.J., J.T. Mortimer, and M.D. Finch. 1996. "Self-Determination As a Source of Self-Esteem in Adolescence." *Social Forces* 74: 1377-1404.

Parsons, T. 1951. *The Social System*. Glencoe, IL: Free Press .

Phelan, T.W. 1995. *1-2-3 Magic: Training Your Children to Do What You Want!* Glen Ellyn, IL: Child Management.

Piers, G. and M.B. Singer. 1953. *Shame and Guilt: A Psychoanalytic and a Cultural Study*. Springfield, IL: Charles C. Thomas.

Rosenberg, M. 1965. *Society and the Adolescent Self-Image*. Princeton, NJ: Princeton University Press.

_____. 1979. *Conceiving the Self*. New York: Basic Books.

_____. 1981. "The Self-Concept: Social Product and Social Force." Pp. 593-624 in *Social Psychology: Sociological Perspectives*, edited by M. Rosenberg and R.H. Turner. New York: Basic Books.

Rosenberg, M., and T.J. Owens. Forthcoming. "Low Self-Esteem People: Collective Portrait." *Extending Self-Esteem Theory and Research: Sociological and Psychological Currents*, edited by T.J. Owens, S. Stryker, and N. Goodman. New York: Cambridge University Press.

Rosenberg, M., C. Schooler, C. Schoenbach, and F. Rosenberg. 1995. "Global Self-Esteem and Specific Self-Esteem: Different Concepts, Different Outcomes." *American Sociological Review* 60: 141-156.

Scheff, T.J. 1979. *Catharsis in Healing, Ritual, and Drama*. Berkeley: University of California Press.

_____. 1988. "Shame and Conformity: The Deference-Emotion System." *American Sociological Review* 53: 395-406.

_____. 1994. *Bloody Revenge: Emotions, Nationalism, and War*. Boulder, CO: Westview.

Scheff, T.J., and S.M. Retzinger. 1992. *Emotions and Conflict: Shame and Rage in Destructive Conflicts*. Thousand Oaks, CA: Sage.

Shott, S. 1979. "Emotion and Social Life: A Symbolic Interactionist Perspective." *American Journal of Sociology* 84: 1317-1334.

Straus, M.A. 1994. *Beating the Devil out of Them: Corporal Punishment in American Families*. New York: Lexington Books.

Stryker, S. 1980. *Symbolic Interactionism: A Social Structural Version*. Menlo Park, CA: Benjamin Cummings.

Stryker, S., and R.T. Serpe. 1982. "Commitment, Identity Salience, and Role Behavior: Theory and Research Example." Pp. 200-218 in *Personality, Roles and Social Behavior*, edited by W. Ickes and E. Knowles. New York: Springer-Verlag.

_____. 1994. "Identity Salience and Psychological Centrality: Equivalent, Overlapping, or Complementary Concepts?" *Social Psychology Quarterly* 57: 16-35.

Stryker, S., T.J. Owens, and R.W. White. 2000. "Social Psychology and Social Movements: Cloudy Past and Bright Future." *Self, Identity and Social Movements*, edited by S. Stryker, T.J. Owens, and R.W. White. Minneapolis, MN: University of Minnesota.

Swann, W.B., Jr., A. Stein-Seroussi, and R.B. Giesler. 1992. "Why People Self-Verify." *Journal of Personality and Social Psychology* 62: 392-401.

Tangney, J.P. 1995. "Recent Advances in the Empirical Study of Shame and Guilt." *American Behavioral Scientist* 38: 1132-1145.

———. 1996. "Conceptual and Methodological Issues in the Assessment of Shame and Guilt." *Behavior Research and Therapy* 34: 741-755.

Tangney, J.P., P. Wagner, and R. Gramzow. 1989. "The Test of Self-Conscious Affect for Adolescents (TOSCA-A)." George Mason University, Fairfax, VA.

Thoits, P.A., and L.K. Virshup. 1997. "Me's and We's: Forms and Functions of Social Identities." Pp. 106-133 in *Self and Identity: Fundamental Issues*, vol. 1, edited by R.D. Ashmore and L. Jussim. New York: Oxford University Press.

Wierzbicka, A. 1992. *Semantics, Culture, and Cognition : Universal Human Concepts in Culture-Specific Configurations*. New York: Oxford University Press.

Wright, E.W., W. Gronfein, and T.J. Owens. 2000. "Deinstitutionalization, Social Rejection, and the Self-Esteem of Former Mental Patients." *Journal of Health and Social Behavior* 41: 68-90.

THE IMPOSSIBLE ME
MISCONSTRUING STRUCTURAL
CONSTRAINT AND INDIVIDUAL VOLITION

Michelle Stem Cook

ABSTRACT

The central dilemma I address in this chapter is the ways in which oppressive social structures complicate subsequent pursuit of authentic identities in a freer structural context. Authenticity is the desired resolution of an individual's struggle to adapt to change, meet needs, and achieve goals without compromising his or her existential identities. The *impossible me* is a category of identities that an individual consciously articulates to be alien to himself or herself. Invoking impossibility eliminates the threat of an identity that seems to be incompatible with the self by inventing a structure that denies the self the option of incorporating that identity. Some Jewish émigrés from the former Soviet Union state that a theistic identity is "impossible" for them. Analysis of the antecedents of this posture exposes the structural compulsion and the individual volition inherent in their *impossible me*, which is founded on the false assumption that they freely chose to act in ways that oppressive social structures actually compelled them to act. Once individuals escape the control of oppressive social structures by migrating or by surviving radical structural

Advances in Life Course Research, Volume 5, pages 55-75.

Copyright © 2000 by JAI Press Inc.

All rights of reproduction in any form reserved.

ISBN: 0-7623-0033-7

change, irrational pursuit of continuity can perpetuate unjust structural constraint in the absence of structural injustice.

In this chapter, I present the *impossible me* as a domain in which a social scientist can assess "the balance of determinacy and indeterminacy in the relationship between person and social structure" (Turner, Hogg, Oakes, Reicher, and Blackwell 1987, p. 120). In essence, the *impossible me* is fabricated social structure that obscures the boundaries between structural constraint and individual volition. When migration or radical structural transformation transfer an individual from one social structural context into another one, options afforded by the new structural context can threaten identities that the individual formed in his or her native structural environment. The *impossible me*, as I define it, can emerge as a coping mechanism when newly acquired, unexplored options tempt or pressure an individual to compromise existential identities formed in a context devoid of those options. Conversely, when an individual suffers a loss of options because the new structural context imposes restrictions, the *impossible me* can become a mechanism of resistance to social control. In both instances, an individual rejects potential modes of adaptation by constructing impossibility. The *impossible me* can be interpreted as a product of individual self-determination, as a product of unconscious individual internalization of social structural constraints, or as a product of complex interaction between self-assertion and structural compulsion. In this chapter I develop the concept of the *impossible me* by analyzing invocation of impossibility among Soviet Jewish émigrés in the context of their adaptation to the United States. Then I briefly discuss the broader relevance of the *impossible me* and provide examples of it emerging as a reaction to unfamiliar freedoms and as a reaction to unfamiliar constraints.

MY FIELDWORK AND THE IDENTITIES OF JEWISH ÉMIGRÉS FROM THE FORMER SOVIET UNION

My ongoing ethnographic research[1] among Jewish émigrés from the former Soviet Union inspired this chapter. I am interviewing and interacting with Jewish veterans of the Great Patriotic War[2] and their children and grandchildren. The term "veteran" is sometimes restricted to people who served in the military in some official capacity, and an even more circumscribed definition links the term only to those who participated in combat. For my purposes, I apply the term "veterans" in its broadest sense, in reference to people who were medical personnel, military staff, partisans, workers in wartime industries, residents of cities under siege, concentration camp inmates, or soldiers during time of war.[3] In February of 1998, I initiated contact with a Soviet Veterans Association and began to regularly attend their meetings and commemorative celebrations. I also began to participate in cultural events sponsored by the surrounding Russian-speaking community. My participant observation is being supplemented by in-depth study of several families.

Although cultural and political shifts occurring over the course of the past three centuries make it difficult to label the population discussed here, the essential qualities uniting this population across time transcend geography. I will use two designations for this population: "Russian Jews" and "Soviet Jews," despite the fact that most of my respondents are actually from territories presently called Byelorussia and Ukraine. I will use the term "Russian Jews" as a term encompassing generations dating from the mid-nineteenth century up to the present.[4] I will use the term "Soviet Jews" when I am speaking of Jews who lived in the Soviet Union during the Soviet period.

The personal characteristics of a qualitative researcher shape his or her communication with respondents; therefore, I disclose some of my own attributes so that the reader can reflect on how they might have affected the validity and content of the data gathered. Members of the Russian-speaking community quickly recognize that I am an *Amerikanka,* an American woman. I am slightly older than most of the grandchildren of the veterans, and this combined with my research interest in intergenerational communication makes my identity as the grandchild of my own grandparents and the child of my own parents salient to my respondents. The most common questions respondents ask me about myself are questions about my family and my education. Sometimes I am asked whether or not I have Jewish ancestors, and more frequently, whether or not I have ancestors from Russia or Eastern Europe. I candidly answer, "No," to both questions, because I am a gentile, and concrete knowledge of my family's origin only traces back to specific farmland in Stem, North Carolina before lapsing into speculation. The fact that I am not Jewish has aroused only minimal distrust among my respondents, but that fact may understandably arouse the concern of readers. I do not share many of the significant attributes of Soviet Jewish émigrés, but I chose them to be my respondents because the universal social processes of loss and change are so intensely manifested in their heritage, their history, and their present situation. My most elderly respondents in particular embody a wealth of experience: they were born before the First World War, were school-age children during the Russian Revolution, survived the entire history of the former Soviet Union, and established a new life in a foreign country at eighty-some years of age.

I have attempted to mitigate the negative effects of the fact that I am not a native of the former Soviet Union or a co-ethnic in a variety of ways. My Russian language skills permit me to independently conduct the interviews in Russian or in English, according to whichever language the respondent feels most comfortable speaking. I still have to endeavor to overcome the language barrier, but even in those moments when I do not understand, my naiveté does carry an advantage: as people have taught me idioms and expressions, I have also learned about the unspoken assumptions underlying them. By listening to my respondents and demonstrating my genuine respect for them, I diminish the awkwardness of age, sex, ethnic, and cultural differences between us. As many "outsiders" have done in other research settings, I have submitted myself to the counsel of "insiders" without sacrificing my own discretion. In fact, the fruitfulness of my research and the great joy I derive from it stem directly from the support of key individuals who champion my cause, acquaint me with informants, provide interpretions of perplexing events, and help me prepare speeches, field guides, and correspondence.

In the context of in-depth interviews I ask members of various generations in these families to tell me about their parents and their grandparents. Their responses enable me to analyze to some extent how their family background affects their identities. The question of the inheritance of authentic individual identities is analogous to the question of the relevance of history to territorial claims. With regard to territorial rights, history leaves many rightful heirs in its wake. Similarly, family history can afford an individual an abundance of identities legitimated by their genealogy. Hareven (1978) used the following story to illustrate that "the length of time over which individuals associate themselves with events which occurred generations earlier" varies considerably across groups:

> Claude Cockburn recalled a meeting with three Ladino-speaking Jews[5] in Sofia, Turkey shortly after the Second World War. They explained that they were not Spaniards, but one of them added, 'Our family used to live in Spain before they moved to Turkey. Now we are moving to Bulgaria.' When Cockburn asked him how long it had been since his family lived in Spain, he responded that it had been approximately five hundred years (Hareven 1978, p. 137).

Individual identity "rest[s] on the linkage of the individual's life history and family history with specific historical moments" (Hareven 1978, p. 137). My fieldwork brings to light that many middle-aged and elderly Jewish émigrés from the former Soviet Union articulate that a theistic identity is "impossible" for them (for similar findings, see Markowitz 1993a; and Ritterbrand 1997). Immigration to the United States or Israel affords Soviet Jewish émigrés the opportunity to appropriate to themselves the collective memory of their distant ancestors, who organized their lives and their communities according to Judaic religious traditions. The question is, now that ex-Soviet Jews can retrieve what some scholars describe as "the authentic, historically legitimated symbols of their ethnicity" (Chervyakov, Gitelman, and Shapiro 1997), to what extent are they even contemplating adoption of new identities derived from adherence to the traditions and beliefs of generations past? And what differences in lived experience account for variation in the extent to which some family members uproot identities that they developed during the Soviet era in favor of traditional religious identities?

Setting aside other complex dimensions of a thorough answer to such questions, in this chapter I address my respondents' belief and disbelief regarding the existence of God. Jewish identity is a very complex concept to measure, particularly among Soviet Jews (Brym 1994; Chervyakov et al. 1997; Levin 1988; Ritterbrand

1997; Simon 1983). Behavioral measures of Jewish *identity*, an actual meaning applied to the self, are not valid unless the behaviors can be shown to be more than Jewish *identification*, or ways of behaving (Herman 1989). So, for the sake of simplicity and clarity I will focus exclusively on one dimension of identity— namely, the theistic, agnostic, or atheistic identity derived from a person's perspective on the existence of God.

It is important to note that my own identity falls at the theistic pole of this dimension of identity, but there are several indicators that my own theistic identity did not significantly distort my perceptions of the beliefs and identities of my respondents. First, the literature on the population resonates with my perception that few of my respondents are theists (Chervyakov, et al. 1997; Markowitz 1993b; Ritterbrand 1997). Secondly, only a few of my respondents were aware of my belief in God. If my theistic identity induced a respondent not only to reveal an agnostic or atheistic identity, but also to vehemently reject theistic identity in terms of impossibility, then I forced expression of the *impossible me*. Alternately, the social desirability factor would suggest that respondents who were aware of my beliefs would try to emphasize the similarity between my beliefs and theirs. My concern about these sources of bias is minimal because the statements of those who were aware of my theistic perspective did not differ from the statements of those who were not aware.

HISTORICAL BACKGROUND

During both the pre-Soviet era and the Soviet era, persecution and radical social change imposed perplexing dilemmas regarding identity on generation after generation of Russian Jews. Ashkenazi[6] Jewry began to develop in Western Europe in the Middle Ages and subsequently spread to Russia and Eastern Europe. In the last decade of the eighteenth century, Catherine II of Russia issued the decree that confined Jews in her kingdom to a region that came to be known as the Pale of Settlement. This region eventually included areas that are part of present-day Poland, Byelorussia, and Ukraine (Heilbronner 1982, p. 190). The Judaic traditions of the Ashkenazim governed life in the *shtetls*[7] of the impoverished Pale of Settlement. The themes that characterized the Ashkenazi pattern of Judaism were "isolation from the non-Jewish world and complete penetration of religious precept and practice into every detail of daily life" (Zborowski & Herzog 1952, pp.32-34). Boys in *shtetls* received religious education (Fishman 1994). Yiddish, a language combining medieval German with Hebrew, was the language of everyday life. Pogroms, unemployment, and restricted access to higher education fueled many secular Jewish movements in the latter half of the nineteenth century. At the end of the nineteenth century, Jews began to escape the Pale of Settlement by migrating either abroad or to urban centers in the Russian empire (Weinberg 1996). Due to these factors both internal and external to Russian Jewry, during the

first two decades of the twentieth century the parents and grandparents of the
World War II veterans suffered the dissolution of the traditional, religious communities in which they grew up (Markowitz 1988, p. 131). In the United States in
later years, the nostalgia of Jewish émigrés from this region was reflected in Yiddish films that highly romanticized *shtetl* life, neglecting to portray the poverty
and violent persecution that the émigrés had fled.

By 1939, 87 percent of the Jewish population in the Soviet Union lived in cities
(Altshuler 1993). The parents of the World War II veterans endured the Commu-
nist Revolution and the Civil War that consolidated the power of the Bolsheviks.
During the years of the Stalinist terror, Jewish cultural leaders and institutions
were annihilated and thousands of Jews were sent to forced labor camps and mur-
dered. The Soviet state and groups like the "League of Unbelievers" harshly
attacked the Jewish religion, especially between 1929 and 1939, using measures
such as enforced labor on the Sabbath and on Jewish holidays, closing of synagogues, and arrests of religious leaders and ritual slaughterers (Pinkus 1988, pp.
98-106). By 1939, "three quarters of those Jews who identified themselves as religious were over fifty years old. Only 23 percent of those aged sixteen to twenty-
nine identified themselves as religious" (Chervyakov et al. 1997). The veterans
became alienated from their grandparents by the enforced prohibition of traditional Jewish practices. Intimate communication between grandparents and
grandchildren regarding religion became a very dangerous endeavor when the
veterans were young:

> The Soviet constitution, which guaranteed both freedom of religion and freedom of anti-reli-
> gious propaganda, prohibited teaching religion to anyone under eighteen years of age
> (Chervyakov et al. 1997).

Because to teach a child about Judaism was to imperil the child's life, many parents and grandparents of the war generation tried not to disclose anything about
Judaic tradition or Yiddish language and culture to their children. The war generation in turn did the same with their children. Ironically, while brutal and unre-
lenting repression of Judaism devastated traditional, religious Jewish identity,
Jewish identity as a nationality became increasingly salient. Beginning in 1933,
all Soviet citizens were required to carry internal passports displaying their
nationality on the fifth line (Levin 1988), and people with Jewish internal passports became marked targets for anti-Semitic persecution. Anti-Semitism gradu-
ally overwhelmed Judaic tradition and dictated what it meant to be Jewish in
Soviet society.

Few of the family members of the veterans survived the Holocaust and the
Great Patriotic War. Many of the veterans survived only because they were not
stationed at home when the Nazis first invaded the Soviet Union. Nazi propaganda escalated anti-Semitism in the Soviet Union during the war, and post-
war discontent escalated it even higher. As in Nazi Germany, this was in spite

of Jewish assimilation; few Jews ascribed to Judaism after the passing of the pre-Soviet generation.[8] For example, in spite of the fact that the children of the veterans were so assimilated that Russian, not Yiddish, was their first language, these children continued to face restricted access to education, discrimination in the workplace, and other forms of persecution. This led to a "paradoxical consciousness":

> The influence of Russian culture and the forcible repression of national Jewish culture spurred assimilation, while anti-Semitism helped preserve national or ethnic identity. Jews lost their original culture but could not lose their identities (Chervyakov et al. 1997).

Jews sought to escape these conditions by trying to emigrate, but throughout the sixties, seventies and early eighties, trying to obtain a visa was a harrowing and often fruitless endeavor. Then, destabilization and the collapse of communism gave way to a massive exodus of Jews from the former Soviet Union. Between 1988 and 1993 alone, more than 460,000 Soviet émigrés were admitted to the United States.[9]

POSSIBLE SELVES

There is a precedent for thinking about identity in the realm of possibility. Paula Nurius, Hazel Markus, and others posit the concept of *possible selves* (Curry, Trew, Turner, and Hunter 1994; Langan-Fox 1991; Markus and Nurius 1987; Nurius 1989, 1991; Oyserman and Markus 1990). Markus and Nurius describe possible selves as identities unrealized in the present, but projected into the future:

> Possible selves represent individuals' ideas of what they might become, what they would like to become, and what they are afraid of becoming....The repertoire of possible selves contained within an individual's self-system are the cognitive manifestations of enduring goals, aspirations, motives, fears, and threats. Possible selves provide specific cognitive form, organization, direction, and self-relevant meaning to these dynamics. (Markus and Nurius 1987, pp. 157, 158)

Individuals strive to achieve some possible identities, and struggle to avoid the onset of others. The *impossible me* defined in this chapter can be seen as a conceptual subset of the identities that Markus and Nurius call "possible selves."

In their concluding recommendations for research on possible selves, Markus and Nurius pose "two difficult questions": one regarding the relevance of possible selves to motivation, and the other regarding the relative influence of negative selves and positive selves on individual action (Markus and Nurius 1987, p. 170). In a more recent article, Nurius (1991) mentions that possible selves are derived in a "particular sociocultural and historical context" and she emphasizes that parameters for possible selves "depend greatly on the nature of the social environment" (p. 246). She states that her conception of a social environment includes "cultural and social identity variables as well as social structural constraints and opportunities (e.g., the constraints of poverty, racism, sexism, ageism, and homophobia)" (Nurius 1991, pp. 256-257). Nevertheless, the development of her ideas makes it clear that for the most part she equates the social with the interpersonal;[10] the social environment she describes is strictly an interpersonal environment of social interactions, reflected appraisals, and internal dialogues with the generalized other (Nurius 1991, p. 250). Richard Brown (1987) incorporates macro social structures into his discussion of how various aspects of political economy define possible selves and affect the realization of possible selves. In this chapter, I also call into consideration the structural antecedents of variation among the possible selves possessed by different individuals. I seek to show how possible selves can serve as windows not only on personal motivation, but also on larger social structures.

IDENTITY AND AUTHENTICITY

Common to most social psychological definitions of identity is the idea that identity refers to "the various meanings attached to oneself by self and others" (Gecas and Burke 1995, p. 42).[11] Gregory Stone described the process by which identities are established in the following way:

> One's identity is established when others *place* him as a social object by assigning him the same words of identity that he appropriates for himself or *announces*. It is in the coincidence of placements and announcements that identity becomes a meaning of the self (Stone 1962).[12]

Neither the self nor others can unilaterally forge a new identity for an individual, because there must be consensus between the two parties. Consequently, identity is largely studied in the context of interpersonal communication, but it is important to consider how this communication is constrained by larger social structures.

I conceptualize development and maintenance of individual identities as the self perpetually struggling to achieve goals and meet needs without compromising its essence. The self asserts itself as both consistency and necessitated innovation. In other words, the self manages the dialectical tension between its *existential* and *instrumental* identities. Existential identities are almost inalienable from the self. These are the identities associated with an individual's deepest beliefs. Existential identities include native cultural and linguistic identities, identities associated with life-long commitments, identities impressed upon an individual during childhood, and identities an individual cannot escape. These identities are mastered to the level of automatic reflex, and afford the individual ease of communication in specific groups. Therefore, individuals who freely express their existential identities within the confines of a group share "roots," "deep understandings, [and] things that don't have to be explained" (Markowitz 1993b). By corporately commemorating various battles, the Soviet Veterans

Association celebrates and honors the existential identities of its members and validates the significance of the catastrophic war that gave rise to these identities. The Great Patriotic War powerfully shaped the lives of the members of the Soviet Veterans Association. Often, the war years predominate over all other aspects of the narratives the veterans supply when asked to tell their life story, apart from a brief prologue and a brief postscript. Elder and Clipp (1988) found that sustenance of ties between survivors of a common traumatic experience produces therapeutic effects. Perhaps this is because a soldier's identity outlasts his period of service and such ties infuse that identity with meaning.

While existential identities are the meanings that define the essence of the self, instrumental identities are the meanings that are learned and adopted in order to achieve goals and adapt to loss and change. One of the elderly respondents expresses his instrumental identity in the form of a *mezzuzah* attached to the right doorpost of the door to his apartment at the prescribed angle and height (Shochet 1999). *Mezzuzot* are boxes containing tiny parchment scrolls inscribed with Deuteronomy 6, pp. 4-9, and Deuteronomy 11, pp. 13-21, the first two passages of the three that comprise the *Shema*.[13] It has been customary since medieval times to touch the *mezzuzah* when entering and exiting a home as a way of marking "the separation between the private, sanctified space within, and the public, ordinary space outside" (Arian 1999). Maimonides explained the intended purpose of *mezzuzot* in this way: "whenever one enters or leaves a home with a *mezzuzah* on the doorpost, he will see it and be confronted with the declaration of God's unity" (Arian 1999). For this respondent, however, the *mezzuzah* serves an instrumental purpose. He does not touch it upon entering and leaving, as is the custom, nor does he believe "...The LORD is our God, the LORD is one...," as is written on the enclosed scrolls. Still, those passing, entering, and exiting his apartment see the display of this traditional Jewish symbol, and are thus informed of his solidarity with the American Jewish community. To his mind, this in no way belies his completely secular mentality; it is clear to everyone he receives in his home, including religious leaders in the local Jewish community, that he believes in Jewishness, but not in God.

The concept of "authenticity" has received great currency of late, but is not necessarily understood by all in the same way. Definitions of the term as rendered in the Oxford English Dictionary[14] elucidate its connotations and facilitate explanation of the conceptual relationship between authenticity, existential identities, and instrumental identities. First, that which is *authentic* is "original, real, genuine; as opposed to copied, imaginary, or pretended." It is understood to be "in accordance with fact" and "true in substance." *Authenticity* implies rightful ownership and authority. "Acting of itself, self-originated, automatic" constitutes another meaning of authentic. Varying perspectives on identity indicate that the self is fundamentally motivated to have, and to be perceived as having, the characteristics associated with authenticity (Burke 1997; Swann 1986). In fact, one of the meanings associated with authenticity equates it with "the quality of being entitled to acceptance."

Gecas and Burke (1995) note that concern about "increasing estrangement from institutional sources of authenticity" figures prominently in literature on self and identity (pp. 53, 57). They go so far as to say, "Perhaps the central problem of selfhood in modern societies...is the problem of authenticity"[15] (Gecas and Burke 1995, p. 57). The history of Russian Jewry supports the idea that "members of oppressed groups are more likely to confront the 'problem' of authenticity than are those who inhabit the world of power and privilege" (Erickson 1995, p. 137). The power of the totalitarian Soviet state was directed towards establishing itself as the *only* institution from which authenticity could be derived. Totalitarian control institutes the ultimate estrangement from sources of authenticity.

Social structural conditions can suppress and eliminate sources of authenticity. Social structure, not personal choice, dictates the *accessibility* of social identities:

> Turner asserts that there is no stable self-categorization or self-concept except to the degree that the social structure itself generates stable contexts or social norms, values, and motives (Turner, Hogg, Oakes, Reicher, and Blackwell 1994), making some social identities relatively more accessible and therefore more likely to be applied in a given setting (Thoits and Virshup 1997, p. 118).

A decline in institutions which support a specific identity and a parallel decline in opportunities for public expression of that specific identity can bring it to extinction, no matter how robust or deeply rooted it once was (Halbwachs 1980, 1926). This is because the identity of a believer is so wrapped up in the expression of belief. In order to be a believer, it is necessary to behave as a believer in conjunction with other believers. Therefore, if all opportunities to express belief can be eliminated, the identity predicated on expression of that belief can be eliminated, too. When individuals stop expressing a repressed belief, they do so in response to coercion that has overwhelmed the power of the individual to choose otherwise.

Ethnographic research among Jewish émigrés from the former Soviet Union suggests that *authenticity* is the desired resolution of the tension between existential and instrumental identities. In her discussion of rituals within Soviet émigré culture in Brighton Beach, New York, Markowitz quotes a woman's explanation of how she arranged a bat mitzvah at a Russian restaurant:

> You know, the main reason, one of the reasons, I picked the Russian restaurant is because I felt—I can't go to a synagogue and then put on a face like I lived this way my whole life. Do you see what I mean? Like our temple—it's Conservative, and I didn't feel I could go there and have the ceremony there because that's not me. And I couldn't ask that rabbi to come to the restaurant because it's non-kosher (Markowitz 1988, p. 133).

This woman sought to express her Jewish identity without pretense. She also wanted to embrace the new freedom her family has to adopt customs like Jewish rites of passage. Markowitz concludes that "the bat mitzvah ceremony that Soviet Jewish immigrants perform in their restaurants works as ritual precisely because it blends and reconciles, rather than disconnects, three powerful aspects of their sense of self—their Jewish, Russian, and American identities" (Markowitz 1988, p. 138). Their innovative way of celebrating the bat mitzvah resolves the tension between who they were in the past, who they are becoming now in the United States, and who they might have been had they been free under Soviet rule to observe evolving Judaic traditions throughout the past century.[16]

Although an individual cannot rightly do so, individuals often take responsibility for willfully relinquishing a belief that was made inaccessible by structural forces. In the former Soviet Union, totalitarian control permeated the directly impinging environment in which individuals formed their existential identities. The woman described above explained that she could not conduct the bat mitzvah in a synagogue because she refused to "put on a face" that would imply she had attended synagogue all her life. The woman says this as if she had freely chosen to avoid synagogue all her life. She holds herself responsible for not making a choice that she never had the opportunity to make, and concludes that she would be generating a fraudulent identity if she were to take part in Conservative Judaic practices now. To adopt a Conservative Judaic approach to the bat mitzvah would corrupt her Russian identity, and asserting her Russian identity in a Conservative Judaic context would not be kosher.

The criteria an immigrant uses to decide which potential identities are "possible" and which ones are "impossible" can be problematic. In the United States, Soviet émigrés sometimes have to choose between identities validated by their life experience and identities validated by freedom and their family background. It is ironic that the effects of Soviet destruction and subsequent repression of synagogues persist in part because those who were denied access to a Jewish religious institutions now defer the opportunity to become involved in them because they were not involved in the past. The central dilemma I address in this chapter is the ways in which oppressive social structures complicate subsequent pursuit of authentic identities in a freer structural context. In the same way that the social is often equated with the interpersonal, decisions constrained by social structure are often characterized as the free personal choices of individuals. The problematic result of action guided by this fallacy is perpetuation of unjust structural constraint completely apart from structural injustice.

THE IMPOSSIBLE ME

Meaningful augmentation of the self takes place within boundaries, because self-definition requires recognition of what the self is not, as well as understanding of what the self is. At some point, existential identities reign in instrumental adaptation. Beyond a person's breaking point, where his or her sense of authenticity expires, lies the *impossible me*. At that point he or she consciously sets himself or herself in opposition to an encroaching potential identity. Pressure to adopt an identity that an individual perceives as a threat to his or her authenticity brings an *impossible me* into sharp focus. It is a reactive response to an alarming impetus to change and it fortifies an individual's existential identities as the individual rises to the demands of necessity. The *impossible me* acts as the first line of defense against a heretofore unthinkable, but now eminently possible, me.

Turner (1987) finds the notion of a "spurious self" to be a complex and real phenomena worthy of significant attention, and he suggests that "true-self and spurious self" are not simply polar opposites along a single dimension, but belong to different dimensions (Turner 1987, p. 127). The identities comprising the *impossible me* are a conceptual subset of Turner's "spurious self" or "not-me." In accordance with Turner's ideas about the origins of the "not-me," it is apparent that the *impossible me* springs "from disruption of underlying order in [the individual's] relations with social structure" (Turner 1987, p. 127). The members of the community of Jewish Soviet émigrés in which I am conducting fieldwork encountered a drastic disruption in their identities when they immigrated to the United States. For example, being labeled as "Russian" upon arrival in the United States took these natives of Byelorussia, Ukraine, and other republics by surprise, but not because they emigrated from republics outside of Russia. As one young respondent explained, this label shocked him because prior to emigrating he had always thought of himself as Jewish, not Russian, because *evreii*[17] was the nationality on his internal passport.

Immigrants confront a barrage of social identities that American society either imposes on them or permits them to explore. As a newcomer to a society, an immigrant is ill-equipped to carry on the internal dialogue whereby the self "privately considers performing a behavior…then imaginatively anticipates other people's reactions to that behavior, then responds to their expected reactions, and so on" (Thoits and Virshup 1997, p. 108). Mead divided the self into the "I," which is the self-proper, and the "me," the self's capacity to see itself from the perspective of others (Mead 1934). The "me" aspect of the self enables an individual to anticipate the reactions of others and then modify his or her behavior accordingly, prior to actually acting. Until an immigrant develops a savvy "me," the perceptions of others will shock and confuse him or her. Immigrants are therefore handicapped in their struggle to manage a bewildering array of newly discovered potential identities.[18] Sometimes new ways of communicating endanger an immigrant's sense of authenticity. As Eva Hoffman exclaimed in the midst of her own immigrant experience, "I think this language is making a new me!" (Hoffman 1989). Instrumental identities include those that emerge out of learning a foreign language and functioning in a foreign culture. While learning the "me" that reflects their new interpersonal context, an immigrant can assert his or her "I" by emphatically placing several identities in the category of the *impossible me*.

COHORT VARIATION IN IMPOSSIBILITY

An immigrant's place in the life course greatly affects how he or she approaches potential shifts in identity, because different cohorts experience different constraints on identity formulation and maintenance:

> Successive cohorts experience the same events at different points in the life span and different events at similar points. This variation and rapid change establish lines of demarcation between the collective experience of cohorts, their life patterns, and options. (Elder 1981, p. 87).

The various generations in these families share a family heritage, but draw on different life experiences as they decide how to interpret valid alternative identities introduced to them by personal religious freedom and by the religious communities now accessible to them.

At present, the tremendous differences between the lives of the veterans and *their grandchildren* are of similar magnitude to those between the lives of the veterans and *their grandparents*. The grandparents of the veterans came of age, for the most part, in confinement in the Pale of Settlement, where the Yiddish language and Judaic traditions predominated, whereas the veterans themselves came of age, for the most part, in large cities, where the Russian language, extreme repression of Judaic traditions, and pursuit of educational achievement predominated. This contrast is mirrored now between the veterans and their grandchildren, who are coming of age in American society, a free and primarily theistic society, where the English language, of course, predominates, and American assumptions regarding Jewish identity differ greatly from those of Russian Jews.

Quite often elderly Jewish émigrés from the former Soviet Union respond in terms of impossibility to my questions about changes in their beliefs since arriving in the United States. The veterans are accustomed to deriving goals, ideals, cultural values, and ethics from secular systems of meaning. Upon hearing someone say that it is impossible for them to "become religious," I sometimes ask, "Why can't you?" or "Why is that impossible?" The essence of the rhetorical question that respondents often ask me in return is, "After all these years, how could I change now?" They explain that their education was not only devoid of traditional Jewish content but infused with atheistic propaganda. Their existential identities, in their view, do not permit them to adopt a theistic identity.

Although middle-aged immigrants also had a secular upbringing, in general, they articulate their own beliefs differently than the elderly. When asked, "Do you believe in God?" one woman in her late fifties replied with a pained expression, "That is a very difficult question, very difficult—(long pause)—All my life I was brought up against God."[19] She then quoted a friend who said, "I did not invent him [God], but neither can I say that he does not exist." In conclusion she said that she did not know what to believe, and then we moved on to another topic. The typical position among middle-aged people in my sample is that of agnosticism, tempered by a sense that it is "too late" for them to learn about the Bible and reevaluate their beliefs. In general, they are more open than the veterans to discovering a basis for deciding that God does exist and has existed all these years that they were taught otherwise.

The grandchildren of the veterans are the most likely generation to introduce theism into these families. Some of these teenagers and young adults have inconclusive or decisively atheistic beliefs, such as those of a high school senior who said, "I am not interested in such things. I want nothing to do with them."[20] On the other hand, many of the grandchildren are deeply involved in religious life within the Jewish community. Judaism appeals to these grandchildren in part because it affords them an identity with continuity in the past and viability for the future. Some teach their elders how to observe Jewish holidays, and many have studied in Jewish educational institutions since their arrival in the United States. The veterans and their children are pleased by the religious activity of the grandchildren.

I am not reporting that age within this population is an infallible predictor of theistic, atheistic, or agnostic identity. There certainly is variation within cohorts with regard to religious belief. One middle-aged male respondent,[21] for example, made the argument that it would be impossible for him to believe and supported it with vivid illustrations. He said that for him to eat kosher now "would be as theater." Furthermore, he said that he was taken aback when he encountered the Hassidim[22] in New York City; he felt as if men from his great grandparents' generation had come back to life. He asserted that it was in no way possible for him to take up the Hassidic way of life of his ancestors. His invocation of impossibility was more common among the war generation than among his own. This variation notwithstanding, what I found remarkable was the recurrence of impossibility in the statements that members of the war generation in particular make about their beliefs. In light of this, I sought to understand why a member of this cohort and population would think it necessary to attest that it would be impossible for him or her to adopt a theistic identity rather than simply saying that they do not believe.

When my elderly respondents say that it would be "impossible" for them to begin to believe in the existence of God, why do they say so? Consider the contrasting attitudes one elderly female has toward religious belief in reference to herself and in reference to her grandson:

> My grandson now attends synagogue. He has become religious. For him, it is good, but for me to become religious? That would be impossible. For me that is impossible.

This respondent is not arguing that theism is impossible for everyone; she is saying that it is impossible *for her*. Similarly, one elderly female respondent in an expression of sympathy for an American elderly woman said that it would be easier for the American woman to deal with her grief than it would be for an atheist because the American will be comforted by her belief in God. She then explained that for the American belief was good, but that for her it is impossible. If the veterans are glad for Americans and their grandchildren to believe in God, then they are not saying that it is impossible for a respectable person to believe in God.

Furthermore, they do not say it is impossible for them to adopt a theistic identity because they are unwilling to participate in public religious rituals. Many who say it is impossible for them to believe in God do participate in public religious rituals. With the shield of a boldly articulated *impossible me*, these elderly Jewish immigrants can invite little children in Purim[23] costumes into their homes, partake of a Passover seder[24] in the home of a friend, and even go to synagogue on the High Holy Days[25] of Rosh Hashanah and Yom Kippur without corrupting their public or private identity by insincerely avowing belief in God. Internal change in belief or the false appearance of change in belief are the dangers inherit in close encounters with religious ritual. The veterans can be part of the religious community on their own terms, because they have adamantly relegated these dangers to the realm of the impossible.

The respondents who say theism is impossible for them have rejected many of the myths perpetuated by the Soviet state. Nevertheless, they do not apply such skepticism to the beliefs about God that they developed in the dogmatic Soviet context. Perhaps they would freely choose to act and think in ways they were forced to act and think after critically evaluating their beliefs, but by neglecting to consider alternative ways of acting and thinking they inadvertently continue to submit to control that is no longer actually exercised over their behavior. The invocation of an *impossible me* is different from a straightforward expression of disbelief. Statements about impossibility reveal an unwillingness to even explore or consider a possibility. The *impossible me* is triggered by the desire to circumvent a possibility. If it were not possible, there would be no need to call it impossible. The elderly immigrants who set up the barrier of impossibility are struggling not to stray too far from who they have been all their lives. When someone refuses to reevaluate an identity they acquired under conditions of oppression, the *impossible me* becomes a mechanism that extends the influence of oppression beyond the existence of the source of oppression. Often people base their determination of what is possible or impossible for them on their past experiences. The effects of structurally imposed constraints accumulate across the life course. It follows that the greater the severity of the oppressive conditions and the longer the period of time over which those conditions constrained life course development, the greater the probability that those constraints will be self-imposed once the structure is no longer influencing experience.

According to Turner (1976), Backman (1985), and others, people generally think that the behaviors that "reveal the 'true self'" are ones whose causes are perceived as residing in the person rather than the situation, particularly when moral issues are at stake" (Gecas and Burke 1995, p. 48). Mead's dichotomy of the self characterizes the "I" as "the active, creative agent doing the experiencing, thinking, and acting" (Thoits and Virshup 1997, p. 108). Even so, confidence that "structural constraints on the self" can be overcome by an indomitable, resilient "I" (Thoits and Virshup 1997, p. 133), must be qualified by recognition of ways that social constraints reverse or obscure that victory. Oppressive conditions obscure the "I" aspect of the self when the liberated self makes decisions regarding matters over which the self had no control in the past. It is difficult to distinguish pursuit of unconstrained authenticity from pursuit of continuity with adaptation to constraint. The *impossible me* denies the "I" the opportunity to determine the behavior of the self.

SOURCES OF IMPOSSIBLITY

One respondent who says that it would be impossible for her to become religious also states that she really doubts the sincerity of her peers who have begun to attend synagogue regularly. Such skepticism is common among ex-Soviet Jews (Ritterbrand 1997, p. 331). Simon (1983) analyzed the answers that 200 Soviet Jews living in Chicago gave to survey questions about their Jewish identity (328). Both parents and children claimed that their religious beliefs had changed since their arrival in the United States. However, when asked about the religious beliefs of their family members, parents did not report significant change in their children's beliefs and their children did not report significant change in the beliefs of their parents (Simon 1983, p. 336). This finding indicates that a Jewish émigré from the former Soviet Union who adopts a theistic identity in the United States often receives little recognition or support from their compatriots. As Stone states in the quote above, identities are established by congruence between self-perception and the perceptions of others. Therefore, an identity shift that does not receive confirmation from the individual's family and community can seem impossible to establish.

My finite definition of the *impossible me* makes it easy to operationalize for research purposes. It truly is impossible for an individual to articulate everything that might be impossible for himself or herself because impossibility is infinite, but an *impossible me* is a consciously delineated identity or set of identities. I concur with Turner in his conclusion that self-conceptions in general are often vague:

> Contrary to Manford Kuhn's assumption, experience with TST and other instruments abundantly demonstrates that people do not necessarily have well-formulated and communicable self-conceptions (Turner, R. 1987, p. 123).

Measurement and analysis of the *impossible me* is facilitated by the fact that the phenomenon captured by that concept is outwardly expressed and decisively articulated. Once a researcher has formed hypotheses regarding possible manifestations of the *impossible me* in their population, the concept can be incorporated into a survey by providing impossibility as a response option to various questions and by posing questions about sources of impossibility.

The concept of the *impossible me* applies in many contexts. Individuals articulate the impossible as a way of coping with possibilities that tempt or pressure them to betray their deepest beliefs and treasured identities. A widow, for example, might say, "To marry again would be impossible for me." Clearly, she is articulating not impossibility, but her opposition to the very real possibility that she might remarry. A child of an alcoholic is likely to attest that it would be impossible for them to develop their parent's uncontrollable drinking habits. Still, if the possibility were not so ominously close, there would be no need to invoke impossibility. Mary Waters observes a defensive posture equivalent to the *impossible me* among émigrés of Caribbean origin in New York City. These immigrants struggle in a variety of ways to distance themselves from negative stereotypes about African Americans. By employing their accent or objects and clothing linking them to their nation of origin, they make explicit their assertion that it would be *impossible* for them to acquire the characteristics that racism has associated with black skin in this country (Waters 1999). In all these examples, the *impossible me* wards off an identity that that threatens to corrupt the self.

Another example of the *impossible me* is suicide in the face of defeat. As the incremental defeat of Japan in World War II reduced its structural context of power and domination to the structural context of a conquered country, many Japanese self-imposed the *im*possibility of surrender. The dynamics of the *impossible me* are also operative in the determination of some Chileans to remember the human rights violations perpetuated by the Chilean dictatorship from 1973 until 1990. Now that a civilian government is in power, some Chileans urge their compatriots to protect current stability by forgetting the past and ignoring the impunity of the guilty. But victims of torture, relatives of the disappeared, and others insist that it is *impossible* to forget. This insistence is necessary because in addition to social pressures, the pain of remembering makes forgetfulness a tempting possibility. In this instance, after passing from the dictatorship into a system with greater civilian control, people self-impose impossibility as a fabricated structure to constrain them to resist injustice (Lira 1997).

In conclusion, this chapter provides evidence that "the very essence of people's selves" cannot be separated from their "position in the social and economic structure of their society" (Kohn 1989, p. 28). Oppressive social structures exercise lasting influence over individual identities through mechanisms like the *impossible me*. Jewish émigrés from the former Soviet Union confront challenges to the Jewish identity to which they were accustomed prior to arriving in the United States, but the effects of oppression on their development constrain their choices about how to change or maintain their beliefs in light of new freedom to do so. The assuredness of some immigrants that that their lived experiences make theistic identity impossible for them exemplifies the structural compulsion inherent in the *impossible me*.[26] Treating structurally constrained decisions as unrestricted personal choices is like the fallacy of equating the interpersonal with the social. The inverse of this fallacy is manifested in the *impossible me*, which presents unrestricted personal choices as structural constraints. The purpose of this chapter was to draw attention to how both the fallacy and its inverse perpetuate the influence of structural constraint even after an oppressive structure is removed.

ACKNOWLEDGMENT

This research is being supported in part by NSF grant SBR-9970765.

NOTES

1. This on-going research is for my doctoral dissertation and is being supported by a grant from the National Science Foundation. My dissertation is entitled, *The Inheritance and Disinheritance of Memory within the Families of Jewish Émigrés from the Former Soviet Union*. The identities of respondents are concealed.

2. Soviet veterans refer to World War II as "The Great Patriotic War."

3. I will sometimes refer to these veterans as "the war generation."

4. For an account of how Russian Jewry coalesced into an identifiable group in the mid-nineteenth century, see (Lederhendler 1995).

5. Ladino, or Judeo-Spanish language, is a dialect composed of a mixture of Spanish and Hebrew elements, used as the vernacular by the Sephardim. The Sephardim are the descendants of the Jews who scattered throughout Turkey, Serbia, Bosnia, Bulgaria, Palestine, and Morocco after being expelled from Spain in 1492.

6. *Ashkenaz* is the Hebrew name for Germany.

7. *Shtetl* is a term used to refer to small Jewish villages in Eastern Europe. See Zborowski and Herzog 1952.

8. Yiddish language and Judaic tradition were retained to a greater degree in the Baltic states and Uzbekistan than in Byelorussia, Russia, or Ukraine.

9. This figure represents the immigrant and refugee admissions recorded in the Annual Reports of the Immigration and Naturalization Service. It includes all émigrés, not only Jewish émigrés.

10. Kohn (1989, pp. 28, 30) discussed this fallacy in his essay on the fundamentals of a sociological approach to social psychology.

11. Backman 1985; Burke 1997; Burke and Tully 1977; Stryker 1994; Thoits and Virshup 1997; and others also define identity in terms of meanings applied to the self by the self and others.

12. This passage is quoted and discussed in Turner 1987, p. 121.

13. The *Shema*, which begins, "Hear O Israel," is of great significance to Jews. Since the Second Temple period, Jews have considered it the essential declaration of faith, to be recited twice daily, every morning and every evening, by every Jew. By tradition, it is the first phrase to be taught to a Jewish child, the last to be uttered by a Jew before he dies, and the prayer to be uttered in times of crisis. *Shema* is Hebrew for "hear." (Goldberg and Rayner 1987, pp. 236, 320, 331; personal correspondence with Carol Brooks Gardner).

14. *The Compact Edition of the Oxford English Dictionary*, 1971, vol. 1, Oxford: Oxford University Press, pp. 569-571.

15. In support of this statement they cite Baumeister 1987; Hochschild 1983; Trilling 1972; Turner 1976; Weigert 1990.

16.   Whereas a bar mitzvah has long been a Judaic tradition, a bat mitzvah, the equivalent ceremony for a girl, has recently been instituted as a practice of Reform and Conservative synagogues.

17.   *Evreii* is the Russian word for Jew or Jewish. Its literal meaning is "Hebrew."

18.   There are immigrants who circumvent this whole process by entrenching themselves in an ethnic neighborhood, refusing to learn the new language, relying on the newly acquired cultural competence of other immigrants when necessary, and flourishing with minimal adaptation (personal correspondence with Carol Brooks Gardner).

19.   Interview, April 11, 1999.

20.   Interview, September 1998.

21.   I interviewed this respondent in the spring of 1992.

22.   Hassidism is a mystical religious movement that was founded in the seventeenth century by the Baal Shem Tov as a reaction to severe persecution from without and excessive legalism from within Ashkenazi Jewry. The Hassidic communities of the *shtetls* were destroyed around the turn of the century, but émigrés established Hassidic communities that still exist in New York City. The Hassidim are easily identified by their peculiar dress. (Potok 1967)

23.   Purim, a Jewish festival based on the Book of Esther, is traditionally celebrated with much merrymaking, including children dressing up in costumes and going door-to-door to receive sweets (Shechner 1989). The festival commemorates Mordechai and Queen Esther's defeat of Haman's plot to kill all the Jews of Persia, and is national rather than religious in character.

24.   Traditionally, observance of Passover includes the ritual of the Passover seder, when family and friends gather around the dinner table and partake of specific foods intended to spark reflection on the deliverance of the Jews from slavery in Egypt. Whereas Purim is a minor holiday, in that work was allowed on that day, Passover is of greater significance.

25.   Rosh Hashanah is New Year's Day according to the Jewish calendar. Yom Kippur is the Day of Atonement.

26.   This is not to say that freedom conditions everyone to believe God exists, or that persecution deprives everyone of belief in God.

REFERENCES

Altshuler, M. 1993. *Distribution of the Jewish Population of the USSR 1939.* Jerusalem: Hebrew University of Jerusalem Centre for Research and Documentation of East-European Jewry.

Arian, R., (Rabbi and Vice President of the Wexner Heritage Foundation). 1999. *Reply to a Question about Mezzuzot.* Union of American Hebrew Congregations.

Backman, C. 1985. "Identity, Self-Presentation, and the Resolution of Moral Dilemmas: Towards A Social Psychological Theory of Moral Behavior." Pp. 261-290 in *The Self and Social Life*, edited by B. Schlenker. New York: McGraw-Hill.

Baumeister, R.F. 1987. "How the Self Became a Problem: A Psychological Review of Historical Research." *Journal of Personality and Social Psychology* 52: 163-176.

Brown, R.H. 1987. "Personal Identity and Political Economy: Western Grammars of the Self in Historical Perspective." *Current Perspectives in Social Theory* 8: 123-159.

Brym, R.J. 1994. *The Jews of Moscow, Kiev, and Minsk.* New York: New York University Press.

Burke, P.J. 1997. "An Identity Model for Network Exchange." *American Sociological Review* 62: 134-150.

Burke, P.J., and J. Tully. 1977. "The Measurement of Role-Identity." *Social Forces* 55: 881-897.

Chervyakov, V., Z. Gitelman, and V. Shapiro. 1997. "Religion and Ethnicity: Judaism in the Ethnic Consciousness of Contemporary Russian Jews." *Ethnic and Racial Studies* 20: 280-305.

Curry, C., K. Trew, I. Turner, and J. Hunter. 1994. "The Effect of Life Domains on Girls' Possible Selves." *Adolescence* 29: 133-150.

Elder, Jr., G.H. 1981. "History and the Life Course." Pp. 77-115 in *Biography and Society: The Life History Approach in the Social Sciences*, edited by D. Bertaux. Beverly Hills, CA: Sage Publications.

Elder, Jr., G.H., and E.C. Clipp. 1988. "War Experience and Social Ties." Pp. 306-327 in *Social Structure and Human Lives*, edited by M.W. Riley. Newbury Park, CA: Sage Publications.

Erickson, R.J. 1995. "The Importance of Authenticity for Self and Society." *Symbolic Interaction* 18: 121-144.

Fishman, D.E. 1994. "Judaism in the USSR, 1917-1930: The Fate of Religious Education." Pp. 251-262 in *Jews and Jewish Life in Russia and the Soviet Union*, edited by Y. Ro'i. Ilford, Essex: Frank Cass & Co. Ltd.

Gecas, V., and P.J. Burke. 1995. "Self and Identity." Pp. 41-67 in *Sociological Perspectives on Social Psychology*, edited by K.S. Cook, G.A. Fine, and J.S. House. Boston: Allyn and Bacon.

Goldberg, D.J., and J.D. Rayner. 1987. *The Jewish People: Their History and Their Religion*. London: Penguin Books.

Halbwachs, M. 1980. *The Collective Memory*. New York: Harper & Row. (Original work published 1926)

Hareven, T. 1978. "The Search for Generational Memory: Tribal Rites in Industrial Society." *Daedulus* 107: 137-149.

Heilbronner, H. 1982. "Pale of Settlement." Pp. 189-194 in *The Modern Encyclopedia of Russian and Soviet History*, edited by J.L. Wieczynski. Gulf Breeze, FL: Academic International Press.

Herman, S. 1989. *Jewish Identity*. New Brunswick, Canada: Transaction Press.

Hochschild, A.R. 1983. *The Managed Heart: Commercialization of Human Feeling*. Berkeley, CA: University of California Press.

Hoffman, E. 1989. *Lost In Translation: A Life In a New Language*. New York: E. P. Dutton.

Kohn, M. 1989. "Social Structure and Personality: A Quintessentially Sociological Approach to Social Psychology." *Social Forces* 68: 28-33.

Langan-Fox, J. 1991. "The Stability of Work, Self and Interpersonal Goals in Young Women and Men." *European Journal of Social Psychology* 21: 419-428.

Lederhendler, E. 1995. "Did Russian Jewry Exist Prior to 1917?" Pp. 15-28 in *Jews and Jewish Life in Russia and the Soviet Union*, edited by Y. Ro'i. Ilford, Essex: Frank Cass & Co. Ltd.

Levin, N. 1988. *The Jews in the Soviet Union: Paradox of Survival*. New York: New York University Press.

Lira, E. 1997. "Remembering: Passing Back Through the Heart." Pp. 223-236 in *Collective Memory of Political Events: Social Psychological Perspectives*, edited by J. Pennebaker. Mahwah, NJ: Lawrence Erlbaum Associates.

Markowitz, F. 1988. "Rituals as Keys to Soviet Immigrants' Jewish Identity." Pp. 128-147 in *Between Two Worlds: Ethnographic Essays on American Jewry*, edited by J. Kugelmass. Ithaca, NY: Cornell University Press.

_____. 1993a. *A Community In Spite of Itself: Soviet Jewish Émigrés in New York*. Washington, DC: Smithsonian Institution Press.

_____. 1993b. "Israelis With A Russian Accent." *The Jewish Journal of Sociology* 35: 97-114.

Markus, H., and P. Nurius. 1987. "Possible Selves: The Interface between Motivation and the Self-Concept." Pp. 157-172 in *Self and Identity: Psychosocial Perspectives*, edited by K. Yardley and T. Honess. Chichester, England: John Wiley & Sons, Ltd.

Mead, G.H. 1934. *Mind, Self & Society: From the Standpoint of a Social Behaviorist*. Chicago: University of Chicago Press.

Nurius, P. 1989. "The Self-Concept: A Social-Cognitive Update." *Social Casework* 70: 285-294.

_____. 1991. "Possible Selves and Social Support: Social Cognitive Resources for Coping and Striving." Pp. 239-258 in *The Self-Society Dynamic: Cognition, Emotion, and Action*, edited by J.A. Howard and P.L. Callero. Cambridge, England: Cambridge University Press.

Oyserman, D., and H. Markus. 1990. "Possible Selves in Balance: Implications for Delinquency." *Journal of Social Issues* 46: 141-157.

Pinkus, B. 1988. *The Jews of the Soviet Union*. Cambridge, England: Cambridge University Press.

Potok, C. 1967. *The Chosen*. New York: Simon and Schuster.

Ritterbrand, P. 1997. "Jewish Identity among Russian Immigrants in the U.S." Pp. 325-343 in *Russian Jews On Three Continents*, edited by N. Lewin-Epstein, Y. Ro'i, and P. Ritterbrand. London: Frank Cass & Co Ltd.

Shechner, M. 1989. "Comedy, Jewish." Pp. 140-144 in *The Blackwell Companion to Jewish Culture from the Eighteenth Century to the Present*, edited by G. Abramson. Oxford, England: Basil Blackwell Ltd.

Shochet, M.A. (Cantor). Temple Rodef Shalom, Falls Church, VA. 1999. *Reply to a question about Mezzuzot*. Union of American Hebrew Congregations.

Simon, Rita J. 1983. "The Jewish Identity of Soviet Immigrant Parents and Children." Pp. 327-339 in *Culture, Ethnicity and Identity: Current Issues In Research*, edited by William C. McCready. New York: Academic Press.

Stone, G. 1962. "Appearance and the Self." Pp. 86-118 in *Human Behavior and Social Processes*, edited by A.M. Rose. Boston: Houghton Mifflin.

Stryker, S. 1994. "Identity Theory: Its Development, Research Base, and Prospects." *Studies in Symbolic Interaction* 16: 9-20.

Swann, W.B. 1986. "To Be Adored or to Be Known? The Interplay of Self-Enhancement and Self-Verification." Pp. 408-448 in *Handbook of Motivation and Cognition*, edited by T. Higgins and R.M. Sorrentino. New York: The Guilford Press.

Thoits, P.A., and L.K. Virshup. 1997. "Me's and We's: Forms and Functions of Social Identities." Pp. 106-133 in *Self and Identity: Fundamental Issues*, edited by R.D. Ashmore and L. Jussim. New York: Oxford University Press.

Trilling, L. 1972. *Sincerity and Authenticity*. New York: Harcourt.

Turner, J.C., M.A. Hogg, P.J. Oakes, S.D. Reicher, and M.S. Blackwell. 1987. *Rediscovering the Social Group: A Self-categorization Theory*. Oxford, England: Basil Blackwell.

Turner, R.H. 1976. "The Real Self: From Institution to Impulse." *American Journal of Sociology* 81: 980-1016.

_____. 1987. "Articulating Self and Social Structure." Pp. 119-132 in *Self and Identity: Psychosocial Perspectives*, edited by K. Yardley and T. Honess. Chichester, England: John Wiley & Sons.

Waters, M.C. 1999. *Black Identities: West Indian Immigrant Dreams and American Realities*. New York: Russell Sage Foundation; Cambridge, MA: Harvard University Press.

Weigert, A.J. 1990. "To Be or Not: Self and Authenticity, Identity and Ambivalence." in *Self, Ego, and Identity*, edited by D. Lapsley and C. Power. New York: Springer-Verlag.

Weinberg, D.H. 1996. *Between Tradition and Modernity: Haim Zhitlowski, Simon Dubnow, Ahad Ha-am, and the Shaping of Modern Jewish Identity*. New York: Holmes & Meier.

Zborowski, M., and E. Herzog. 1952. *Life Is With People: The Culture of the Shtetl*. New York: Schocken Books.

THE DEVELOPMENT AND TRANSFORMATION OF FEMINIST IDENTITIES UNDER CHANGING HISTORICAL CONDITIONS

Pamela Aronson

ABSTRACT

This study examines intra-cultural differences in political identity, and the ways in which identity can be transformed. I compare women who came of age and began to be politically active in quite different historical eras—those involved in the League of Women Voters during the 1950s and 1960s, and those active in the National Organization for Women (NOW) during the 1970s and early 1980s. These findings illustrate that the identities of these two distinct "political generations" reflect the cultural and historical context in which they came of political age. However, existing notions of political generations in the social movement literature do not address the conditions under which someone of a particular generation transforms and takes on a world view different from that of her contemporaries. This study finds that identity transformation has the potential to occur at later points in the life course, when turning points in individual lives intersect with a rapidly changing social and cultural context.

Advances in Life Course Research, Volume 5, pages 77-97.
Copyright © 2000 by JAI Press Inc.
All rights of reproduction in any form reserved.
ISBN: 0-7623-0033-7

INTRODUCTION

Why do women embrace different types of feminist and political identities? What is the impact of the cultural and historical context in this process? What forces lead to identity transformation? This study examines the feminist identities of two distinct generations of women activists to understand the ways in which identities develop and transform as a result of the changing cultural context.

I compare feminist identities during two distinct cultural periods by studying women who were active in the League of Women Voters during the 1950s and 1960s, and those active in the National Organization for Women during the 1970s and early 1980s. These organizations differed in their points of intersection with the second-wave women's movement, as the League peaked beforehand, and NOW peaked during its height. This chapter illustrates that the identities of these two distinct "political generations" reflect the cultural and historical contexts in which they came of political age. Additionally, I argue that existing notions of political generations in the social movements literature need to be expanded, since they do not address the conditions under which someone of a particular generation transforms and takes on a world view different from that of her contemporaries. Applying the concept of "turning points" (Strauss 1959), I argue that identity transformation can result when events in one's personal history intersect with a rapidly changing cultural and historical context, particularly one that emphasizes personal change.

Social Movements and Political Generations

Social movements develop within particular political opportunity structures, which may create favorable conditions for activism (Meyer and Staggenborg 1996). In the late 1960s and 1970s, new public policies and governmental bodies, focused on women's issues, created opportunities for the development of the women's movement (Costain 1992; Harrison 1988; Meyer and Staggenborg 1996). The women's movement is located within a broader cycle of protest (including other social movements of the time period, and past women's movements), and arose in part because the demands of other groups helped to transform previous ideological frames (Tarrow 1989). Such times of rapid social and political change expand the potential for shaping new identities (Aminzade 1993).

The "political generations" approach helps to explain why individuals embrace particular identities. Mannheim (1952) conceptualizes a generation as having common social and cultural experiences which structure its world view. A political generation, persons "coming of age" in a particular historical period, shares a similar consciousness, and represents "a way of seeing the world" (Schneider 1988, p. 6). Activists' perspectives thus result from the intersection of the trajectory of an individual's life course and that of a particular cultural and historical moment (Ginsburg 1989a, 1989b).

Periods of rapid social change serve as "crystallizing agents" to produce common experiences and identities among people of the same generation (Mannheim 1952, p. 310). Mannheim (1952, p. 298) suggests that the most formative period for the development of such a perspective is during youth, since "early impressions coalesce into a *natural view* of the world." Others have suggested such perspectives may also develop during early adulthood, as events experienced during adolescence and early adulthood influence identity and life choices (Stewart 1994).

The political generations concept is quite relevant to the women's movement, as women from different political generations view feminism differently.[1] For example, Freeman (1975) illustrates the ways in which generational differences within the early women's movement led to distinct ideologies—the older "women's rights" branch took a "liberal" approach, while the younger "liberation" branch was more "radical." Similarly, Whittier (1995) found that women who joined the movement at the same time developed a shared collective identity. However, within one political generation, there were several "micro-cohorts" whose definitions of themselves as women and feminists differed (Whittier 1995). These subtle variations in attitudes and identities between members of different micro-cohorts resulted from entering the movement at different points in time. Chodorow (1989) also offers support for the political generations approach in her interviews with women who had gone through psychoanalytic training in the 1920s, 1930s and early 1940s. These women believed in sex equality in the public sphere, yet did not discuss the ways in which gender inequality occurred on a personal level in their own lives. Chodorow (1989, p. 217) saw the "generation gap" between herself (a "70s woman") and her interviewees as arising because "the salience and meaning of gender were products of one's time and place."

Identity Transformation and Turning Points

The political generations approach assumes that formative social and cultural conditions lead to the development of a particular world view; it does not attempt to explain why some individuals come to be out of sync with their own political generation as a result of identity transformations. However, identity is influenced not only by social and cultural contexts, but also by the life course and individual experiences. Wells and Stryker (1988, p. 209) argue that identity transformations result when "master statuses" (such as gender and race) "take on new meanings under changing historical circumstances." For example, the meanings of being a woman may change when women's movement ideology challenges previous conceptions.

Similarly, "turning points" (Strauss 1959) result from events in one's personal history, such as changes in relationships, handling a new role unexpectedly well, and betrayal. At such times, "an individual has to take stock, to re-evaluate, revise, resee, and rejudge" (Strauss 1959, p. 96). Thus, changes in life circumstances can lead to identity change.

This exploratory study combines insights from social movement and social psychological literatures to examine the ways in which feminist identities develop differently in different cultural and historical contexts. In addition to finding support for the political generations approach, this research also suggests that identity can be transformed during later phases of the life course. This appears to happen most readily during periods of rapid social and cultural change.

METHODOLOGY

This chapter compares the experiences of women who were active in the Twin Cities Chapter of NOW during the 1970s and early 1980s, with those active in the Minneapolis League of Women Voters during the 1950s and 1960s. As I will discuss later, both of these are local affiliates of national organizations, yet had differing mobilizing frames, ideology, goals, strategies, and tactics, and varied in their points of intersection with the women's movement.

I examined organizational archival materials during peak periods in the organizations' histories—from the Minneapolis League from the early 1950s through the late 1960s, and from Twin Cities NOW in the 1970s. These organizational peaks, occurring in two quite different cultural periods, reflect similar stages of organizational strength and appeal. Comparing these organizations at the two time periods means that I am comparing two different points of intersection with the women's movement, or two distinct cultural periods. The League came before the peak of the women's movement, and this is reflected in League ideology, goals, strategies, and tactics. In contrast, NOW was integral to the women's movement and peaked during the period of its greatest influence.

I interviewed nine women who were involved in these organizations during their peak periods. Following Smith (1990, p. 28), my research began with "women's experience as it is for women," in women's everyday lives. This method helps to recognize the diversity of the types of activism which women consider important, as it leaves space for them to develop and recount their own definitions of the activism in their lives.

The first round of participants (five women) was located through the two organizations. Names and phone numbers were provided from past membership lists. The second round of interviews (with four participants) were conducted a few months later, using a snowball sample method. In all, I interviewed three women from each organization, and three who belonged to both organizations during each organization's peak membership period. Interviews were conducted face-to-face, in a place chosen by each participant. The interviews were "structured conversations" (Taylor and Rupp 1991, p. 126), and allowed space for participants to bring up the issues they found most relevant and important. I asked a

Table 1. Characteristics of Activists in the League and NOW

Organization	Years of Birth	Average Age When Joined Organization	Years When Joined Organization
League	Mid-1920s to Mid-1930s	24	Late 1940s to Early 1960s
NOW	Early 1940s to Mid-1950s	23	Late 1960s to Mid-1970s
Both	Late 1910s to Early 1930s	League: 29 NOW: 44	League: Early 1950s to Early 1960s NOW: Late 1960s to Mid-1970s

wide range of questions about their biographies, organizational histories, political and feminist identities, and conducted follow-up interviews when clarification was needed.

The women I interviewed represent different generations (see Table 1), yet they are comparable because their life course trajectories and experiences were similar in many respects. The League-only and NOW-only women joined and were most active in their respective organizations at similar points in their lives—early adulthood (see Table 1). However, this period of the life course meant quite different things as a result of the changing cultural context—the League women were married and beginning to have children, whereas the NOW women were focusing on career development. All nine women work or worked in professional, middle-class jobs; all graduated from college (although one did so later in her life than the others). Additionally, they were involved in a wide range of leadership positions in their respective organizations.

All of the women were white and middle to upper-middle class. Since race, class, and gender identities are intertwined and interlocking (Collins 1991; Hooks 1990; Spelman 1988), the meanings of feminism and politics for these activists should be seen in relation to their racial and class background. While this means that this study focuses on a select group of women, nearly all of the interviewees indicated that they were similar demographically to other members of their organization(s).[2]

WOMEN'S ACTIVISM AND FEMINIST IDENTITIES, 1950s AND 1960s

The Cultural Context

During the 1950s and early 1960s peak of the Minneapolis League of Women Voters, the social context for American women was slowly shifting. During the 1950s, the United States was filled with "fears about the changing place of women and changing sexual norms" (Evans 1989, p. 244). McCarthyism and the cold war were linked to conceptions of the traditional family and sexuality, and women, when in their "proper" place, symbolized security and safety within the social

order (Evans 1989). This reaffirmation of domesticity, reflected in increased marriage and birth rates and declining age at first marriage, emphasized traditional
gender and family roles (May 1988). The dominant ideology about white, middle
class, suburban women was the "feminine mystique," which defined women
primarily in terms of being wives and mothers (Friedan 1974).

At the same time, white, married women with children were entering the paid
labor force at a rapid rate—from 17 percent in 1950 to 30 percent in 1960 (Evans
1989). Still, women's work was "legitimate only as an extension of traditional
family responsibilities," thus lessening the threat of women's autonomy and
power (Evans 1989, p. 262). The situations of African-American and working
class women were quite different, as they had been more likely to be in the labor
force before this shift.

Overall, middle-class life was apolitical and people were encouraged to take a
private, therapeutic approach to problems (May 1988). Women still participated
in organizations such as church groups, PTAs, and the League, on "the sidelines
of political life" (Evans 1989, p. 247). While these organizations allowed for
activism, they "could not provide a base from which to challenge the complexities
of women's place" (Evans 1989, p. 261). Taylor and Rupp (1991) argue against a
monolithic characterization of this time period, as their research found that the
women's rights movement continued to operate despite its small size, homoge
neous makeup, and limited objectives (such as a primary focus on the Equal
Rights Amendment passage). However, the League rejected identification with
feminism, and thought that women should "think of themselves as citizens first
and as women incidentally" (Rupp and Taylor 1987, p. 49).

History of The League of Women Voters

The League of Women Voters was formed in 1919 as an auxiliary of the
National American Woman Suffrage Association, and became an independent
organization in 1920. After the suffrage Amendment was passed in 1920, the
League's goals were to get "women legally and intellectually ready to be full cit
izens" (Black 1989, p. 261). The Minneapolis League began in 1919 or early
1920.[3] The goal was to "increase the effectiveness of women's votes in furthering
better government" (Minneapolis League undated-c). The League was nonparti
san, as the suffrage movement and experiences of European feminists illustrated
the hazards of women's involvement in partisan politics (Black 1989).

Framing its issues of concern in terms of "good government" promoted the non
partisan image. It represented an attempt to distance the organization from those
which were focused on reform and social change issues. The League was "'ser
vice oriented' rather than 'political or change-oriented'" (Black 1989, p. 296). It
"aim is NOT reform in government but promotion of the democratic process
whereby many citizens are informed about their governments and actively partic
ipate in it" (Minneapolis League of Women Voters 1953). The organization'

main goal, educating citizens, did not attempt to change the "structure or environment of power, let alone its distribution" (Black 1989, p. 295). It sought to work within existing governmental institutions and processes, rather than focusing on changing the existing political system.

Reflecting these goals and tactics, the Minneapolis League sought to have a study group in every ward in the city to educate women about citizenship issues. Called "units," these study groups became the focus of the organization (Tsouderos 1951), and were typically comprised of women who knew each other. Discussion focused on issues from the local, state, and national programs (League of Women Voters of Minnesota 1975). In 1951, unit discussions were monitored by a liaison who made sure the conversations stayed on track (Tsouderos 1951).

After an issue was studied, League members considered establishing "consensus," which represented substantial agreement on an issue. Once consensus had been reached, the League took action by either building public opinion or supporting legislation (Minneapolis League undated-a). Thus, as a document says: "League action is threefold: 1. assembling and disseminating facts. 2. building public opinion. 3. supporting or opposing legislation" (Minneapolis League undated-b). Some of the issues which were studied over a wide range of years (e.g., 1946-1978) include: atomic energy, candidate's meetings, citizen power programs, citizen's community centers, housing, Minneapolis public schools, neighborhood elections, voter registration, Indian affairs, and reapportionment.

In the 50s and 60s, the Minneapolis League was engaged in a wide range of activities. Many of these centered on voter education and voter service, and fit closely with the League's stated purpose. For example, this included: voter service booths, candidate's meetings, publishing a Voters' Guide in the *Minneapolis Morning Tribune*, and having "observers" on a wide range of city boards (to inform members about what was occurring on these boards). The League was also involved in sponsoring a foreign student program (which recruited wives of foreign students to become active in the League), and urban renewal.

In terms of women's issues, the national League concentrated on ending discrimination and achieving legal equality for women (Black 1989). Yet the organization never called itself a feminist organization, and sharply distinguished itself from feminists during the 1950s and 1960s (Rupp and Taylor 1987). For example, a 1951 article in the national organization's magazine said that it represents "work by women but not for women" (Black 1989, p. 275). The League had originally opposed the ERA because it might eliminate protective labor legislation for women (Rupp and Taylor 1987), and in 1940, lobbied against the ERA, calling its support by the Republican National Convention "the shock of the century" (Harrison 1988, p. 19). The organization withdrew this opposition in 1954, as the membership did not know much about the ERA, and it did not seem "important enough to oppose" (Rupp and Taylor 1987, p. 49). By 1974, women's movement ideology had influenced the League, and passage of the ERA became a high priority (Black 1989). Following the national League, the Minneapolis chapter did not focus on women's issues during the time period under consideration.

Women's Life Courses and Feminist Identities

The League members I interviewed joined the organization between the late 1940s and early 1960s (see Table 2 for more specific information.). They all were married and had children when they became active in the League. Based on analysis of archival data, it appears that nearly all of Minneapolis League members were married (Minneapolis League 1953).[4] Although none of the interviewees worked outside the home when their children were young, all of these women worked outside the home later in their lives, when their children were older. It is interesting to note that these women all had a higher number of children than the national average of 2.34 (U.S. Bureau of the Census 1960). Quite different from my "NOW-only" interviewees, the League members (including those who belonged to both organizations at different times) had an average of 3.7 children.

All of the League activists I interviewed were housewives when they joined, and each said that involvement provided a way to get out of the house and provided important social connections. For Ann,[5] "It provided me with the intellectual stimulation which I needed. And it put me in touch with another world other than the world of children and housework." Francine noted how common a reason this was for involvement: "I really fit...the picture of the average person, who is

Table 2. The Women Activists

Pseudonym	Organization	Year Joined	Marital Status when Joined	Total Number of Children	Year Began Work
Ann	League	Late 1940s	Married	5	Early 1970s
Betty	League	Late 1950s	Married	5	Late 1970s
Carole	League	Early 1960s	Married	3	Early 1960s Late 1970s
Dorothy	League NOW	Early 1950s Late 1960	Married	4	Late 1960s
Emma	League NOW	Mid-1950s Mid-1970s	Married	3	Mid-1970s
Francine	League NOW	Early 1960s Early 1970s	Married; later divorced	2	Late 1950s Early 1970s
Gail	NOW	Late 1960s	Married	1	Mid-1960s
Holly	NOW	Mid-1970s	Single	0	Early 1970s
Iris	NOW	Mid-1970s	Single	2	Mid-1970s

a woman, who is a homemaker, had a child, and who has been active previously in some job or whatever, and is feeling kind of suffocated, and talking only baby talk." These statements are reflective of the culture of the 1950s and 1960s, since many women did not work outside the home. As a period focused on domesticity, these women's lives also focused on their families and the domestic realm.

When asked about their relationship to feminism, the League women I spoke with all defined themselves as feminists. To them, feminism referred to public policies and legislation, such as the Equal Rights Amendment, "equality of opportunity," and equal pay. Like others who came of age in the 1940s and 1950s, they did not define feminism in relation to their personal lives or the domestic sphere (see also Chodorow 1989).

For example, both Betty and Carole concentrated on issues such as equality of opportunity, the ERA, equal pay for equal work, abortion rights, and women in leadership roles. They both compared their own conceptions of feminism with what they viewed as a different type of feminism. As Carole put it:

> I'm not as rabid on these subjects as some people are. I work very well with men as well as with women, and I don't take the attitude that every man is an obstacle or every man is a bad person, as some people who are involved with feminism really seem to believe—that...men are the enemy. But I'm certainly supportive of a range of initiatives here that I would consider to be a progressive feminist program.

Betty mentioned a similar distinction when discussing the issues that were important to her: "I don't feel strongly about semantics and I think some of those things are tempests in teapots. But I feel very strongly about the real issues—about women's equality of opportunity and the role [women] play." These distinctions seem to be directed at parts of the women's movement which they consider to reflect a different type of feminism than they endorse.

The lack of feminism's *personal* relevance was also expressed by Emma, who "led a very traditional life" at the time she joined the League. After describing how she had performed well in college, she said:

> And yet, with that kind of background it never crossed my mind to have a career or go to graduate school or do anything. All I wanted to do was to get married, which is what I did, and then I stayed at home for 20 years raising children because that's what people did in the 50s and 60s, well, until the mid-60s when things started popping open.

When she talked about the early 1970s, which was prior to her own coming to feminism, she mentioned having a friend who was running for political office and emphasizing women's issues. Emma said: "and I can remember thinking 'that really is kind of trivial.'" Francine, who experienced a profound transformation in her view of feminism later in her life, described her League experience as follows:

> In that period, I would be Mrs. [Bob Jones], and it would be Mrs. [Joe Smith], and Mrs. [Tom Wright], and we were accepting this....the reason I got [involved in the topic of] population

and the environment, it was a lady bountiful kind of approach. I mean, let us worry about other people's problems. I didn't perceive it as my problems.

Defining feminism in terms of public policy and legislation rather than personal issues reflects the cultural context, as these women came of age before the 1970s "personal is political" feminism of the women's movement came to predominate.

Similarly, Dorothy discussed how her conception of feminism changed over time: "Well, probably it's gotten stronger. I mean I was always a feminist but didn't know it. I was raised by feminists. They didn't know it either." This suggests that feminism was not a salient issue or identity for Dorothy until later in her life, indicating how the historical period of the late 1960s and 1970s may have influenced her realization of her feminist identity.

Supporting the political generations approach, the League activists fit within the cultural context of the 1950s and 1960s in terms of both their life course trajectories and their feminist identities. Their lives during young adulthood were focused on marriage, children, and domesticity. These activists articulated their feminist identities primarily in terms of public-realm issues, such as equality of opportunity, equal access, comparable worth, and the ERA. These women were politically active and went through early adulthood before the women's movement of the late 1960s and 1970s, and were most influenced by the ideology and paths open to them during the period in which they came of age.

WOMEN'S ACTIVISM AND FEMINIST IDENTITIES, 1970s

The Cultural Context

The "feminine mystique" context began to shift during the 1960s, as the civil rights and then later, anti-war movements, emerged and gained momentum. Evans (1989, p. 267) says that "for all kinds of women changes in the 1960s paradoxically generated stresses, new possibilities, and new consciousnesses." The small, spontaneous groups which arose to confront women's personal concerns in the 1960s and 1970s challenged both home and workplace roles. Activism was often sparked by anger. As Evans (1979, p. 218) puts it, "for most American women only a movement that addressed the oppression at the core of their identity could have generated the massive response that in fact occurred." The women's movement thus addressed issues rooted within women's personal lives. Scholars discuss the convergence of women's rights and women's liberation groups in the late 1970s, indicating a radicalization of the women's rights section (Rossi 1982; Gelb and Palley 1982). This reflects the spread of feminist liberation ideology, which also influenced traditional women's organizations, such as the League.

History of The National Organization for Women (NOW)

NOW's founding was linked to the emergence of the women's movement in the early 1960s, when the Presidential Commission on the Status of Women was formed to assess women's place in the family, the economy and legal system (Evans 1989). NOW was formed in response to frustration over the Third National Conference of State Commissions in 1966, as delegates learned that the conference would not allow any resolutions or actions to be submitted (Evans 1989). This new organization was formed with an awareness of the limitations of governmental bodies, and sought to create a "civil rights movement for women" which could confront laws and customs (Harrison 1988, p. 197).

The first statement of purpose was "to take action to bring women into full participation in the mainstream of American society now, exercising all the privileges and responsibilities thereof in fully equal partnership with men" (National Organization for Women undated). At NOW's first national conference in Washington, D.C. in 1967, a Bill of Rights was enacted, demanding: the passage of the Equal Rights Amendment (ERA); the banning of sex discrimination in employment; the granting of maternity leave and child care expenses for parents; the establishment of national child care centers; the elimination of sex discrimination in education; equal job training for women in poverty; and reproductive freedom (Morgan 1970).

NOW encouraged the formation of local chapters, and frequently worked in coalition with other women's movement organizations (Harrison 1988). In 1970, a Twin Cities NOW chapter was formed. A membership pamphlet listed its priorities: politics and legislation; employment; "help wanted ads listed by occupation, not sex"; image of women; education; abortion law repeal; family law; child care; and religious institutions. NOW also invested a great deal of time and energy on passing the ERA.

The local chapter's four main tactics and goals emphasized changing women's position in society. The first tactic was education—public speaking to groups such as schools and teachers to raise awareness about sexism. These educational workshops were often met with hostility by those in the audience who were reluctant to recognize sexism (Interview July 7, 1994). The second tactic involved protests and demonstrations, including: protesting against an Old Gold billboard advertisement on a busy street (which "showed the letters O and G on a woman's prominent breasts"—Twin Cities National Organization for Women, undated-a); burning a copy of the constitution on the steps of the federal building; picketing two movies and a sexist rock group; and taking over a restaurant at an upscale department store, which was then men-only (Interviews February 10, 1994 and July 8, 1994). The third type of tactic was focused on the legislative arena, and included continued work on the Minneapolis City Council affirmative action program, educating women about the Federal Equal Credit Act, political organizing for the ERA, and letter-writing to public officials (Twin Cities NOW undated-a). Finally, reflecting a significant radicalization by the late 1970s,[6] consciousness raising groups were established (Twin Cities NOW 1975). The consciousness raising task force proposal stated the objectives as bringing "women from NOW and the community together to help them find their common ideas and build strong ties of sisterhood, to promote NOW, to take people from the personal to the political" (Twin Cities NOW undated-b).

NOW's primary focus of changing women's position in society greatly contrasts with the League's organizational ideology, since the tactics and goals were aimed at altering existing political and social institutions. This concern for creating structural change is distinct from the League's ideology, which promotes democratic process within established governmental institutions. The issue of readiness distinguishes the organizations: the League's ideology and tactics were oriented to getting women (as well as other citizens) *ready* (through education and studying issues) to take part in politics, while NOW's ideology and tactics were designed to alter patriarchy, "now." Comparing NOW and the League in 1977, Rossi (1982, p. 215) describes the differences between these organizations as follows: "NOW is the most representative feminist organization, with a very broad agenda of feminist commitments, whereas the League is a good representative of an equally sophisticated political organization of women that has no central feminist ideology or commitment to work for increased sex equality." She found that the members of NOW had stronger feminist positions, and higher individual and group consistency on feminist issues than did those of the League. Thus, NOW fits within the historical context of the women's movement of the late 1960s and 1970s, as it emphasized social change to eliminate sexism and employed a wide range of protest tactics.

Women's Life Courses and Feminist Identities

The NOW-only women I interviewed joined between the late 1960s and the mid-1970s (see Table 2). In contrast to the League members, they worked outside the home before, during, and after the time they had children. As already mentioned, they graduated from college and developed their careers while in their 20s, and had relatively small families. Challenging traditional notions of being a woman, these women's lives centered on education and careers instead of domesticity during a period when this became increasingly acceptable. The character of their early adult life courses thus reflected larger cultural changes in women's lives in general.

Whereas the League women felt that social connections in the organization provided a way for them to get out of the house when their children were young, the NOW activists felt that their relationships with other women made them realize that they weren't "crazy." As Emma put it, the women's movement "was that great sense of discovery—that great sense of 'I'm not crazy, the world is crazy. There's nothing wrong with me, it's a patriarchal society.'" An important aspect of knowing "I'm not crazy" was acceptance of oneself in the face of patriarchal conditions, which constrained women's roles. These activists found support in NOW for controversial political views, such as criticism of patriarchy.

Like the League activists, the NOW women defined themselves as feminists. However, their conception of feminism included both the public and the personal realms. They mentioned legislation, like the ERA and sex discrimination in education and athletics, as well as personal issues, such as intimate relationships, independence, appearance, and anger. The NOW-only women both reflected, and probably influenced, the ideology of the women's movement of the late 60s and 70s, as they came of age during this period.

For example, Iris, who was in her young adulthood during the 1970s, was heavily involved in NOW's consciousness raising groups. She saw feminism as a very personal issue at that time in her life. To her, feminism encompassed a wide range of personal issues—intimate relationships, how she was raised, her career, and making changes in her life. She said that NOW helped in:

> just understanding what feminism has to do with you as an individual person. That had a very, very strong impact on me....It was real close to home kinds of stuff....It was a real support group. It wasn't just a meeting to air political views or to work on equal rights legislation. It was helping people in their daily lives.

This is closely tied to the "you knew you weren't crazy" theme. Connecting with other women lessened feelings of isolation which came from family members "who don't understand." Iris said of her family: "They finally learned, after screaming tirades from me, that it's different to talk about a public policy that doesn't really affect you than to hit something that was at the core of who I am." This distinction between policy and "the core of who I am" suggests that Iris' feminist identity was deeply tied to personal issues.

Similarly, Holly saw personal and public issues of feminism as intertwined, and emphasized each at different times during the interview. Emphasizing the personal aspects, she said:

> I think it's hard for someone to be an activist without having any personal experience. I think it's hard to look at it purely on an intellectual basis—you really need to have something you've seen or experienced....I think a lot of women found themselves in NOW and made some major decisions about their lives—decided to leave marriages, or restructure their marriages, demand more equal partnerships, and for some there were lesbian issues....There were a lot of personal changes that came out of it....As you start to work within it you start to realize things about yourself. It's more of an outgrowth.

A sense of solidarity which developed from the support of others in the organization may have encouraged these women to continue to make changes in their lives.

The NOW women emphasized the process of coming to feminism, and the ways in which the cultural context influenced this process. For example, Holly did not remember there being any women's rights organizations when she was in college. Then later,

> People were raising issues that I hadn't really thought about....The rules [for athletics and dorm hours] were just totally different [for men and women] and I hadn't really thought about it. All these flags started coming up, and I started to realize the unfairness of it all, that women really didn't have the same opportunities, and that became important to me—important enough that I was willing to spend a lot of my time to try to make things better....[NOW] gave me a feminist perspective.

Iris said that involvement with the organization made feminism "more of an integral part of me." This illustrates a strengthening of her personal conception of feminism.

Gail discussed a wide range of both public and personal realm issues, but she also mentioned a time when she decided *not* to make a dramatic change in her life:

> I sat with a very reflective time with myself somewhere in [...the early 1970s], and thought how possible it would have been for us to end up divorced and dealing with custody issues if I was *really* out there, going to the national NOW in the national office in D.C....I had known other people then, I'd have to look at lists to remember their names, whose lives did go like that. And there were divorces and there was a whole shift of a life, and that basically was a plausible option. And I'll always look at all of these kinds of decision points and say, "you never exactly know the unknown path."

It should be noted that Gail came of age and was active in NOW in the mid-1960s, prior to the height of the women's movement. Perhaps Gail's experiences, as an early "micro-cohort" member (Whittier 1995), differed from those who joined later.

Again in support of the political generations approach, the NOW activists' life course trajectories and feminist identities fit within the cultural and historical context of the late 1960s and 1970s. In contrast to the League women during the 1950s and early 1960s, their early adult life courses were focused on pursuing their education and careers rather than having families. In addition, their feminist identities centered on personal issues which began to be raised by the women's movement during the late 1960s and 1970s.

IDENTITY TRANSFORMATION

Moving beyond the political generations approach in the social movements literature, this study illustrates how experiences in some women's lives led them to break with the ideology of their own generation, and take on new identities later in the life course. These identity transformations occurred as a result of the intersection of "turning points" (Strauss 1959) in personal history with ideological currents in the cultural context, namely the emergence of the women's movement. That is, the movement's emphasis on personal change, along with events in these women's lives, created the conditions for new identity possibilities and identity transformation.

Identity change occurred for two activists. These women came of age and joined the League between the mid-1950s and early 1960s, and later joined NOW in the early- to mid-1970s. Contemporaries of the League activists, and previously leading very traditional lives, these women experienced transformations in their identities in ways that other League activists did not. In doing so, their feminist identities became quite similar to those of the younger women who came of age during the peak of the women's movement. However, the process by which they arrived at these identities was quite different than it was for the younger women.

For example, Emma saw a difference between her own coming to feminism and the path that other women her age took, as they did not bring feminism into their personal lives. After she discussed the difference that feminism made in women's personal lives, she told me "our life has really, really changed." When I asked her how, she responded:

> I know people who were my contemporaries who consciously chose not to be feminists because they had a comfortable marriage and a comfortable life and they didn't want to jeopardize that. I feel terribly sorry for them, their lives.... I can't imagine what my life would have been like without the women's movement.

These activists relate their identity transformations to particular turning points. Emma pinpointed the early 1970s as a time of many "clicks" in her thinking. One occurred when a public office holder encouraged her husband to run for office instead of her, and another was the way she was treated after she got elected. Despite her success in this new role, she was not treated as a "co-equal" in the position. As Strauss (1959) suggests, these turning points may have been transformative as a result of both betrayal (in terms of how she was treated) and the successful handling of a new role. These experiences were part of her transformation, and were a "real consciousness raiser." She said:

> It took me a long time to realize that it was patriarchy and that it was everywhere....It was a gradual awakening of a number of different things....[Patriarchy] is so much a part of the culture that you don't see it—it's like smog in Los Angeles. Then of course once your eyes are open, you see it everywhere. The more you see it, the angrier you get, and that's why I think women get more radical when they get older.

This radicalization with age suggests a need to go beyond the standard political generations model.

Another activist, Francine, pointed directly to the effects of the historical and cultural period on her feminist identity. Suggesting that her initial orientation was "lost along the way" as a result of her experiences in the 1950s, she later went through a dramatic identity transformation. She described how she was "diverted" as follows:

When I graduated from high school I was going to be a psychiatrist. I had bets with people that I wouldn't get married before the age of 30....And at that time, this was in the 50s, there was this [college] dean who believed in gracious living, which is straight feminine mystique. The reason why we were [in college] was because we were going to marry Harvard men and have children and raise them to be literate leaders. It was absolutely not the thing to do to think about going out and having a career. And it was just amazing how quickly I was done in....I think it goes to show that it's real easy to get diverted.

In the early 1970s, Francine experienced a dramatic transformation as a result of her divorce. She suddenly had to support herself economically and end her "emotional dependence" on her husband. Her transformation may have resulted from her adjustment to the relationship change, her husband's betrayal, and the new roles she had to jump into (Strauss 1959). It is also possible that this identity change represented a return to the earlier orientation described above.

In the early 1970s, she joined NOW. Other NOW activists, unlike League women, were supportive of her when she got a divorce:

I don't know how much the independence that I had gained as a result of [the NOW conscious-ness raising groups]...had influenced [my husband]....The blessing was...that I had this net-work, both through the League, and also, and more important, through NOW, because the League ladies were all married. And let's face it, they did not invite me to dinner as a single woman, any of them. It was just the beginning of the point, of the era, when everyone was get-ting a divorce, and everyone was scared to death....The married women were really nervous. See, change was about to occur and they had been totally dependent....The NOW support group is fabulous, just fabulous. And I didn't have money, and I had this big house, and my husband took all the furniture, which had been his family's antiques, so I turned it into a com-mune...Feminism was really big in my life after about three years, and I basically dropped the League at that point.

In this woman's experience, the NOW activists were supportive of her during life changes like divorce, and were not "scared to death" of dramatic personal change. Support for personal change in relationships, and a new social network, helped her cope with her divorce and establish a new identity. Francine emphasized the importance of transformation when she compared these two different times in her life, and the two organizations:

So that...was for me like the end of one life and the beginning of another life, a totally fasci-nating transition....The reason why I was in the League was kind of like a diversion, to talk about those issues in this kind of neutral, objective, and passive, not passive, but it was good citizenship. NOW got me where I lived, in my gut....I was able to show anger, which I had never shown before....It's interesting, because I feel that there's a huge gulf sometimes between me and my friends who stayed with the League and never went beyond it, so to speak....They're still in that, and I know that they have a lot of fear.

These experiences suggest that identity transformation which coincides with changing cultural circumstances may be sparked by particular life events. These identity changes may also represent a return to earlier orientations and previous identities which felt more genuine.

The experiences of these activists illustrate how their own transformations were different from many other women their age, who were afraid of the personal changes which this conception of feminism might bring into their lives. Each experienced important turning points which helped to produce identity transformations, and their lives changed in both family and work arenas. These turning points occurred in a rapidly changing historical context which emphasized women's personal change, suggesting that these conditions together can lead to identity transformation.

CONCLUSIONS

As proposed by the political generations approach, this study found evidence that feminist identities develop in relation to the cultural ideologies predominant at the time when one comes of political age. Women active in the League of Women Voters during the 1950s through the mid-1960s came of age before the peak of the women's movement and conceptualized "feminism" largely in terms of public-realm issues. These activists came to early adulthood during the 1950s, when the dominant cultural ideology emphasized a disjuncture between the public and private realms. In contrast, the women activists who were most readily influenced by "the personal is political" ideology of the women's movement were those who were involved with the National Organization for Women during the 1970s and early 1980s, and came of age during the peak of the women's movement. Focusing on personal and societal change, these activists' feminist identities were linked to a cultural ideology which challenged the separation between the public and private realms and opened up the issue of personal change.

However, these findings also suggest a need to expand the political generations concept to include the possibility of identity transformation later in life. Experiencing profound changes in their identities, some interviewees were influenced by the women's movement during middle age. These activists, formerly involved in the League and embracing similar feminist identities as League members, later joined NOW and began to focus more on issues of personal and social change. These women came of age before the women's movement, but then took a path very different from their contemporaries, largely due to particular turning points in their personal histories which led them to change both the shape of their life courses and their feminist identities.

These identity transformations occurred in a rapidly changing cultural context. The conditions of women's lives were in flux and new identity possibilities were emerging. While it was mainly women who came of age during the height of the women's movement who were influenced by its concern with personal change, women who came of age in the 1950s and early 1960s were sometimes influenced as well, resulting in identity transformation. The combination of the women's movement, which created the conditions for new identity possibilities with its emphasis on personal change, and events in these women's lives led to identity transformation.

This study has several implications for thinking about identity across the life course. First, it supports previous studies in revealing the long-lasting influence of the cultural context when one comes of age. The formative period of young adulthood becomes a key to understanding identities at later points in the life course. At the same time, these findings suggest a process of identity change coinciding with a rapidly changing cultural and political context. These profound identity transformations reveal the fluid and changing nature of identities in response to new cultural conditions. However, it is not new cultural conditions alone which spark identity change, but rather the corresponding influence of particular life-altering events in one's biography.

DIRECTIONS FOR FUTURE RESEARCH

These exploratory findings, while illustrative of the process by which an individual's identity is transformed at later points in the life course, suggest that future research in this area is necessary. Several questions emerge as a result of this study. First, precisely who undergoes identity transformations, and what are the specific conditions under which this occurs? For example, is it only political activists who experience such transformations, or is this process generalizable to a broader population? Related to this issue, which changing cultural conditions are most influential for identity transformation? And finally, what effect do different types of turning points have on identity change?

Future research could address these questions in several ways. First, it would be beneficial to interview a larger number of activists from these two organizations, and to do so over a wider period of activism. In particular, it would be useful to study a more diverse sample, particularly in terms of racial and class background and marital status. For example, it is possible that marital status and organizational affiliation are confounded in the present study. Expanding the sample size would also provide greater insight into potential differences in organizational activism and organizational change over time.

Second, these findings should be explored in relation to a wider range of social movement organizations. In particular, it would be interesting to examine other types of social movements in relation to identity transformation. It might be the case that the women's movement, with its emphasis on "the personal is political," engenders identity transformations as a result of personal turning points in ways that other social movements do not. This research could deepen our understanding of the types of movements which have the potential to lead to identity change at diverse points in the life course. Thus, the generalizability of these findings to other social movements and organizational contexts is an important area of future research.

A third direction for future study is an examination of different types of turning points and different forms of identity change. It might be the case that only particular turning points alter identity. Furthermore, identity change may only occur at certain times in the life course. These directions for future research will help to more fully explicate the process of identity transformation under changing cultural conditions.

Studying women's political activism has important implications for both historical understanding and future change. Women's political power has made a tremendous impact in this country, and the past thirty years have seen a cultural revolution. Women are getting elected to political offices in increasing numbers, many people discuss the "gender gap" in voting, and women's activism in the women's movement of the 1960s and 1970s transformed the workplace, the family, and their own lives. Change in women's identities is important both historically and for its power to alter the future. This is nicely captured by a quote from one of the activists:

> Well in a way, it felt like you were a part of history...you look back and you read about the suffragist movement and think "well that was us"...just working on the Equal Rights Amendment instead....And [it means a lot to know]...it's changed—things are better for my daughter than they were when I was seven.

ACKNOWLEDGMENTS

This research was partially supported by a National Research Service Award from the National Institute of Mental Health (Training Program in Identity, Self, Role, and Mental Health—PHST 32 MH 14588). The author would like to thank the following people, who all provided comments and contributed insights to this project: Ronald Aminzade, Ronald Aronson, Sara Evans, Barbara Laslett, Jeylan Mortimer, Timothy Owens, Todd Paxton, Kimberly Simmons, and Heather VanderLey.

NOTES

1. A full discussion of the antecedents of feminist attitudes is beyond the scope of this chapter. It should be noted, however, that higher levels of education and income are related to less traditional gender role attitudes, and that employed women are more likely than nonemployed women to express feminist attitudes (Hunter and Sellers 1998). Other studies suggest that women who have experienced discrimination more frequently identify as feminists (Renzetti 1987). This "liberation consciousness" (Flacks 1988) develops when people begin to doubt the moral rightness of their accustomed subordination, and begin to formulate new demands which correspond to new identities. Sexism in the civil rights and antiwar movements, for example, sparked the creation of the women's liberation branch of the women's movement (Evans 1979).

2. There was no available archival information about members' class or racial backgrounds.

3. Some documents suggest the originating date as 1919, while others cite it as January 1920. Thus, the precise founding date remains unclear.

4. Members were listed by their husbands' names (e.g., Mrs. Bob Jones) in the 1950s through the mid-1960s.

5. All names have been changed to maintain confidentiality.

6. This information is based on a personal conversation with Marcia Neff, a graduate student in American Studies at the University of Minnesota and former member of the Twin Cities National Organization for Women.

REFERENCES

Aminzade, R. 1993. *Ballots and Barricades: Class Formation and Republican Politics in France, 1830-1871*. Princeton, NJ: Princeton University Press.

Black, N. 1989. *Social Feminism*. Ithaca, NY: Cornell University Press.

Chodorow, N. 1989. *Feminism and Psychoanalytic Theory*. New Haven, CT: Yale University Press.

Collins, P.H. 1991. *Black Feminist Thought: Knowledge, Consciousness, and the Politics of Empowerment*. New York: Routledge.

Costain, A. 1992. *Inviting Women's Rebellion: A Political Process Interpretation of the Women's Movement*. Baltimore: John Hopkins University Press.

Evans, S. 1979. *Personal Politics: The Roots of Women's Liberation in the Civil Rights Movement and the New Left*. New York: Vintage Books.

_____. 1989. *Born For Liberty: A History of Women in America*. New York: Free Press.

Flacks, R. 1988. *Making History: The American Left and the American Mind*. New York: Columbia University Press.

Freeman, J. 1975. *The Politics of Women's Liberation*. New York: Longman.

Friedan, B. 1974. *The Feminine Mystique*. New York: Dell.

Gelb, J., and M.L. Palley. 1982. *Women and Public Policies*. Princeton, NJ: Princeton University Press.

Ginsburg, F. 1989a. "Dissonance and Harmony: The Symbolic Function of Abortion in Activists' Life Stories." In *Interpreting Women's Lives: Feminist Theory and Personal Narratives*, edited by Personal Narratives Group. Bloomington: Indiana University Press.

_____. 1989b. *Contested Lives: The Abortion Debate in an American Community*. Berkeley: University of California Press.

Harrison, C. 1988. *On Account of Sex: The Politics of Women's Issues, 1945-1968*. Berkeley: University of California Press.

Hooks, B. 1990. *Yearning: Race, Gender, and Cultural Politics*. Boston: South End Press.

Hunter, A., and S. Sellers. 1998. "Feminist Attitudes Among African American Women and Men." *Gender and Society* 12(1)(Feb): 81-99.

League of Women Voters of Minnesota. 1975. *Let's Talk League*. St. Paul, MN: Minnesota Historical Society.

Mannheim, K. 1952. *Essays on the Sociology of Knowledge*. London: Routledge & Kegan Paul.

May, E.T. 1988. *Homeward Bound: American Families in the Cold War Era*. New York: Basic Books, Inc.

Meyer, D., and S. Staggenborg. 1996. "Movements, Countermovements, and the Structure of Political Opportunity." *American Journal of Sociology* 101(6): 1628-1660.

Minneapolis League of Women Voters. Undated-a. "How to Keep Membership." *Let's Talk League*. St. Paul, MN: Minnesota Historical Society.

_____. Undated-b. "The Why, the What, the How."St. Paul, MN: Minnesota Historical Society.

_____. Undated-c. ("1920 or 1921" written in pencil). *Constitution of the Minneapolis League of Women Voters*. St. Paul, MN: Minnesota Historical Society.

_____. 1953. *Orientation Outline for New and 'Old' Members.* St. Paul, MN: Minnesota Historical Society.

Morgan, R., (Ed.). 1970. *Sisterhood is Powerful: An Anthology of Writings from the Women's Liberation Movement.* New York: Vintage Books.

National Organization for Women. Undated. *The First Five Years: 1966-1971.* St. Paul, MN: Minnesota Historical Society.

Renzetti, C. 1987. "New Wave or Second Stage? Attitudes of College Women Toward Feminism." *Sex Roles* 16(5/6): 265-277.

Rossi, A. 1982. *Feminist in Politics: A Panel Analysis of the First National Women's Conference.* New York: Academic Press.

Rupp, L., and V. Taylor. 1987. *Survival in the Doldrums: The American Women's Rights Movement, 1945 to the 1960s.* New York: Oxford University Press.

Schneider, B. 1988. "Political Generations and the Contemporary Women's Movement." *Sociological Inquiry* 58: 4-21.

Smith, D. 1990. *The Conceptual Practices of Power: A Feminist Sociology of Knowledge.* Boston: Northeastern University Press.

Spelman, E. 1988. *Inessential Woman: Problems of Exclusion in Feminist Thought.* Boston: Beacon Press.

Stewart, A. 1994. "The Women's Movement and Women's Lives: Linking Individual Development and Social Events." In *The Narrative Study of Lives, Volume 2: Exploring Identity and Gender,* edited by A. Lieblich and R. Josselson. Thousand Oaks, CA: Sage.

Strauss, A. 1959. *Mirrors and Masks: The Search for Identity.* Glencoe, IL: The Free Press.

Tarrow, S. 1989. *Struggle, Politics, and Reform: Collective Action, Social Movements, and Cycles of Protest.* Occasional Paper No. 21, Western Societies Program, Center for International Studies, Cornell University, Ithaca, NY.

Taylor, V., and L. Rupp. 1991. "Researching the Women's Movement: We Make Our Own History, But Not Just As We Please." In *Beyond Methodology: Feminist Scholarship as Lived Research.* Bloomington: Indiana University Press.

Tsouderos, J. 1951. *Case History No. 1: Minneapolis League of Women Voters.* Unpublished. St. Paul, MN: Minnesota Historical Society.

Twin Cities National Organization for Women. Undated-a. *Twin Cities NOW: 10 Years Ago.* St. Paul, MN: Minnesota Historical Society.

_____. Undated-b. *Consciousness Raising Task Force Proposal.* St. Paul, MN: Minnesota Historical Society.

_____. 1975. *Annual Report.* St. Paul, MN: Minnesota Historical Society.

U.S. Bureau of the Census. 1960. *Census of the Population: Detailed Characteristics of the Population.* Washington, DC: United States Department of Commerce, Bureau of the Census.

Wells, E., and S. Stryker. 1988. "Stability and Change in Self over the Life Course." In *Life Span Development and Behavior,* edited by P. Baltes, D. Featherman, and R. Lerner. Hillsdale, NJ: Lawrence Erlbaum Associates.

Whittier, N. 1995. *Feminist Generations: The Persistence of the Radical Women's Movement.* Philadelphia: Temple University Press.

THE CROSS-CULTURING WORK
OF GAY AND LESBIAN ELDERLY

Melvin Pollner and Dana Rosenfeld

ABSTRACT

Homosexuals wend their way through a hostile culture in which an understanding of the attitudes and actions of the dominant heterosexual culture is necessary for practical, emotional, and even physical survival. By virtue of their life-long experiences in such a culture, gay and lesbian elderly provide a perspicuous opportunity to examine practices through which people define and engage other cultural groups—practices we call "cross-culturing." Our analysis of in-depth interviews with a sample of gay men and lesbians over the age of 65 showed that, for them, cross-culturing is complicated by divisions within the homosexual community regarding the appropriate response to the "heterosexual other." We examine how our subjects use their relation to both heterosexual culture and to the alternative paradigms within the homosexual community to define and evaluate the self over the life course. We conclude the paper by suggesting the possibilities and concerns for exploring the response to cultural diversity among future cohorts of elderly, homosexual or otherwise.

Advances in Life Course Research, Volume 5, pages 99-117.
Copyright © 2000 by JAI Press Inc.
All rights of reproduction in any form reserved.
ISBN: 0-7623-0033-7

The increasing recognition of the cultural diversity of aging has brought attention to the gay and lesbian elderly (Adelman 1991; Dorfman et al. 1995; Lee 1987; Quam and Whitford 1992). Because issues pertaining to sexual orientation reverberate throughout the life course (George 1996), these elderly may be expected to have concerns and experiences different from their heterosexual counterparts. A number of studies have explored differences (and similarities) between hetero- and homosexual elderly in terms of social relationships and sense of well-being (e.g., Dorfman et al. 1995). An appreciation of the methodological consequences of the diversity of aging, however, requires more than comparisons of dominant and minority groups, especially comparisons framed in terms of concepts drawn from the former. The experiences of minority groups—homosexual or otherwise —may be so distinctive that the imposition of mainstream categories can obviate the unique and meaningful features of their life worlds. In lieu of assumptions and frameworks derived from the perspective of dominant groups (Grigsby 1996; Calasanti 1996), researchers in the interpretive tradition (Gubrium and Sankar 1994) suggest that respect for diversity requires attending to the concerns and contexts of the elderly as they are defined and experienced by the elderly themselves.

In considering the implications of diversity for the study of aging, it is also important to recognize that cultural diversity is not merely an analyst's construct. Although social gerontology appreciates that various communities may develop distinctively different ways of defining and enacting their social worlds, it has yet to fully appreciate that social actors encounter, interpret and adapt to such differences in their everyday lives. Globalization, immigration, and demographic change increase the likelihood that the everyday worlds of the elderly will include groups different from their own. Thus, cultural diversity does more than mark the social scientific recognition of the variety of contexts of aging: it refers as well to everyday encounters with cultural others.

Because cultural diversity is a feature of the life world—"the self-evident and taken-for-granted experience of the individual, grounded in both the cultural and natural environments" (Kaufman 1994, p. 135)—comparisons and contrasts of heterosexual and homosexual elderly risk neglecting how members of minority and dominant groups typify and engage one another in everyday life. Indeed, members may conduct their own "comparisons and contrasts" as they characterize and evaluate one another. Thus, a methodology mindful of diversity as a feature of the life world examines social actors' representation of and response to cultural others. We refer to the everyday practices of typifying and taking into account other cultural groups as "cross-culturing."

In addition to providing a version of cultural others and their likely actions, the practices of cross-culturing have implications for actors' sense of self and personal identity. Hewitt (1994, p. 165) has suggested that:

> Each way of talking about the self and relating concrete thoughts, feelings, and actions to
> self-conception is also a way of imagining the social order and thus establishing a place for
> oneself in it.

In turn, a particular imagining of the social order is a way of talking about the self. As individuals represent other cultures in their life worlds, they generate the resources for identifying their own social location through contrast and comparison: I am like (or not like) the other. Moreover, the version of the social order developed through cross-culturing is insinuated in the assessment of personal and moral qualities. If cultural others are represented as corrupt, for example, relations with them may occasion self-attributions of moral integrity or failure. Constructions of what is "out there " in terms of cultural others, then, provide the basis for imputations of what is "in here" in terms of character and self.

The gay and lesbian elderly afford a perspicuous opportunity to examine cross-culturing. If, as Dowd (1986, p. 180) suggests, the elderly are "immigrants in time" whose looks, behaviors, and values are so different that they appear as "strangers in our midst," then members of the current generation of gay and lesbian elderly are akin to illegal aliens. As Wolfe's (1998) recent survey of the moral tenor of the middle class shows, despite tolerance for alternative values and behaviors, many Americans still regard homosexuality as a moral, psychological, or physical pathology. Thus, the gay and lesbian elderly wend their way through a hostile culture in which an acute understanding of the attitudes and actions of the dominant heterosexual culture is necessary for practical, emotional, and even physical survival.

The cross-culturing work of the elderly is complicated by the emergence of major ideological and cultural divides within the gay and lesbian community itself. During their lifetimes, many homosexuals witnessed a revolutionary change regarding the meaning and expression of homosexual identity due to the emergence of the gay liberation movement sparked by the Stonewall uprising of 1969 (Duberman 1994). The pre-Stonewall culture of the homosexual community cultivated an understanding of homosexuality as an emotional-erotic attraction confined to private relations (Faderman 1991). The paradigm emerging in the post- Stonewall period, by contrast, emphasized homosexuality as constituting a self whose authentic expression required public declaration and political action (Marotta 1981; D'Emilio 1983).

Ironically, the new identity paradigm created yet another cultural rift. Tensions between the two paradigms, each with its own standards for action and self-assessment, emerged alongside a new homosexual identity politics. For some of the current cohort of gay elderly, the new definition and demands of being gay or lesbian seemed naive or dangerous in the context of a punitive dominant culture (Grube 1991; Lee 1987). For others, however, the earlier understanding was an unacceptable accommodation to heterosexual oppression (Stein 1997). In some measure, segments of the gay community became alien to one another—

finding themselves on opposite sides of a new cultural divide, this time within the gay community. Thus, members of the current cohort of gay elderly were (and are) enmeshed in positioning themselves in regard to both the dominant culture *and* alternative perspectives regarding how to position oneself in regard to that culture.

We examine the cross-culturing work of a sample of gay and lesbian elderly by first describing our subjects' typification of heterosexuals.[1] Almost without exception, heterosexuals are portrayed as threatened by homosexuals and prepared to end relations with them—indeed, even to banish them from the community. The consensus on the attitudes and likely reactions of heterosexuals, however, belies markedly different understandings of the risks of disclosure and of appropriate precautionary measures. For most in our sample, passing as heterosexual was the most practical way to avoid the personal costs of public identification. For others, however, passing was itself an intolerable betrayal of the "real" self. For these individuals, the appropriate response to the heterosexual threat was not to pass as heterosexual, but to disclose one's homosexuality to heterosexuals. We then examine how these relations to the dominant heterosexual culture and the alternative paradigms within the homosexual community were used by our subjects to identify and evaluate themselves. In stipulating their stance toward the heterosexual community—to pass or to disclose—subjects explicitly and invidiously distinguished themselves from those who did otherwise. Relatedly, they used their stance as the source of criteria for evaluating the integrity and efficacy of their actions.

METHODS

A snowball sampling technique (Bailey 1994) was used to secure a sample of noninstitutionalized gay and lesbian elderly over the age of 65.[2] The initial respondents were contacted at programs and events for the gay and lesbian elderly in the Los Angeles area. Although some of those approached declined to be interviewed, most—including those most concerned with keeping their identities secret—agreed once they were assured of their confidentiality. (Subjects' names have, of course, been changed.) At the conclusion of an interview, subjects were asked if they knew other gay and/or lesbian seniors and, if they did, to contact them to determine if they would participate in the study. A total of 25 men and 24 women were interviewed.[3]

The sample ranged from 65 to 89 years old with a mean of 73.2 years. Three quarters of the sample is retired, but there is considerable variation in yearly income: 18 percent receive less than $10,000 while a similar percentage has an income in excess of $40,000. Similarly, while 14 percent of the sample did not go beyond college, almost a third were enrolled in and/or completed a graduate program or professional school. Other distributions are noteworthy for their skew:

more than three quarters of the sample lives alone, was never in a conventional marriage, and did not have children. Finally, despite a considerable effort to secure an ethnically diverse group, all but 14 percent of the sample is Anglo.

Through the interviews we sought to understand subjects' life worlds by combining questions seeking demographic information (e.g. birth date, education, income, marital and relationship status, etc.) with more open-ended questions (e.g. "Do you think being gay has influenced your life in significant ways, and if so, how?"). These allowed subjects to introduce experiences and concerns of importance to the subjects themselves and often elicited lengthy accounts and/or exchanges. Most interviews lasted between two and three hours. With the exception of two interviews conducted with different lesbian couples, all interviews were conducted in private.

Dana Rosenfeld recruited and interviewed the subjects. Her personal knowledge of and public identification with the homosexual world made it relatively easy for her to develop rapport and to pursue topics that subjects raised in the course of the interview. Separated from subjects by at least one generation, the differences between subjects' and Rosenfeld's experiences provided opportunities to explore cross-culturing work through extensive discussion. Moreover, the generational differences created an occasion for the transmission of subcultural knowledge from "old-timers" to a perceived neophyte. As in all in-depth interviews, these differences and similarities allowed data to "emerge in the process of dialogue, negotiation, and understanding" (Kaufman 1994, p. 128).

SENSE OF OTHER AND SELF IN A HETEROSEXUAL WORLD

Representations of the Heterosexual Other

Our respondents' narratives often demarcated themselves and other homosexuals as confronting the "rest of society" in a tense and precarious relationship. Many subjects anticipated that the disclosure or discovery of their sexual orientation could rupture or terminate whatever level of emotional support or civility had been achieved with neighbors, coworkers, and even friends and family. Indeed,

> You can't go outside the stream of things and for things not to be, you know, like, society all functions in a certain way. We don't function that way—gay people and lesbians, you know, and so you have to expect that we're going to face a lot of challenges because we're not in that social movement that everybody else is in. We're a minority (Maria, age 65).

To respondents, this segregation was based on the heterosexual tendency to see homosexuals as threatening and polluting agents: as, in Rhoda's, 89, words, "an untouchable, almost like a disease." Tony, 70, for example, recounted his mother asking if he had "made" his lover "this way." Subjects treated the image of the

predatory or polluting homosexual with disdain. Constance, 74, described heterosexuals' fear that homosexuals will recruit children into a homosexual life.

> The straight people they worry a lot. When they're married they worry about kids getting
> involved in gay life and all that and you'd think that the gay people would go there and say
> "Hey! Come on, you're going to be gay." You know they worry about that. Yeah, they're
> scared. It's fear. That's what's wrong with the straight people. They're fearful of gays.

Similarly, Leonard, 72, who oversees a local gay senior group's outreach to old
gay men and lesbians in a downtown senior housing complex, found residents'
suspicion of him ridiculous:

> I've been denounced as a, you know, devil's advocate or something of the sort, I'm "recruiting
> innocent senior citizens." Can you imagine?

Subjects characterized heterosexuals who have homosexual thoughts, acts or
contacts of their own as most likely to condemn homosexuals. This condemnation, respondents explained, was designed to prevent others from identifying them
as homosexual on the basis of these connections—indeed, even to produce the
appearance that they have no such connections in the first place. Poor treatment of
homosexuals is thus driven by heterosexuals' own concern for self. One subject
spoke of explaining this to a heterosexual friend:

> She don't ask me if I'm gay—she's asked me a lot of questions about gays, she'd say "Some
> of the women in the group are forever criticizing gays." I said "Emma when you hear someone
> blabbing off about gays you can be sure they're either gay themselves or they have a child who
> is gay and they're trying to act so strong against them to make it appear that they're not gay or
> have no gay connections." So I said, "Keep your mouth shut," and she does (Ryan, 81).

Some form of exclusion or disenfranchisement was assumed to follow disclosure or discovery regardless of the length or intimacy of the relationship. Even
those with whom respondents were closest—including family members and children—were seen as capable of terminating relations should they learn of others'
homosexuality. Subjects saw exclusion on the basis of sexual orientation to be a
burden, unique to homosexuals, greater than any that heterosexuals endure.

> If I were straight there would never be any question about revealing myself to somebody else.
> Being lesbian or gay [you] make a conscious decision whether or not you reveal to another per-
> son something very very very personal and which may or may not—well depending upon
> whom you select to say—which may terminate the relationship. And that has [an impact]
> beyond uh anything probably anything in the straight world (Marilyn, 66).

Apprehension about heterosexuals' treatment of known homosexuals was
grounded in personal experience and observation. Respondents offered vignettes
and anecdotes to illustrate how disclosure or discovery precipitated reactions

including discrimination and dismissal by employers and withdrawal by friends and family. Maria, 65, feels her poverty was caused by heterosexuals' refusal to hire or promote her "no matter where I went."

> There's that general harassment and the fact that I could never get ahead no place because I was such an obvious [lesbian]. No matter where I went the other guy had the better deal, whether they were smarter or not. I never did get good-paying jobs.

Another subject explained that his coworkers created a "barrier" to acceptance and trust which contributed to his alienation and constrained his potential for leadership. Had he been "openly heterosexual," he explains, he would have been treated as an equal and able to achieve the level of personal and professional excellence of which he felt he was capable:

> I think that being gay in a straight world has been negative in my life. I feel that I should have been a better professional person if I would have been straight. Because my relationships, that feeling that I have that I don't belong in their world has created some sort of a barrier in my life. I think I should have become a leader—my leadership would have been different if I would have been you know openly heterosexual with a family perhaps, kids and everything else. I think it would have been different. Because there was a barrier there and that barrier created some sort of suspicion [in their minds] (Ricardo, 66).

Some used their own experiences of personal and professional discrimination to extrapolate to the universality of both the threat of exclusion and its consequences. A subject who had lost his job at the State Department during the McCarthy era spoke of the unavoidability of disclosure and the havoc it inevitably wreaks:

> It's the centerpiece of your life and it has affected you since you were at least a teenager. And if you're not aware that it has affected you, you just haven't a picture of what would have happened if you weren't gay. I mean it can affect your choice of occupation, it affects what your social life is, it hits you everywhere you go! There's nothing that you can do that isn't affected by being gay. And if you think that you're hiding it from people, you're not. I know [my life is] different because I'm gay. I've got it demonstrated to me by being fired for being gay. My career ended for being gay. I mean I've seen it, I've seen it (Leonard, 72).

These experiences contributed to what Bech (1992, p. 138) called the "existential uneasiness" and sense of "injury and of feeling watched" characteristic of contemporary homosexuals. For our subjects, to be homosexual was to be vulnerable to public identification and to an ensuing disenfranchisement from work, friends, or family. Tony, 70, likened this identification to being "marked with the scarlet letter" by "homophobics" in the family and in the community at large.

> You got family and you have the homophobic too within family. A straight person doesn't have that problem. You have more people concerned about you [when you're] straight than

you would being gay, within the family. So you multiply that and the people that you don't know that are homophobic, you really have nothing but [stage whisper] "goddamn faggot." Or, "she's a lesbian." It's like, "hey, you!" You're marked with the scarlet letter. You're homosexual. So certain things happen to you.

This unease pervaded respondents' everyday relationships, including those with unknown others. Some spoke of the "general harassment" described by Maria and Tony; others feared more violent reprisals. Greg, 75, for example, was especially concerned that were his homosexuality widely known, some "redneck" heterosexuals in his neighborhood might vandalize his property: "I don't want somebody, you know, straight people, rednecks, pointing a finger at me or writing on my garage door, spraying my garage door."

In addition, subjects felt that even heterosexuals to whom they were personally close were capable of rejecting them should they learn of their homosexuality. Several named heterosexual friends with whom they had never discussed their homosexuality out of fear that the practical and emotional support on which they had come to depend would be withdrawn. Barbie, 67, explained that

The ones that I'm closest to now [are] straight people. Church family, that's become a family. If I need help, they'll help. Or if they need help, I'll help. Be supportive. Except if they knew what I was, I don't know how they would feel towards me. I don't know.

Respondents also described their fear of being rejected by relatives. They cited an inability to "really" know the inner feelings of family members regarding homosexuality in general and their own homosexuality in particular. Assumptions about the tenacity of family ties—the commitment of family members to maintain relations despite internal conflicts or problems—were reflexively modified to apply only to heterosexuals. Homosexuality is thus seen as an exception to the rule of unequivocal family acceptance.

If I said anything there might be rejection. You can read everything you can lay your hands on and it'll say, "your family loves you," but you really don't know. It's an unknown quantity. 'Cause you always keep in the back of your mind that blood is thicker than water, but sometimes it's not (Abby, 70).

In sum, respondents understood heterosexuals to be capable of excluding homosexuals from whatever level of community had been achieved regardless of the intimacy of relations they had established. They depicted their relations with heterosexuals as akin to walking on thin ice, that is, as perilous journeys in which a misstep might shatter the relationship.

Responding to the Other: Passing and Disclosing

While subjects were unanimous in their characterization of the potential consequences of the discovery or disclosure of their sexual orientation, they differed markedly about how this threat should be managed. On the one hand, most committed themselves to passing as heterosexual, noting that homosexuality was a "private" matter:

> I've always been very closeted about my lifestyle. Closeted means that I'm not wearing a sign on my back, I'm not willing to announce my sexuality to the world. I don't go walking around and telling who I am and what I am, it's my business; it's none of your business. I consider it very private (Lillian, 69).

These subjects also suggested that explicit disclosure was unnecessary. Several noted that homosexuals were able to recognize one another—as Barbie, 67, put it, "It takes one to know one." They noted that family members also frequently "knew" that the respondent was homosexual without explicit discussion. Further, explicit disclosure might selfishly subject family members to an ordeal they would prefer to avoid. Patricia, 77, explained that she

> never mentioned it. They all know that I am. My sisters know I am but we've never talked about it. I'm sure my dad and mother [knew but] we never discussed it. They knew when I went to live with June, especially my mother. But we never discussed it. It was just something that [they] didn't want to have to go through [or] live with.

Respondents mentioned a variety of practices through which they assured their "privacy." These ranged from adeptly avoiding situations which might lead to discovery of their homosexuality to actively constructing the appearance of heterosexuality. Subjects, for example, described "side-stepping" direct questions regarding their own sexuality with ambiguous or evasive responses. When asked how she would respond to someone asking if she were homosexual, for example, Betty, 74, answered "I would say only my hairdresser knows." Lillian, 69, described having laughed when business associates asked if she was gay, characterizing their question as "ridiculous":

> Well someone would say "oh you're not married, you don't have any children, are you gay?" Well I would never think of answering a question like that! I would laugh! "Oh don't be ridiculous!" I wouldn't say, I would not get defensive "oh it's none of your business" because I don't wanna really put myself in that position so there was always a pat answer I had, I don't remember what they are, but it was enough to get me off the hook. And that's all I was interested in.

Others responded to queries about marriage by providing accounts consonant with typical heterosexual concerns and motives. Franz, 86, for example, when asked why he had not married, depicted his "single" status as caused by his "choosiness":

> My family and everybody else, it's two and two is four: 86 and never got married. So people ask me "How come you didn't get married?" I say "Because when I came to the country I was 40, and then I was already too choosy."

In addition to minimizing evidence of homosexuality, some used the trappings of heterosexuality as a protective facade. Three of our subjects had married (in two cases to other homosexuals) specifically to allay suspicion regarding their sexual orientation. Constance, 74, explained that she had been married "in name only" to a heterosexual merchant seaman who benefited from the arrangement by having, through the marriage, a place "to come home to":

> When I was in San Francisco I got married to some merchant seaman. He was never home, he'd take off and maybe stay two, three years out at sea. And the reason I got married was because I got caught with this woman. Threw the books at us, you know. So I says "Oh bullshit." So when he came in he asked me if I'd marry him. I says "All right but I'm gonna tell you something, we're gonna get married and I'll get married in name only." I said "That's all."

In contrast to those who understood their homosexuality according to the precepts of the pre-Stonewall culture, a smaller group understood their homosexuality according to the tenets inhering in the post-Stonewall ideology.[4] While they appreciated the wrenching practical and emotional consequences of disclosure, they saw the failure to disclose sexual orientation as more damaging to the sense of self. Specifically, for these subjects, attempting to pass as heterosexual was a suppression or distortion of the "real" self. On the one hand, they explained, the other's knowledge of the individual's homosexuality could terminate the relationship. On the other hand, passing saved the relationship only to damage its integrity. Because passing was a denial of the authentic self, it rendered relationships based on passing inauthentic as well. The "real" threat posed by the heterosexual other, therefore, is the latter's seduction of the homosexual into a life of duplicity in exchange for what is ultimately an inauthentic relationship. As Marilyn, 66, noted, she cannot exist authentically—cannot "be" herself—in the context of a relationship in which her lesbianism is not known.

> A friend to me is somebody who I have selected whom I want to be with whom I enjoy mutual experiences with, somebody I really would like to you know to enjoy their presence. Acquaintanceships I enjoy, but I wouldn't necessarily make an effort to continue the relation. Am I making myself clear at all? So if I have a straight friend I can enjoy their presence in going out and being social but I wouldn't be completely *me* if I'm not out to that person.

These subjects viewed disclosure to both homosexuals and heterosexuals as a moral obligation pursued in the interest of personal and relational authenticity. Rather than rely on family members' tacit recognition, for example, they disclosed their homosexuality to them. Susan, 75, who divorced her husband once she began to define herself as a lesbian in her forties, described her need to "discuss" her lesbianism with her children in order to have her family "aware of who I am":

> My whole family's fully aware of who I am and that's what's important to me. After the divorce, I thought it was time to set them down and really discuss the situation, who I was. My oldest two knew. They had an inkling of what was going on. But they were very accepting.

Similarly, while those disposed to passing might evade discussions and questions pertaining to homosexuality, those who felt disclosure was central to authenticity used them as opportunities to do so.

> I came out to [my aunt] just six, eight months ago. What made me decide on the spur of the moment to do it, over supper she was talking about some people in her family, and problems that a niece and nephew of hers are having, one kid was on drugs and that was a problem, and another kid was a homosexual and that was a disappointment and de da de da de da and I said "Well, it's not always you know a tragedy," and she said "I realize but they were unhappy." And I said "You realize of course that I'm a lesbian." And she said "No! Are you?" And I said "Yeah." And she said "Oh." And she didn't ask any questions, she probably figured she wasn't supposed to (Kate, 76).

Subjects thus understood the threat of exclusion in very different ways. Most saw it as a threat to social relations and social status, and responded to this threat by keeping their homosexuality secret from heterosexuals. Others, however, saw passing as heterosexual, while a solution to this threat of exclusion, as constituting a more dire threat to the authentic self. This smaller group managed this threat to self by adopting a policy of disclosure to heterosexuals.

Positioning and Evaluating the Self

Subjects defined different stances that could—and "should"—be taken toward others; stances which, they emphasized, they themselves adopted but which other homosexuals did not. Those committed to passing criticized those who did not "recognize" the threat of banishment as the most severe danger they faced, while those committed to disclosure condemned homosexuals who failed to see the more onerous threat to authenticity of passing. Subjects applied these evaluative standards to their own actions as well, presenting their actions over the life course as consonant with—or in conflict with—policies of passing or disclosing. Just as subjects variously distinguished themselves from or claimed fellowship with other homosexuals who manage relations with heterosexuals in particular ways, they also distinguished themselves from or aligned themselves with their own past actions.

Having adopted a policy of passing, most subjects contrasted their own passing practices with policies of disclosure. Ryan, 81, for example, described how his gay church group does and does not advertise itself. While the existence of the group is mentioned in the church bulletin, members do not "wear badges or any-thing": in short, do not mark themselves as homosexual, a practice which would publicly express an "essentially private" matter. Similarly, Betty, 67, both con-demned and distanced herself from policies of disclosure, which she depicted as effectively declaring one's homosexuality to "the whole world." She specified that her refusal is not due to her lack of self-knowledge—on the contrary, she "knows who she is"—but to the fact that it "offends" her. She thus contrasted herself with others who, she said, neither recognize the difference between private and public "business" nor respect the boundaries between them.

> I don't want to tell the world I'm gay! It's my business to do. I resent that term coming out, I do. It offends me. I know who I am but I don't like to go up to someone and say "Oh I've come out of the closet!"

Finally, Rhoda, 89, subtly distinguished herself from homosexuals whose disclosure caused them to be identified and ridiculed. She noted that she had successfully passed with minimal or no effort (she just acted "natural") and that she associated with "good" heterosexuals who displayed contempt for homosexuals in her presence because they thought she was "one of them." That passing was "natural" for her constructs her as not only capable of but predisposed to behaving like a "normal" person. This enabled her to socialize with "good" heterosexuals despite their derision of homosexuals (a practice she tolerated but in which she did not participate.) Moreover, her ability to pass allowed her to witness even "good" heterosexuals' contempt of gays and confirmed her view that failing or refusing to pass invites insult.

> So many people did not know that I was gay you know, and I associated with a lot of good people who were not gay. And especially with the very feminine boys [they] pointed the finger at them and talked to me about them, you know thinking I wasn't gay.

Others understood those committed to disclosing their own homosexuality as equally committed to forcing others to do the same. Gabrielle, 87, and Betty, 67, spoke of being offended by the term "coming out" because of its prescriptive emphasis:

> Gabrielle: It's an offensive term to me. Because people have used it in the sense that "Oh I'm so glad that she came out or he came out, and why don't they come out?" We take it as forcing, or thinking people should.

> Betty: It's what we read about, about making people come out. Who's that asshole that says, "This one's gay, that one's gay?" That's repulsive.

Just as those committed to passing criticized those committed to disclosure as foolhardy and self-destructive, those committed to disclosure castigated those committed to passing as "dishonest." Tex, 72, distinguished himself from those who "aren't being honest with themselves" as a way of displaying his own beliefs and practices regarding disclosure:

It just irks me because these people aren't being honest with themselves. I think if you are or believe in one way and you project a belief or an idea what you are contrary to that, then you're not being honest with yourself or them. I mean you can't have it both ways. Because you do have to interact with other people.

Similarly, Leonard, 72, condemned the efforts expended upon passing as heterosexual as ultimately futile, depicting those who pass as deluded about both the efficacy of their own passing techniques and the decoding capacities of others:

If you think that you're hiding it from people, you're not. I mean, how many people do you know that are in the closet that are not really known anyway? And the people who are in the closet with all that scurrying around, throwing sand up in this direction and sand up in that direction in order to keep people from figuring out that they're gay! I mean the amount of effort that's put into that sort of thing? Enormous amounts go into that!

Kate, 76, raised this issue as well when she described her ex-lover Jan's refusal to accept the "fact" that, despite her best efforts, others knew of her homosexuality and talked about it amongst themselves:

She's quite butchy in appearance now and eventually ended up having a relationship with Nell, a teacher on her faculty, and when they broke up Nell said "Jan thinks that nobody knows, but the kids call her Lizzie,[5] and they all know." And I said to Jan "Do you really think that people don't know?" And her response then was the same she had said years before—she said "I don't care what people think they know, as long as they don't catch me in the act or I don't tell them, they don't know." And it matters to her, it matters very much to her.

Because these subjects considered homosexuality to be relevant in the context of close relationships, they depicted the refusal of intimate others to come out to them as an insult to the relationship. Sharon, 66, for example, portrayed her brother's failure to discuss his homosexuality with her as an astonishing, almost "unbelievable" affront to the close relationship they had established, and contrasted her brother's commitment to passing with her own, preferred commitment to disclosure:

My brother is not married. He has never said anything to me about being gay. Ever. Can you believe it? And he and I were just this close; we grew up like twins, there was a year difference. We were very close, he and I were raised very close. Yet he will not tell me he's gay. Oh yeah, he knows about Val and I, in fact I sent him a copy of my will telling him if anything happens that you know to tell Val whatever he wants and she'll give it to him and she's getting this and this.

The competing ways of managing relations with heterosexuals outlined above also presented different standards through which to assess the self's performance over the life course. For most subjects, a positive evaluation of the self centered on how well they had managed to pass as heterosexual and to thus preclude negative sanctions for their homosexuality. Ryan, 81, positively evaluated his life because he protected himself from harassment and ridicule by avoiding being identified as homosexual. If he had his life to live over, he explained, he would pursue the same policies as he had followed when working in a supermarket:

> I oftentimes think if I had my life to live over, I would probably do it about the same as I did because I think I've been smart to stay away from it and not make myself obvious. When you were working you had to be very careful that way. We would have some people come into work, we would hire them, why I don't know because it was obvious they were gay. And they would get them in there and just make fools out of them. They'd try to make them do the dirtiest work and the hardest work. Well they didn't pull that on me. And I think it was because they weren't sure about me.

Relatedly, for these subjects, minimizing the impact of homosexuality on their own lives was a central goal. Indeed, when asked how their homosexuality had affected their lives, subjects committed to passing noted that it had not, and that this was because they had passed throughout their lives. Franz, 86, for example, answered the question this way:

> It didn't affect my life so far because what my business concerns I achieved what I wanted, being gay or not being gay. It has nothing to do with being gay, because I never put it on the platter and told them "Here, I'm gay." So how should it affect me, it didn't affect me.

For those committed to disclosure, however, positively assessing the self over the life course hinged on the degree of openness they had managed to achieve in their relations with heterosexuals—an openness essential to authentic relations on the one hand and an authentic self on the other. For these subjects, evaluating the self over the life course was more complex: because disclosing one's homosexuality to others invited rejection, they explained, they had often failed in their quest for authenticity. When asked how her homosexuality had affected her life, for example, Marilyn, 66, explained that it had been both a "moral problem" and "struggle" in which she had often failed. Because she had not been "entirely herself" with some heterosexuals, she had deceived them, and was now "living with" the moral consequences of her decision:

> It's a moral problem that I've struggled with for some time about coming out, because of being deceptive with other people if I'm not entirely myself. I have a difficult problem, but I live with that because that's the decision I've arrived at, not to come out to them.

This group of respondents assessed the degree of personal and relational authenticity they had achieved by balancing successful disclosures with perceived failures to do so. Subjects offered concrete instances or situations in which they could have disclosed their homosexuality, but did not. Abby, 70, while proud of having defended her gay friends, condemned her failure to take advantage of the opportunity to disclose her lesbianism as a "cop-out":

> Somebody did say something at a family gathering once and I jumped right in. I said I don't want to hear anything like that about my two close friends who are gay. I have a lot of gay friends. And that was a cop-out because that would have been a perfect opportunity to say, "You're talking about me."

This is not to say that these subjects only produced negative evaluations of self. In these accounts, their ongoing commitment to authenticity by way of disclosure overrode the significance of discrete instances of failure. Marilyn, 66, for example, emphasized the fact that, while she "censored" herself in the past, she was becoming more comfortable disclosing her lesbianism to (in this case, unknown) heterosexuals.

> Last Sunday there were four of us that went down to the Santa Monica Pier and we were sitting waiting for the program to begin. And I found myself talking about being gay and lesbian without any thought about it until I stopped and looked around and said "Hmm!" Here I was in public talking about being gay and lesbian—I might not have done that at one time, but I felt comfortable doing it on Sunday. And I didn't care—it was very easy to do and not something I censored myself doing, which at one time I might have.

Moreover, while subjects committed to passing cited their freedom from the negative consequences of disclosure as proof of their success, subjects committed to disclosure cited their liberation from the perceived worries associated with passing as proof of their own.

> For the first time in my entire life, I am so comfortable with being who I am. I never even think about it anymore. It feels great! I never worry about what other people think. I never worry about who I'm with, what they look like or anything (Abby, 70).

DISCUSSION

The gay and lesbian elderly are an especially perspicuous population for examining representations of and responses to cultural others. As we suggested earlier, while "self and identity across the life course in cross-cultural perspective" is typically understood to entail exclusively *social scientific* comparisons and contrasts of the life course in different cultural contexts, it is also an everyday concern for social actors. Our research has shown that the gay and lesbian elderly themselves make such comparisons with both the dominant heterosexual culture and with regard to alternative identity paradigms within the homosexual community. As part of negotiating their social worlds, the gay and lesbian elderly developed typifications of the attitudes and reactions of heterosexuals and articulated policies and practices regarding an appropriate response.

While respondents anticipated that the disclosure or discovery of their sexual orientation could rupture or terminate their relationships to heterosexuals, they responded to this threat in different ways. Most stated their life-long commitment to passing as heterosexual, and described how they had artfully evaded or avoided situations in which their sexuality became topical. Although appreciative of the emotional, relational, and material consequences of disclosure, a smaller number expressed a commitment to disclosing their homosexuality to others in the interests of personal and relational authenticity. Indeed, they interpreted others' failure to disclose their homosexuality to *them* as an affront to the relationship. If the former group focused on the loss of relations that occurs as a consequence of disclosure, the latter group emphasized the loss of integrity that accompanies passing.

Stances towards disclosure provided the criteria for evaluating subjects' own actions and those of other homosexuals. Evaluating the self over the life course did not just involve applying the criteria inhering in their own stance to their own actions. Rather, it involved distinguishing the self from the policies and practices of their counterparts on the other side of the Stonewall schism. Those who understood themselves from the perspective of the pre-Stonewall identity paradigm, for example, prided themselves on having avoided the costs of identification as homosexual by passing and derided the foolishness of those who proclaimed their homosexuality. Those who adopted the post-Stonewall paradigm, however, savored the episodes in which they disclosed their sexual orientation. They rebuked both themselves for having failed to do so consistently and other homosexuals for failing to recognize that passing betrays the authentic self.

The examination of cross-culturing work among the gay and lesbian elderly suggests possibilities and concerns for exploring the response to cultural diversity among future cohorts of the elderly, homosexual or otherwise. Indeed, the *first* suggestion is that cross-culturing work is increasingly likely to be found among all populations of elderly. In urban environments, the elderly find themselves in neighborhoods whose socio-economic and ethnic composition has radically changed. Newly arrived or displaced immigrant elderly are thrust into cultural contexts profoundly different from their native land (see "The Impossible Me," this volume). In retirement homes and hospitals, the elderly may be placed among others with diverse backgrounds. Indeed, as Dowd (1986) suggested, to be "elderly" itself is to be a cultural stranger in the midst of the ideas and institutions of another generation. To the extent that encounters with cultural others are increasingly prominent features of their life worlds, then cross-culturing work is likely to be an increasingly common practice among the elderly.

Second, while the consideration of marginalized groups is essential to a respect for diversity, such groups may themselves be riven by fissures that make members seem "other" to one another. As we have seen, among the gay and lesbian elderly, positions regarding self, homosexuality and disclosure constituted a schism across which proponents seemed variously foolish or repressed to one another. Other groups may, of course, orient to other divisions (e.g., class, ethnic, religious, and political) in the course of their cross-culturing work, making it all the more important to examine the endogenous understandings and internal conflicts of distinctive groups. Accordingly, the methodological realization of cultural difference entails not only recognition that various sub-groups have distinctive concerns, but recognition that the community may itself encompass—or be divided by—a variety of perspectives.

Third, while the presence of others with different values, norms, and practices promises to be an increasingly prominent feature of the life worlds of young and elderly alike, the specific fault lines along which internal and external divisions develop will reflect changing socio-historical circumstances. Historically emergent fissures are particularly evident among homosexuals, who continue to witness—and be implicated in—radical reformulations of homosexuality during their lifetimes. As ideological tensions within and cultural debates about homosexuality change, so will the nature and content of cross-culturing that occurs within and across cohorts. As a result, standards through which to evaluate self in later life will be different for each generation of homosexuals, and for groups within each generation. The current generation of gay and lesbian elderly, for example, is likely to be the last generation for whom pre- and post-Stonewall constructions of homosexuality comprise the basis of distinctions within the homosexual community (save as the source of historical references to "the way things used to be"). The current middle-aged cohort of homosexuals will likely use different standards for self-evaluation in their old age than have our subjects: specifically, AIDS and the debate over sexualities that it fostered, rather than Stonewall and the debate over disclosure and identity to which it gave birth.[6] Homosexuals who are now middle-aged may, in later life, evaluate how they reacted and related to the cultural-political debates surrounding AIDS, in addition to considering issues of disclosure of both homosexuality and HIV-status (see Edwards 1991). Those who were born during or after the debates sparked by AIDS may, of course, evaluate themselves in later life according to a yet different set of standards.

Fourth, and finally, as the purview of social science expands to recognize the cultural diversity *of* the social world, it is important to recognize that cultural diversity is also *in* the social world. Thus, the analyses that might have been the prerogative of the social sciences are made by social actors as they make sense of, construct and negotiate their life worlds. In surveying the cultural landscape and its faultlines, actors chart their life worlds, assay the costs and dangers of proceeding in one direction or another, specify the coordinates to position themselves, and establish the criteria for evaluating how well they navigated the terrain.

ACKNOWLEDGMENTS

An earlier version of this paper was presented at the 1998 annual meeting of the American Sociological Association. Funding for our research was provided by the UCLA Center on Aging.

NOTES

1. While the lesbian-feminist movement distinguished itself from gay liberation (Faderman 1991), both movements provided a virtually identical challenge to the pre-Stonewall world's commitment to passing on the one hand and an essential, authentic homosexual self on the other. Thus, for present purposes, we have combined our male and female subjects.

2. For a comprehensive treatment of methodological procedures, see Rosenfeld (1999a).

3. Because of the unintelligibility of several audio tapes and interviewees' memory lapses, a number of interviews were not employed in the current analysis.

4. Rosenfeld (1999a, 1999b) examines differences between individuals adopting either the pre- or post-Stonewall identity paradigm.

5. A vernacular—and derogatory—reference to lesbianism.

6. AIDS constituted a socio-political crisis to which those currently in their thirties, forties and fifties were forced to respond. In Plummer's words (1991, p. 149), "both as disease and symbol [AIDS] has played a powerful part in the reshaping of gay and lesbian communities throughout the 1980s."

REFERENCES

Adelman, M. 1991. "Stigma, Gay Lifestyles, and Adjustment to Aging: A Study of Later-Life Gay Men and Lesbians." *Journal of Homosexuality* 16: 7-32.

Bailey, K.D. 1994. *Methods of Social Research.* New York: Free Press.

Bech, H. 1992. "Report From a Rotten State: `Marriage' and `Homosexuality' in 'Denmark'." Pp. 134-150 in *Modern Homosexualities: Fragments of Lesbian and Gay Experience*, edited by K. Plummer. London: Routlege.

Calasanti, T.M. 1996. "Incorporating Diversity: Meaning, Levels of Research, and Implications for Theory." *The Gerontologist* 36: 147-156.

D'Emilio, J.D. 1983. *Sexual Politics, Sexual Communities: The Making of a Homosexual Minority in the U.S. 1940-1970.* Chicago: University of Chicago.

Dorfman, R., K. Walters, P. Burke, L. Hardin, T. Karanik, J. Raphael, and E. Silverstein. 1995. "Old, Sad and Alone: The Myth of the Aging Homosexual." *Journal of Gerontological Social Work* 24:1/2: 29-44.

Dowd, J.J. 1986. "The Old Person as Stranger." Pp. 147-190 in *Later Life: The Social Psychology of Aging*, edited by V.W. Marshall. Beverly Hills, CA: Sage.

Duberman, M. 1994. *Stonewall.* Middlesex: Plume.

Edwards, T. 1991. "The AIDS Dialectic: Awareness, Identity, Death, and Sexual Politics." Pp. 151-159 in *Modern Homosexualities: Fragments of Lesbian and Gay Experience*, edited by K. Plummer. London: Routledge.

Faderman, L. 1991. *Odd Girls and Twilight Lovers: A History of Lesbian Life in Twentieth-Century America.* New York: Penguin Books.

George, L.K. 1996. "Missing Links: The Case for a Social Psychology of the Life Course." *The Gerontologist,* 36:2: 248-255.

Grigsby, J.S. 1996. "The Meaning of Heterogeneity: An Introduction." *The Gerontologist* 36: 145-146.

Grube, J. 1991. "Natives and Settlers: An Ethnographic Note on Early Interactions of Older Homosexual Men with Younger Gay Liberationists." Pp. 119-135 in *Gay Midlife and Maturity*, edited by J.A. Lee. New York: Haworth Press.

Gubrium, J.F., and A. Sankar, A. 1994. *Qualitative Methods in Aging Research*. Thousand Oaks, CA: Sage.

Hewitt, J.P. 1994. "Self, Role, and Discourse." Pp. 155-173 in *Self, Collective Action, and Society; Essays Honoring the Contributions of Ralph E. Turner*, edited by G.R. Platt and C. Gorden. New Haven: JAI Press.

Kaufman, S.R. 1994. "In-Depth Interviewing." Pp. 123-137 in *Qualitative Methods in Aging Research*, edited by J.F. Gubrium and A. Sankar. Thousand Oaks, CA: Sage.

Lee, J.A. 1987. "What Can Homosexual Aging Studies Contribute to Theories of Aging?" *Journal of Homosexuality* 1 13:4, 43-71

Marotta, T. 1981. *The Politics of Homosexuality: How Lesbians and Gay Men have Made Themselves a Political and Social Force in Modern America*. Boston: Houghton Mifflin Company.

Plummer, K., ed. 1991. *Modern Homosexualities: Fragments of Lesbian and Gay Experience*, edited by K. Plummer. London: Routledge.

Quam, J.K., and G.S. Whitford. 1992. "Adaptation and Age-Related Expectations of Older Gay and Lesbian Adults." *The Gerontologist* 32: 367-374.

Rosenfeld, D. 1999a. *Identity Work Among Lesbian and Gay Elderly*. Ph.D. dissertation, Department of Sociology, University of California, Los Angeles, CA.

_____. 1999b. "Identity Work Among Lesbian and Gay Elderly." *Journal of Aging Studies* 13(2): 121-144

Stein, A. 1997. *Sex and Sensibility: Stories of a Lesbian Generation*. Berkeley: University of California Press.

Wolfe, A. 1998. *One Nation, After All: What Americans Really Think About God, Country, Family, Racism, Welfare, Immigration, Homosexuality, Work, The Right, The Left and Each Other*. New York: Penguin.

GENERATIVITY IN THE LIVES OF ELDER CATHOLIC WOMEN RELIGIOUS

Susan Perschbacher Melia

ABSTRACT

Generativity is an important component of late life identity development and of graceful aging in the lives of elder Catholic women religious. Life review data from forty women religious (mean age of 80) reflect the importance of ongoing service to others into late life; much of their current satisfaction as elder sisters derives from their continued ability to help others. The qualitative data, in the tradition of grounded theory research, inform the theoretical debate about whether generative behavior occurs in staged developmental sequences of identity formation or recurs continuously through life. The findings from this subculture of women support the claims of Kotre and McAdams, among others, who have found that generative "urges" or "scripts" promote ongoing patterns of generative behavior. The lives of elder women religious support a growing body of research showing that the ability to contribute in late life is part of what gives life meaning and helps people to age gracefully.

Advances in Life Course Research, Volume 5, pages 119-141.
Copyright © 2000 by JAI Press Inc.
All rights of reproduction in any form reserved.
ISBN: 0-7623-0033-7

119

INTRODUCTION

Generativity is an important component of graceful aging in the lives of elder Catholic women religious.[1] Life review data from interviews with forty women religious, ages 68 to 98 (mean age of 80), reflect the importance of the theme of ongoing service to others into late life. Much of their current satisfaction as elder sisters derives from their continued ability to help others and to benefit society, which, in turn, gives their lives meaning, purpose, and fulfillment. The evidence of ongoing contribution can be seen in several areas: their views and positions on retirement, their descriptions of their daily lives, their conviction that elder women religious have contributions to make to society, and their affirmation that their ability to contribute is part of what gives life meaning and helps them to age gracefully, that is, with acceptance of their age, of the life they have lived, and of the person that they have been. First the concept of generativity and its importance in the formation of identity will be discussed, and then a rationale will be established for focusing on a sociological ideal type, a subculture of women religious, as a case study of the role of generativity in graceful aging.

GENERATIVITY

Generativity as a concept is often associated with Erikson's staged theory of developmental psychology (Erikson 1963). In his early work Erikson conceptualized generativity versus stagnation as the seventh stage of eight developmental tasks in identity formation. Reached in mid-life, this task involved the conflict between contribution to the next generation and to society as opposed to self-absorption. At this time, according to Erikson, the individual, having resolved the six previous developmental tasks, is motivated by an interest in establishing and guiding the next generation, thereby creating and maintaining human life and social institutions. Generative acts rest on a belief in humanity and on a sense of hopefulness for the future. Because he viewed this task as foremost in identity development during the middle-adult years, Erikson initially posited that generativity declines in old age. In a later work (Erikson, Erikson, and Kivnick 1986) he revisited his staged developmental theory and used the term grand-generativity: caring for what one has generated, for example involvement with one's children and grandchildren, can be meaningful for the ongoing identity development of elders and can contribute to successful aging.

Subsequent theorists studying generativity have found that it is not a staged developmental task resolved at a single chronological point in time. Two prominent theorists have each written about generativity: Kotre (1984), wrote about it as an impulse released at various times, in moments and episodes; and McAdams (1990) wrote about it as running through individual life story narratives as a dominant and recurring theme in their identity. Both of these men argue that the concept of generativity merits further development through both qualitative and quantitative studies.

Kotre (1984), arguing that "the particularities of individual lives elude even the most ambitious of theories" (1984, p. 3), develops a theory of generativity significantly different from that of Erikson. Kotre writes of the generative impulse, an urge or desire, which can occur throughout one's lifetime. It is "a desire to invest one's substance in forms of life and work that will outlive the self" (1984, p. 10). Four kinds of generativity can be identified in different people's stories: biological, parental, technical (passing on of skills), and cultural (creating, renovating, and conserving a symbol system of a culture). In addition, generativity can be in two different modes: agentic, having more to do with the self, and communal, participating in a mutual reality. Kotre recorded and studied in-depth biographies of people whose lives contained acts of generativity. He found generative threads throughout their lives and concluded that the staged theory of development poorly fits these stories. Instead Kotre postulates that the generative impulse is released at various times in one's life, and that different types of generativity are released at different moments and episodes. Furthermore, he finds that generativity represents a fortuitous match of individual needs and social continuity. In a later work Kotre (1995) also states that "cultural generativity is the most far reaching of the four types" (p. 36).

McAdams (1990) developed a life story model of identity in which generativity becomes part of identity through the composition of a generativity script. "The generativity script is the adult's plan or outline specifying what he or she hopes to do in order to leave a legacy of the self to the next generation" (McAdams and de St. Aubin 1992, p. 185). This generativity script must also make sense in terms of the person's framework of beliefs and values, images of self, and events from the past. Through this plan the individual can attempt to leave a legacy of self to the next generation. Generativity includes behaviors such as parenting, teaching, leading, nurturing, and doing things that benefit the community and promote its continuity: "The generative adult commits him- or herself to the continuation and even the improvement of society as a whole, through the next generation" (McAdams and de St. Aubin 1992, p. 186). Like Erikson, McAdams believes that the motivation toward this generativity is founded in a basic faith in the goodness of human life. The person must have hope and trust for the betterment of human life, as well as a belief in progress. Like Kotre, McAdams states that mature generativity involves both agency and communion. "In summary, the generative man or woman must first fashion a legacy of the self (a highly powerful agentic act) and then offer it up to others as a gift (an act of self-surrender and communion)" (McAdams and de St. Aubin 1992, p. 187).

McAdams and de St. Aubin (1992) find that generativity runs through some life stories as a dominant and recurrent theme. "The generativity script is an inner narration of the adults' own awareness of where efforts to be generative fit into his or her own personal history, into contemporary society and the social world he or she inhabits, and, in some extraordinary cases, into society's own encompassing history" (1992, p. 1012). The generativity script is a significant aspect of a larger life story that the individual constructs for identity, and it provides that life with a sense of purpose and unity (McAdams, de St. Aubin, and Logan 1993). Through this script the individual person is linked to the social world.

In his various studies McAdams and his colleagues (McAdams, de St, Aubin, and Logan 1993) have found that older adults show surprisingly high scores on generative commitments in their life stories. These researchers found that the highest predictor of both life satisfaction and happiness was generative concern. Generative actions stem in part from commitments adults have made to generative goals. Assessed through thematic analysis of narratives, he found evidence of highly generative adults whose stories detail great commitment to contribute in positive ways to the next generation. Fisher (1995) found that generativity is one of the contributing factors of successful aging, and is a vital developmental task in later life. Hart (1997) found that generativity leads to social involvement for those interested in offering to and investing in others. They show higher evidence of social support, religious participation, political participation, and community involvement in their lives. For generative people there are several benefits of religious belief: self preservation through hope and strength that helps one get through life with peace of mind; connection to others with a sense of community and belonging; structure with rules to live by and a path to follow; transcendence involving the meaning and purpose of life; and faith.

Alexander, Rubinstein, Goodman, and Luborsky (1991), cultural anthropologists, theorize that generativity is a cultural construct situated within a particular cultural system. We can only understand it within our cultural system, because "generative behavior is inextricably tied to a constellation of American beliefs about the nature of the self, the meaning of death, and attempts to attain immortality that are informed by the ideology of individualism" (1991, p. 417). Generative action in the United States seeks to create a legacy for the individual which is not created by social structure or by the culture itself (as it occurs in other cultures). Thus the content of generativity is also culturally determined. "In American culture the parental model is the dominant idiom in which individuals express generativity" (1991, p. 426). For women, generative expression most often comes through their dominant role of motherhood. "Almost all women without children of their own whom we interviewed consciously and systematically sought out parental roles as outlets for generativity, whether through their jobs, neighbourhoods, churches, or with nieces and nephews. These relationships were very important in their lives" (1991, p. 429). Women without children also express generativity through continuity of tradition and institutions such as the church. This was seen as the culturally appropriate way of attaining generativity and of creating permanence and continuity of the self.

CATHOLIC WOMEN RELIGIOUS: A CASE STUDY OF GENERATIVITY IN GRACEFUL AGING

Before discussing generativity in the life stories of elder women religious it must be determined that data from subjects working in such an unusual vocation and living in communal settings have any relevance to the ongoing theoretical debate about generativity. This group of women constitute a subculture with values and beliefs separate from mainstream culture. Can their experience and example inform on the life course development and successful aging of people from other segments of the population? If Alexander and colleagues (1991) are correct, generativity means something different to them than to other groups in our society. What then is their subcultural value system? Is this so different from mainstream American culture that these data offer no insight on existing theory, no lessons that can be applied to the lives of lay people?

In her study of quality of life for elderly nuns in convent care centers, Wood (1996) argues that research on this population is extremely valuable.

> Elderly nuns are a subculture of American women whose concerns are located at the intersection of several major trends in research. Examples include emphasis on elderly women's health as an emerging specialty; the specific research interest in women exemplified by the Women's Health Initiative; emphasis on inclusion of minority and under-researched groups; efforts to investigate those who make up the oldest-old; and attention to social, political, and economic relationships that influence the health of women and elderly persons (Cowan, 1992; Healthy People 2000, 1991; Lonergan, 1991; Pinn, 1992). Studies focusing on elderly and oldest-old nuns specifically, or including elderly and oldest-old nuns and identifying them as participants, can inform and enrich the diverse but small body of existing research pertaining to nuns (p. 15).

Margraff identified this subculture as a valuable study sample in order "to consider aging in a rapidly changing subculture in our society" (Margraff 1986, p. 47). Mercier, Powers, and Daniewicz (1991, p. 27) examined adjustment to retirement among Catholic sisters "who represent one subculture of the aged population." Clearly studies of the subculture of elder women religious are fruitful in our understanding of the aging process.

As a subculture, women religious forgo traditional women's roles and responsibilities of childrearing and homemaking. Becoming a "bride of Christ" means they leave their families of origin, forgo marriage and children, enter into communal life, take vows of chastity, obedience, and poverty, and work in missions such as teaching, nursing, or administration of religious orders, schools, hospitals, and social service agencies and programs. Their entire calling, to serve God, represents both generative commitment and action. The chosen lifestyle of women religious is a generative one, based on faith in God's goodness and on belief in the teaching of Christ. Each of the elements of their lifestyle is to this end: vows, religious formation, communal living, missionary work, and belief in the gospel of Christ. In their work they are not only serving God, they are promoting God's church here on earth. Their generativity serves to maintain the institution that represents God through activities of teaching, nurturing, leading, and benefitting the Catholic community and world as a whole. It is also evident that women religious remain generative on into their later years. Because they live with many dynamic roles models they have access to examples of positive aging to which other groups in society do not have available. Also, they have not readily accepted retirement (Magee 1987; Margraff 1986; Mercier, Powers, and Daniewicz 1991; Wolf 1989, 1991). Instead, they see their vocation as a lifelong commitment. Wood (1996) found that a major theme of her study of elderly nuns in long-term care was their need to remain involved in meaningful activity: "It kept elderly nuns connected to the work of their communities and provided an opportunity to do something for others. Sometimes the activity was of a spiritual nature, while at other times it was active work" (1996, p. 27). Generativity continues in the form of prayers for others (Magee 1987). Elder women religious think of others, pray for the world, and serve God, on into late life.

Literature on women religious points to their value as subjects for research on development of identity and on making of meaning across the life span. Women religious live on average 3.5 years longer than other women in the United States with increasing numbers of members in their communities who are among the old-old and the oldest-old. Study results show that these sisters are a valuable source of information because of their life choice. In the Nun Study out of the Sanders-Brown Center on Aging at the University of Kentucky, they were picked as subjects for an ongoing alzheimer's study because nuns have the advantage of similar lifestyles, environments, and social support. They are, as a group, highly educated and have a sense of purpose (Snowden 1989). Recent studies relate their accomplishments as strong women (MacHaffie 1986; McNamara 1996). They are also noted for their flexibility in adapting to changes to Vatican II, after which they created new lifestyles and working arrangements (Deedy 1984; Neal 1984; Wittberg 1985).

Studies show a connection between the religious faith and commitment of religious sisters to their self-esteem (Doyle 1986; Wolf 1990b). Wolf posits that their deep sense of commitment produces a sense of autonomy. Religious commitment transforms losses due to aging into gains because of attentiveness to spiritual life, to prayer, and to one's relationships with God (Magee 1987). Mercier, Shelley, and Powers (1996) found that religious sisters maintain rewarding social relationships which positively affects their self-esteem. Daniewicz, Mercier, Powers, and Flynn (1991) found that sisters with social support and with a high degree of control in their lives exhibit positive self-esteem. Mercier and Powers (1996) in their study of control, produced these same results.

Wolf (1986) conducted a series of life review studies of women religious which revealed their growth and continued development through themes of family, endurance, caring for others, and mission work. In a study of their call to vocation (Wolf 1990b) she identified common themes of: childhood, call to vocation, novitiate, friendships, life in community, habits as symbols, and legacy. Wolf (1990a) also found that women religious are concerned with their personal legacy, hoping to die with grace, and are not devastated by the loss of legacy related to diminishing religious orders of sisters. In another study (Wolf 1991) she examined sources of meaning for elder sisters: fidelity, spirituality, routine, and practice. "Meaning for the sisters involves contributing" (1991, p. 9). Meaning is also rooted in community, in faith, in commitment, and in love of God.

Studies of women religious in late life show that withdrawal from social activity and work do not bear on their life satisfaction. They "see themselves as having chosen their life-style in response to a call from God and thus remain invested in their daily routine of reflection and prayerfulness" (Magee 1987, p. 46). Magee found that their spirituality offers meaning in late life and helps sustain them through the decline and losses of age. "The older women religious can daily offer their prayer and devotions, their infirmities and losses, for the success of the works carried on by their younger colleagues" (1988, p. 46). Mercier, Powers, and Daniewicz (1991) found that elder women religious adjust to retirement as a process over time rather than as a one-time event. "To sisters, retirement meant that there will be more time for relaxation, prayers, and to help others" (1991, p. 31). Wolf (1991) found that spiritual development was an organizing goal for elder women religious. "The routinization of prayertime, focus on structure of the day, and spiritual discipline were important to the population studied" (Wolf 1991, p. 8). This search for spirituality is "the extension of a life-long process, a vocation" (1991, p. 11).

In her study of the elders of her congregation (75 years and older) Jacques (1997) asked: "What it is like for you to be an aging Sister of Saint Anne?" She determined that these sisters "are aging well. Their attitudes are positive yet realistic. They struggle or have struggled with most aspects of the aging process and, as a result, are happy and fulfilled" (1997, p. 6). She invited older sisters into reminiscence groups to share significant aspects of their life stories and to articulate some of the wisdom they acquired during their years of religious life. "What is particularly striking to me is the great faith in God that has nourished and sustained these women throughout their lives" (1997, p. 9). Jacques concludes that "their lives are based on such strong faith and such deep love of God," and that theirs is a "ministry of prayer and presence" (1997, p. 19). "For the aging Sister of Saint Anne, the post-retirement years offer her more time for prayer; more time, that is, for deepening her relationship with God, with her sisters, and with the world" (1997, p. 24). In responses Jacques received from twenty-nine women, twenty (69%) mentioned that aging brings time for prayer and to be with God. "Aging can be years of peace and growth in the Lord."

> I find joy in praying and in talking to God. I believe I never took the time to really see religion in this way and I find beauty and closeness to God that I never had. Not only for myself, but for those with whom I come in contact. I try to be alive with the joy of loving God and

letting this flow out of me. I also do my best to be positive and pleased with what I have,
what I can do, and I thank God for it all. I get closer and closer to the trumpet sound of God's
call (1997, p. 24).

Life review interviews of elder Catholic women religious for this study provided data that were rich in application to several theoretical discussions in gerontological literature. Identity development for these women religious followed the
tenets of the continuity theory rather than the staged life span development theory
proposed by Erikson (Melia 1999). Continuity of self was promoted by the reliance on several themes weaving throughout the individuals' lives on into later
life. This finding supports Kaufman's (1986) notion of an "ageless self" that is
organized around themes that are the building blocks of identity. As a group these
women also show remarkable similarity in the continuous themes that run
throughout their individual lives: faith, family, education, friends, community of
religious sisters, service to others, and prayer (Melia 1999). In addition, these
women age gracefully because they continue to develop as sisters and as individuals due to strong social support and mentoring into positive aging roles (Melia
1998). The women religious positively disengage from life in order to experience
the presence of God (Melia forthcoming). For them aging brings with it more time
for prayer and a deeper sense of God's closeness. Their prayers, part of their vocation, are sources of continuous activity and structure in their lives from which they
never retire. Closeness to God means their later years are more often filled with
solitude than with loneliness (Melia forthcoming).

Another main finding is that generativity is an important factor in their graceful aging. Generativity is a theme in all of the life stories of the women religious that were interviewed; all of the 39 women had service to others as a
major theme upon which their identity was formed. Wolf (1986), in her study of
elder Catholic women religious, found this to be true as well. This is a major
way that they believe they serve God and live out their religious vows. A noteworthy contribution to the discussion about generativity in older adults is its
role in successful aging; generativity in older women religious seems to foster
or accompany other behaviors which are factors in quality of late life: positive
attitude, sense of support and belonging, psychological strength, and connection
to a larger purpose or belief system (Day 1991; Hart 1997; McAdams 1990).
While the connection between these factors and generativity cannot be statistically proven in this qualitative research, the study of highly generative women
can produce interesting questions about the role and value of generativity in late
life. It is because these women reflect subcultural values endorsing service to
others that they are an excellent case study in generativity in late life. Women
religious are members of a subculture that has an emphasis on generativity that
is incorporated into their religious calling and communal lifestyle. They are an
interesting group to study as a sociological ideal type demonstrating of the
existence of generativity throughout the adult life span, of the value of

generativity in late life, and of its role in graceful aging. As McAdams (McAdams and de St. Aubin 1992) advocates in his ambitious study of the topic, we need a wider and broader definition of generativity. He suggests we need a "thick description" of generativity (1992, p. 1013). Who better to study then women who are highly generative?

METHODOLOGY

This qualitative research study, formulated in the grounded theory tradition (Strauss 1987), was based on an interest in the factors that contribute to the successful aging of older women on into late life. The work is conducted as interpretive social science (Weiland 1995), using narrative data to identify both the patterns and the meanings embedded in human development. The model of "thick description" identified by Clifford Geertz (1973) is a valuable tool in interpreting cultural meanings of behaviors (Weiland 1995).

Interview Sample

The respondents for this study were drawn from the population of sisters of three religious orders. Forty women ranging in age from 68 to 98 (mean age of 80) were recruited using a convenience sampling technique. Some women were contacted directly by the interviewer because they were mentioned by other interviewees, some were approached by leaders in their order, and others volunteered based on an announcement and/or sign-up sheet circulated by the leaders. All of the women volunteered to be interviewed with the knowledge that it was an intensive life review interview which included questions regarding issues in aging.

The subjects have been in religious life from 45-75 years. They are highly educated, all but one having at least a teaching or bachelors degree, over 50 percent with masters degrees, and five with PhDs. The majority of the women were educators. Others were nurses, administrators in their orders, and social service workers. The women live in independent apartments, convents of varying sizes (10-60 women), assisted living facilities, and longterm care centers. They rate themselves as having generally good health, thus indicating positive attitudes towards health; among them they have a wide range of health conditions associated with aging including diabetes, advanced osteoporosis and arthritis, arterial sclerosis, stroke, cancer, blindness, and hearing loss. As Wolf (1990a) found, the women are remarkably diverse in their life stories. As Mercier and Powers (1996) found, the majority of the sisters are working, although most of them at reduced levels. Many of them remain active as volunteers or assist in the places where they live.

Interview Process

An in-depth interview process was used. The interview schedule was a modified reminiscence tool which guided the respondents through memories of their personal histories and life stories. This was intended to draw out themes and turning points in their lives. They were also asked about their aging process, retirement, and work. Questions were asked that would allow the coders to analyze the existence of developmental stages, generativity, and ego integrity.

The interviews were conducted with the participants in their homes or rooms or in a private area, and lasted from two to four hours. It was a concern that elder women religious, trained not to focus on themselves, might be reticent to speak of their own lives. However, the majority of women responded at length, and clearly the women were comfortable and open in discussing their lives. The women volunteered for the interview because they saw it as a contribution; they could demonstrate how aging can be done with a positive spiritual outlook and with support from their communities. Due to the nature of the life review interview and of the sampling technique, the results portray an ideal type of successful or graceful aging.

Data Analysis

Interviews were tape recorded and transcribed. Four independent coders reviewed the life review transcripts to determine if the individual women were successful agers. Using criteria from Day (1991) they were evaluated in ten areas to determine successful aging: autonomy and control, positive attitude towards health, managing daily activities, social relationships and support, comfortable environment, meaningful activity, commitment to larger cause, psychological strength, prescription for living a long life, and optimism about aging. Responses to several questions having to do with generativity and the aging process were compiled and analyzed to determine common patterns and elements in ongoing contribution and service to others. Responses to the following questions provided the data for this paper: Have you retired? What is a typical day like for you? What brings happiness to you? What do you tell people about how to live a good life? What kinds of things have given you the most pleasure? What has given and continues to give your life meaning? What sustains you through difficult times? How do you live your faith at this time? When is God present to you? Do elder women religious have anything to contribute? Is their contribution valued? What do people need to do to grow old gracefully? What kinds of things do you pray for? Has your prayer changed as you've grown older?

Interviews were also analyzed to discover emerging themes. Four independent coders systematically examined the narratives to determine the themes in the individual stories. This same procedure of analyzing individual themes was used by Wolf (1990a) in her life review interviews with elderly women religious, and by

Cox and Parsons (1996) in their study of the late life relationships between women. The coders also evaluated whether ego integrity had been achieved. Attainment of ego integrity was operationalized as having a sense of peace, of satisfaction with one's life, of acknowledgement of death, of a philosophy of life, and of sharing of wisdom.

Themes were coded in a process developed by Kaufman (1986) who argues that there are four to six themes for each life story which represent conceptions of meaning that emerge over and over in the life stories. They are identifiable because of their repetitive nature. Through close examination of the life review interviews these themes emerge. First substantive codes are generated from topics or words mentioned frequently during the life review. These codes are grouped into categories or themes based on their similar meaning in the interview. Coders were trained to systematically examine the life review narratives to determine themes related to how the women sustained themselves and made meaning in late life. The coders were also trained to assign the women to categories relating to gerontological theories of activity, reciprocity, and disengagement. Assignments were based on time spent interacting with people, involved with work and volunteering, and/or engaged in hobbies and social events; on levels of exchange and emphasis on sharing with and providing services to other people; and on the degree of withdrawal or slowing down that is mentioned by the individual woman. The women were assigned this designation based on self-described activity levels and types of interactions.

FINDINGS

Generativity or ongoing service to others is continuously demonstrated in the lives and identities of elder Catholic women religious. Throughout their life review interviews this theme is present. Much of their satisfaction in late life is derived from their ability to help other people and thus demonstrate they still have something to offer, both as individuals and as a group. When they contribute to others they feel validated by the recognition they receive. Even without societal recognition there is self-satisfaction that life remains fulfilling with meaning and purpose. The evidence for ongoing contribution can be seen distinctly in several areas which will be developed in this paper: their views and positions on retirement, their opinions on the contributions elder women religious have to make to society, and in their descriptions of their daily lives. They also state that the ability to contribute is part of what gives life meaning and helps them to age gracefully and live a good life. In the next sections these areas will be looked at separately. Because the women are so articulate and insightful, whenever possible, their voices are used to present the main findings.

Retirement

I retired from teaching a few years ago, four or five years ago. But I haven't retired from living. I'm very happy in retirement. I thought I would miss teaching so much that I might be lonely about it, but I really wasn't. I'm living in a teaching area; the school is right there. And I'm living with teachers too. I do go over to the school a lot, reading in the library. I have been involved for about 20 years in an organization called "Bread for the World," and I'm on their board of directors. It's just a little group. It's hard work, the hunger issues, the welfare. So that is an interest to me. And I've really kept up my interest in reading. And then I have a kind of letter writing mission. I like to write, so I'm not being heroic in doing this. But I have a lot of elderly people and some friends that are no longer able to get around as much as they used to. And I keep up correspondence with them and I find that very lifegiving to me in the sense that it's nice to be doing something for somebody else that probably isn't as able to do as you are yourself. Then I like to help keep the house running and do things that are very simple and ordinary. I love to bake bread. That's a very lifegiving experience. Now I have time to do some of the things that I love, things that I didn't have time to do. I like to go and sit in the chapel quietly and pray and think, which is good (93 years).

Well, you don't tell yourself everyday, "I'm retired." You tell yourself, "I'm alive and glad and in love with life and interested in life." If that's retired, I don't read that as retired. I think retirement is a state of mind more than anything. See retirement connected with sisters is an unknown word. You never retire as a sister. You still have your prayer life, your liturgy, your office; and if you have a leg under you at all you're there participating (86 years).

Being asked, "Have you retired?" brought some laughs, some regret, some relief, and an emphasis on ongoing service to others in the lives of the women religious. Some of the women were not yet retired, some worked part-time, and others emphasized their volunteer work. Clearly, for this subculture, retirement and the accompanying leisure have not become long awaited rewards after years of work. When they do retire, their lifestyles are similar to elders who demonstrate the "busy ethic." Their business is in the service of others. "If you saw my book of appointments, the pages are crazy. I tire more easily and I think I'm more crazy, but I don't give up. I don't want to retire. What would I do? What does a nun do if she's retired?" (71 years). Whether or not they consider themselves retired, each of the women remain active as best they can. "It depends on what you mean by retired. I have abandoned the responsibilities of an office which I had for 41 years. But I have not retired my mind. I hope I will never do that. And I have not retired from activity either. I enjoy working. I enjoy doing things that stimulate me and I have not retired from that kind of activity either" (78 years).

Maintaining a high level of activity and involvement with others is rewarding. These women feel their work is recognized and that the recognition they receive is very valuable to them, especially in late life. Thus they continue working and volunteering as much and as long as possible. "Especially when you've got your health, where you like your work, when you're recognized in your work. I'm always surprised at how I'm recognized. It surprises me that people have fairly high expectations of me; it surprises me but I really am grateful for it" (71 years). The gratitude they receive stems from their continuing contribution to society.

These activities allow one to feel useful and needed. They stay involved, semi-retired by working part-time, volunteering, and helping each other out in the community.

> Do you call it retired when you work all day? I haven't earned any money for a long time. I can tell you that. I retired from teaching, but I didn't retire from any volunteer work. There's always something I have to do. I don't feel I'm retired. 'Cause I'm working all the time. But if I were retired and I didn't have some type of a schedule, I think I'd be very bored (82 years).

Some enjoy the benefits of retirement, spending their days doing what they wish.

> I define retirement as continuing all kinds of things that you're interested in, but getting no pay. So I've retired. I love it 'cause I've got time to do the things I want to do. I'm volunteering for all the programs I'm working with and so I can call up and say, "I'm sorry, I don't feel good. I can't go today. I'm sorry that I can't go to that meeting. Let me know what happened." I am retired. Sure. And I enjoy every minute of it. And I can do the crewel work and the embroidery and the leather work that I didn't have time to do. Now I can do it. A lot of time to read and to catch up on things that I never had a chance to do. Catch up on the things that I said, "I'll do that later." Now is later (74 years).

The enjoyment comes mainly from remaining active, involved, engaged. Their interest in various activities reflects a generative interest in life. "Oh, 92! However, I spend my time knitting, crocheting, sewing. I make aprons. We have this bazaar every year. I buy towels and crochet the tops. I do that. I have a supply of things I've made. I do some reading. I don't sit there and do nothing. I'm able to use my hands" (92 years). Most of their volunteer and retirement activities contribute to others.

> You can call me semi-retired. I'm really not retired because I volunteer over there at the assisted living house. I go over there every week. And I go down to longterm care. I have my lunch with them. And then I go down and visit with the people. And I teach; I still teach. But I only have one class. It's very challenging. I don't fear retirement because I think I'll keep doing. I'm seventy-six years old. So, it might be my last year of teaching. But I'll keep volunteering and perhaps more of it. Because I don't feel seventy. I don't fear it or anything because I think the volunteering is good. I have plenty of hobbies to do. I love sewing. That cross stitch stuff. So I like crafts. I've been into that for awhile (76 years).

A major advantage of retirement is the sense of freedom that the women feel, because they can determine how to organize and spend their time and establish their daily schedule more independently.

> It's wonderful. It gives me time. First of all, it gives me time to visit many of the sisters whom I seldom saw. And I like to go to the infirmary and visit the sick. Extra time for the chapel. That's because before the days were so full. Get home, go to school, whatever. Yes, you'd like to spend some time, but then there were a lot of other things that had to be done. But now it's no, nothing in the way. I mean it's a peaceful atmosphere (82 years).

In the words of one woman, they "retire to" an activity, because they know they can devote time to whatever they choose.

> Now I can do what I want, when I want. But I want to feel useful. I just don't want to hang loose. I don't feel I'm responsible the way I was when I had a job. I mean I had to be there on time. It's too much. I'm not what I used to be. So I can go visit them. I can take time out....Religion goes on forever. So I can pray better now. I can even pray more which is an advantage for my life. And that's a plus. I can still do; I can still do if I want to do it. That want is still there which is the plus side of it. I can go over and do something. They can still ask me and they do. So I'm still able. But I don't have to (78 years).

The women can occupy their time as they see fit, with hobbies, crafts, music, reading, and prayers; but of foremost importance is feeling useful and being available when needed.

> I could not retire as such and live the life of Reilly. If I retire I know I could not sit here all day. Maybe God is going to ask me some day to be a contemplative and maybe my prayer life will be the main theme in my life. But right at this moment I do have pretty good health. I'm sharing my joy and my love with little children. I love to go to nursing homes. I like to bring communion to shut-ins. For the school I collect soda cans. I run a store. I have a snack bar. Since 1986 I've collected over $17,000. I type all the teachers' papers, the attendance cards. I'm there as they need me" (76 years).

Retirement is a process, a slowing down or altering, but not a new direction. The women continue to be engaged in meaningful contribution to others. Generativity runs throughout their later years: "I will continue to do as long as I can, a little bit of service that will be some kind of a blessing on humanity or something". (71 years).

Contributions of Elder Women Religious

The elder women religious value their ongoing service to their church and to society. They believe that they contribute largely through their faith and prayer as well as through their volunteer activities. In response to the question about whether this contribution was valued by society, the women said that they are uncertain; nonetheless, they themselves recognize the value of their contribution to society, to the religious community, and to the individual. It is through their service that elder women religious express and recognize their own sense of worth. It is of less significance whether or not they receive recognition by society at large.

> I'm not thinking of any particular contribution, but I'm sure they are powerful in their prayer life, their suffering life. I mean their physical diminishment. They're well taken care of and therefore they last longer. My sister who was a nurse said they live so long 'cause they get such good care. So just the fact that they are surviving and people know that they're living as older women now. They're probably praying for all those kids they had in school.

Hoping that they're leading good lives and doing anything good. They have that spirit. It just flows (75 years).

I think by their being there, by their prayer. I think prayer is so important. And their ministry is prayer, the real older sisters who are now at the provincial house and some of them even confined to wheelchairs. But they still, prayer is such a support. They certainly can contribute to the church that way. Some of them are capable of expressing their opinions by writing. Some of them can speak out at times. But I think prayer is their main way of helping, not only the church, but the world. Some of them go to visit others, elders. We had one sister who retired at ninety-one, but she used to go visit elderly [people] who were much younger than she was. She used to go visit regularly and bring them things and used to go to nursing homes, two or three nursing homes. But then she became hard of hearing so she gave up doing that (71 years).

Much of their generativity is expressed through prayer for the world: "Praying for conditions in the world. Praying for one another, for those that are in trouble" (86 years). Their prayers are for people they come in contact with: "I think that their prayer life can contribute to the church, and to the community, and to the surrounding areas, the neighborhood, by prayer. Prayer is so powerful" (77 years). No matter how frail a sister may be, she can continue to pray: "I think prayer is an important offering, one I believe that most elder religious pray for a larger cause. That's a vocation. Even if others can't go out and help the sick or the poor, we can pray" (94 years). The prayers of women religious are contributions in their eyes because through lives prayers they spread their faith. "The basics are love the Lord and love your neighbor, and faith, hope, and charity. And most of them have experienced that throughout their life and are continuing. And especially in the experience of prayer. They may have had more time to pray and it's more of a contemplative type of contribution" (69 years).

They have faith that their prayers work. "Just by their prayers and not only their own personal prayers. You can pray and you can pray. But I really believe you can pray and God will help and touch somebody" (78 years).

They believe that elder women religious serve as role models of graceful aging, showing by example what it is like to live a satisfied and content life. In this way they also contribute.

By showing that they're content, that they're, I can almost say that they're happy in their way of life or anything else, people seem to get a message. I think that by being, you know, sometimes when you get older, sometimes you get very selfish too. You know what I mean. But being there for others, I think is a big thing (75 years).

These women religious believe that they demonstrate a way of coping with life. "Their whole life, their attitude, their reactions to things. All those things have an effect. Their reactions to things that come up" (92 years). They are models; by the way they live their elderly life they show it can be a positive experience. Their lives demonstrate the need for ongoing service to others. "They have weathered the storm and have growth in their spiritual life. Grown wise. Grown mellow. A great help to those coming after them" (82 years).

The volunteer contributions performed by elder women religious into late life represent a commitment to society and to others that move these sisters outside their own lives. "By being there for others, I think is a big thing" (75 years).

> Definitely; through their prayer life. There are so many sisters that feel they can't do much of anything but pray. But it's very, very important. Miracles have come about as a result of prayer. The AIDs situation all over the world. Only prayer will help to at least minimize. At least I think that some of our sisters really think, "This is a mission, something very good that I can do right now." Pray the rosary. Pray for young people who think they know it all, have all the answers. Help the people in programs to get around; to spread aid through prayers. We had a sister who was bedridden for 36 years. I think that woman did more on her bed praying then all the rest of us who were running around doing things. That woman was so devout. She says, "This is all I can do. I can't do anything more." Thirty-six years. We used to have to go help turn her. She couldn't move herself. She helped more people through prayer than the rest of us running around (82 years).

These women help the church by attending meetings, being involved in parish life, and also being a spiritual presence. They are wisdom figures who share the wealth of experience. "They give even their presence at meetings. Some of them attend meetings. They may not contribute as much verbally, but I think in a one-on-one with someone else that is there they can get their thoughts across" (82 years).

> Besides their prayer life, and I emphasize their prayer life is a priority. And that's their priority to the church, I think, as a whole. To pray for the church. To pray for the church in the difficult times that it's going through. And I find many of the older religious are more open to the changes in the church than the others. They've had experiences they can share. And many of the older sisters are on various committees and commissions that they can share their knowledge and experience" (71 years).

> I think their prayer life. I'm sure they're praying for themselves and the whole world too. And some, even a little older than I am, I'm amazed at the closeness they have to God, the way they're close to God at times. "I was talking to God and He said...." I think the encouragement that they give young people. Cheer them up sometimes. To show an interest in their work. Urge them on and encourage them (88 years).

Meaningful Lives

In the sisters' daily lives, which for each woman now consists of individually structured routines and practices, service to others is a common and frequent occurrence. They teach English to immigrants, provide spiritual direction to inmates, visit elders and sick people who are homebound, work with orphans and troubled youth, help teen parents, serve the homeless and AIDs victims, and feed the poor. They help religious sisters who are less independent than they are themselves. Their sewing and crafts are for the benefit of others. Their prayers are for the world and for the intentions of others. Thus their days are structured through semi-retired activities and volunteer work as well as by faith practices and prayers. Their lives are given meaning by ongoing contribution to others, by their generativity.

While their individual lives are given meaning by their community life and the support they receive, it is in community that the value of helping others, within and without the community, is promoted. When asked what gives life meaning, one woman captured popular sentiment:

> Still being able to do things for other people. Being able to see the big picture. Knowing that there are others that can help you. It still relates to looking beyond the self, you know, to see that everyone contributes in some way to the whole. You can't look down because they're not able to do what you can do. You can't expect them to do what you can do. You have to take people the way they are. Let them make their contribution. People have their differences. People listen to one another. It all works out together. It keeps you from thinking that what you're doing is the "real thing (74 years).

For the women religious it is important to continue to have the ability to be able to do something that's of service to someone else:

> I think my life would be really cut short if I were crippled or in the infirmary or had to be. The quality of my life would change. And maybe it wouldn't. Maybe I'd find some other ways to pray for others and to pick up another apostolate of some sort. I'm not going to worry about that 'til I get to it (74 years).

When asked what is required for aging gracefully, service to others is frequently mentioned. Through service the elder women religious can think of others and not be thinking of themselves all the time: "See what they can do to make others happy" (92 years).

> Live in the times that you're living. Don't look back at what was in the past. And don't look too much in the future. Just live and be happy where you are and when you are. I would say to keep busy. I would say to keep busy 'cause that's where loneliness sets in. Real loneliness I'm talking about. Lonely almost to the point of depression. When you're just sitting there. Find there's always a little thing you can do. Keep busy. Stay in the now. Don't look back. And we're caught looking back often. Sometimes we have to look back, it's good for us. But what can I do to improve my life? I can make my happiness or break it. I can be happy. Even with all the health problems, with the work load, I can be happy if I want to. And I think, also, looking at what others do and comparing is very bad. Do it because you want to do it. Do anything because you like it and you enjoy it. I've got to do something. I've got something to do. So just take what you have around you and be. One of the things I would say is be, not overly busy, but busy. And you'll never be bored. When you're aging there are different ways to be busy. You can help someone else that can't do what you can do. You can read to them. Write for them. Do their little errands, or washing. There's so much you can do just to cheer them up. You don't ever have to be bored (82 years).

The elder women religious believe that contribution to others is necessary in order to live a good life: "Judging from myself I find you have to be a giving person and you have to be a good listener and from there you know you can't be on the receiving end all your life. It has to be give and take" (75 years). Helping other people gives helps them to be open and flexible.

> Share. Share. That's one thing. If you don't want to share you won't get anywhere. Be. That's part of being open. Be able to give of, share of your talents. If you can do something, do it. Don't wait 'til they squeeze it out of you. Come forward. What I can do? Don't save yourself. Give (78 years).

Thinking of other people rather than of oneself also helps women religious to be positive in their thinking and in their approach to life. This is what they feel they have been called to do: "And as a woman religious continue to be a mission. Our lives are meant to be a blessing to humanity. Don't stop being a blessing to humanity in some way, whether it's writing a letter for Amnesty International or whatever" (71 years). The call of service to others through action and prayer, to being open and challenged to grow as one ages, continues on into late life for these elder women religious.

DISCUSSION

Women religious have service to others as a main theme throughout their life stories, and it is continuous in their identity formation through the years. It is for the love of God and their wish to do God's work on earth that they enter religious life. Their desire to serve their fellow human beings, primarily through teaching in these three orders, is a calling stronger than parenthood. Theirs are highly generative lives or life scripts. The impulse to generativity occurs frequently throughout their stories, and their contributions are often in the forms of technical or cultural generativity. They are teachers and healers and creators; their behaviors benefit and improve the church as well as the community and society-at-large. They also nurture the next generation by doing this work based on personal and religious beliefs of faith and hope that are positive and life-affirming (Van De Water and McAdams 1989, p. 437). Kotre (1984) included a biography of a middle-aged nun in his study. He found her to be capable of cultural generativity, more so than any other subject, because she transmitted the highest values of society. She demonstrated the generative potential in childlessness and cared for the culture as a keeper of meaning, sharing principles and truth. She exemplified a communal orientation (as opposed to agentic) in her efforts to participate in a mutually shared social reality. The women religious in this study are equally impressive in their generativity, more so because they are years beyond midlife. They demonstrate the value of continuous service to others as an important factor in ongoing identity development and in meaningful and graceful aging.

The elder Catholic women religious in this study have devoted their lives to God and therefore to service to others, to generativity. Theirs is a life framed by a unique subculture of beliefs and values that call them to lives of nontraditional roles and activities. In their demonstration of graceful aging, these women provide a picture of identities formed with continuous patterns of generativity; generative themes run throughout their lives. Generativity is present in their early family values; it is operative in their choice of vocation which emphasizes service; it framed their middle years when service to God replaced family roles; and it is of major importance in their later years as they continue serving others, most particularly through their prayers. This unique subculture demonstrates several points emphasized by both Kotre (1984) and McAdams (1990) that generativity, whether an impulse or part of a life script, is ongoing in people's identity formation and lives. The benefits of generativity with regard to life satisfaction and happiness (noted by McAdams, de St. Aubin, and Logan 1993), are vividly demonstrated in the lives of these elder women religious. Service to others gives them a reason to be, a sense of purpose and meaning, and a feeling of self-satisfaction. Perhaps Alexander and colleagues (1991) are accurate that this type of generativity in American culture serves the self as much as society, even in this religious subculture; but the satisfaction these women derive is largely related to their sense that they are doing God's work here on earth. Their generativity is connected to their fears and hopes related to dying, death, and entering heaven. Their generativity, in part, is based on an accountability to God. There are both agentic and communal elements involved in their actions. This is similar to what Alexander and colleagues (1991) found in the late-life generativity of childless women.

This case study of the generativity of elder women religious is not without problematic aspects. The subculture that has been promoted by religious life is threatened by the lack of new initiates into religious orders. Many older women religious mentioned that the lifestyle they lead will cease to exist because women no longer choose the path they took fifty or sixty years ago. Despair and stagnation could result if this generative subculture is discontinued. The women might wonder, "What does my life matter?" As in the study conducted by Wolf (1990a), these women did not appear devastated by the loss of legacy related to diminishing religious orders of sisters. This was readily discernible in the life review transcripts. They seemed to be able to resolve this dilemma in several ways. Some believe new forms of religious orders will evolve, some rationalize that they are serving God through the Church which will go on, and others conclude that it is "in God's hands, and He won't disappoint them." Wolf (1990a) found that the elderly women religious in her study did not focus on the external crisis in facing what she identified as a crisis of legacy. They were concerned instead with their own personal development. The theme of death was identified by Wolf. "They were concerned with dying as they have tried to live: charitably and without complaint. They wanted to be remembered well by the women they leave behind and by the cohort that follows" (p. 77). While this social and cultural dilemma is potentially problematic, their positive belief systems and generative outlooks help these particular women interviewed to avoid pitfalls of despair and stagnation in their continuous development of identity. In a way theirs is a more selfless view of generativity than Alexander and colleagues (1991) suggest. These women are accountable to God rather than to the individualistic culture. Indeed, as these authors suggest, there are competing ideologies, both religious, humanitarian, and philanthropic within our American culture which promote generativity.

Finally, while they strongly identify more with their religious communities and subcultural beliefs in a vowed life of obedience, poverty, and chastity, in serving God, these sisters are also aware of the status of older women in our society. We continually devalue older women as having little contribution to make to the over-all maintenance of society (Browne 1998; Friedan 1993). Childless, unmarried women are particularly suspect. These women religious chose to enter a vocation that did not include these roles and duties, often making this choice in part because they wanted to be teachers, nurses, and/or social workers, as well as become religious sisters. It is through these activities that they fulfilled themselves while following their religious vows and nurturing others. In old age they again recognize the consequences of this choice as they do not have offspring in a culture where generativity is most often biological and parental (Kotre 1984; Alexander et al. 1991) They do not have offspring to care for them in late life, or with whom to express their generativity in late life (Erikson, Erikson, and Kivnick 1986). Here again is a potential source of despair and stagnation. But the women interviewed believe that their lives of service nurture their religious communities and the church, as well as their own families and society. Their prescription for generativity, in Kotre's terminology, is technical and cultural. They demonstrate, through their choice of vocation and lifestyle, that a variety of forms of generativity exist together, each providing means of fulfillment as well as motivated by positive and hopeful belief in the future of humanity.

This has been a "thick description" of generativity in the lives of forty elder Catholic women religious whose vocation and lifestyle represent a subculture based on communal and spiritual beliefs. These findings about women religious in late life match those found in other studies of religious sisters described earlier in this paper. Studying the late life generativity of these sisters contributes to the literature about the lifestyle of this unique subculture. What conclusions can we reach about generativity for the larger culture? Generativity is definitely important for identity formation throughout the lives of elder women religious, and a source of great satisfaction and meaning in late life for them. Because other groups and individuals share this theme of contribution through service to others from a rich variety of traditions as well as from an American cultural emphasis on volunteerism, this study would also have value for a great number of older individuals in this country. Studies of the oldest-old among other groups in the population indicate that generativity, perhaps through an emphasis on volunteering, serving others, or helping within the family, is important to other elders as well (Fisher 1995). Service to others, generative acts, get us outside of ourselves and help place our own lives in a context of greater meaning; it is harder to focus on oneself and one's problems, aches, pains, and losses, while one is engaged, actively or passively, with the wider community. This is what the women religious demonstrate. A qualitative study such as this cannot answer which comes first, positive belief and hope for the future, or generativity; it is beyond the scope of this methodology and exploration. But generativity exists in the life stories of elder women religious and contributes to the continuation of a positive outlook and in the conviction that one's life, including the later years, has meaning and purpose.

NOTE

1. The term "religious" when used in reference to a member of a religious community (i.e., a group of individuals who live together as sisters or brothers and publicly profess religious vows) is a *noun* and "women" would designate the gender of the group. Although the term "nun" specifically refers to a member of a religious order whose chief purpose and work is to worship in a cloistered setting, it is properly used to refer to any woman religious. Therefore, throughout this paper the terms "sister," "nun," and "woman/women religious" are used interchangeably.

REFERENCES

Alexander, B.B., R.L. Rubinstein, M. Goodman, and M. Luborsky. 1991. "Generativity in Cultural Context: The Self, Death and Immortality as Experienced by Older American Women." *Aging and Society* 11: 417-442.

Browne, C.V. 1998. *Women, Feminism, and Aging.* New York: Springer Publishing Company.

Cowan, M.J. 1992. "Facts About the National Center for Nursing Research." *Cardiovascular Nursing* 28(2): 9-14.

Cox, E.O., and R.J. Parsons. 1996. "Empowerment-Oriented Social Work Practice: Impact on Late Life Relationships of Women." *Journal of Women & Aging* 8(3/4): 129-143.

Day, A.T. 1991. *Remarkable Survivors: Insights Into Successful Aging Among Women.* Washington, DC: The Urban Institute Press.

Daniewicz, S.C., J.M. Mercier, E.A. Powers, and D. Flynn. 1991. "Change, Resources and Self-Esteem in a Community of Women Religious." *Journal of Women & Aging* 3(1): 71-91.

Deedy, J. 1984. "Beyond the Convent Wall: Sisters in the Modern World." *Theology Today* 15(4): 421-425.

Doyle, J.C. 1986. "Commitment in a Religious Order: A Sociological View." *Review for Religious* 45(2): 188-204.

Erikson, E.H. 1963. *Childhood and Society* (2nd ed.). New York: W. W. Norton.

Erikson, E.H., J.M. Erikson, and H.G. Kivnick. 1986. *Vital Involvement in Old Age.* New York: W. W. Norton.

Fisher, B.J. 1995. "Successful Aging, Life Satisfaction, and Generativity in Later Life." *International Journal of Aging and Human Development* 4(3): 239-250.

Friedan, B. 1993. *Fountain of Age.* New York: Simon & Schuster.

Geertz, C. 1973. *The Interpretation of Cultures.* New York: Basic Books.

Hart, H.M. 1997. *Generativity and Social Involvement.* Unpublished doctoral dissertation, Northwestern University, Evanston, IL.

Healthy People 2000: National Health Promotion and Disease Prevention Objectives. 1991. U.S. Department of Health and Human Services Public Health Services. Washington, DC: DHA publication no. (PHS) 91-50212.

Jacques, M. 1997. *Drawing on the Wisdom of SSA Sages.* Unpublished final paper, Geriatric Pastoral Certificate, Luther Seminary, St.Paul, Minnesota.

Kaufman, S.R. 1986. *The Ageless Self: Sources of Meaning in Late Life.* Madison, WI: University of Wisconsin Press.

Kotre, J. 1984. *Outliving the Self: Generativity and the Interpretationof Lives.* Baltimore: Johns Hopkins University Press.

_____. 1995. "Generative Outcome." *Journal of Aging Studies* 9(1): 33-41.

Lonergan, E.T. (Ed.). 1991. *Extending Life, Enhancing Life.* Washington, DC: Institute of Medicine, National Academy Press.

MacHaffie, B.J. 1986. *Her Story: Women in Christian Tradition.* Philadelphia: Fortress Press.

Magee, J.J. 1987. "Determining Predictors of Life Satisfaction Among Retired Nuns: Report From a Pilot Project." *Journal of Religion & Aging* 4(1): 39-49.

Margraff, R.L. 1986. "Aging: Religious Sisters Facing the Future." *Women and Politics.* New York: The Haworth Press.

McAdams, D.P. 1990. "Unity and Purpose in Human Lives: The Emergence of Identity as a Life Story." Pp. 128-200 in *Studying Persons and Lives,* edited by A.I. Rabin, R.A. Zucker, R.A. Emmons, and S. Frank. New York: Springer Publishing Company.

McAdams, D.P., and E. de St. Aubin. 1992. "A Theory of Generativity and Its Assessment Through Self-Report, Behavioral Acts, and Narrative Themes in Autobiography." *Journal of Personality and Social Psychology* 62(6): 1003-1015.

McAdams, D.P., E. de St. Aubin, and R.L. Logan. 1993. "Generativity Among Young, Midlife, and Older Adults." *Psychology and Aging* 8(2): 221-230.

McNamara, J.K. 1996. *Sisters in Arms: Catholic Nuns Through Two Millennia.* Cambridge, MA: Harvard University Press.

Melia, S.P. 1998. *The Encouragement of Friends: Modeling of Graceful Aging Among Elder Catholic Women Religious.* Unpublished paper.

_____. 1999. "Continuity in the Lives of Elder Catholic Women Religious." *International Journal of Aging and Human Development* 48(3): 173-187.

_____. Forthcoming. "Evidence of Positive Disengagement in Late Life: Prayer and Solitude." Manuscript accepted by *Journal of Religious Gerontology.*

Mercier, J.A., and E.A. Powers. 1996. "Sense of Control Among Women Religious." *Journal of Religious Gerontology* 9(4): 7-26.

Mercier, J.A., E.A. Powers, and S.C. Daniewicz. 1991. "Aging Catholic Sisters' Adjustment to Retirement." *Journal of Religious Gerontology* 8(2) 27-39.

Mercier, J.M., M.C. Shelley, and E.A. Powers. 1996. "Religious Commitment and Social Relationships: Their Relative Contributions to Self-Esteem of Catholic Sisters in Late Life." Pp. 91-111 in *Relationships Between Women in Later Life,* edited by K.A. Roberto. Binghamton, NY: Harrington Park Press.

Neal, M.A. 1984. *Catholic Sisters in Transition.* Wilmington, DE: Michael Glazier, Inc.

Pinn, V.W. 1992. "Women's Health Research: Prescribing Change and Addressing the Issues." *Journal of the American Medical Association* 268: 1921-1927.

Snowden, D.A., S.K. Ostwald, and R.L. Kane. 1989. "Education, Survival, and Independence in Elderly Catholic Sisters, 1936-1988." *American Journal of Epidemiology* 130: 999-1012.

Strauss, A.L. 1987. *Qualitative Analysis for the Social Sciences.* New York: Cambridge University Press.

Van De Water, D.A., and D.P. McAdams. 1989. "Generativity and Erikson's 'Belief in the Species.'" *Journal of Research in Personality* 23: 435-449.

Weiland, S.. 1995. "Interpretive Social Science and Spirituality." Pp. 589-611 in *Aging, Spirituality, and Religion*, edited by M.A. Kimble, S.H. McFadden, J.W. Ellor, and J.J. Seeber. Minneapolis, MN: Fortress Press.

Wittberg, P. 1985. "Transformation in Religious Commitment." *Review for Religious* 42(2): 161-170.

Wolf, M.A. 1986. "Growth and Development with Older Women Religious: An Exploration in Life Review." *Lifelong Learning* 9(4): 7-10, 28.

_____. 1989. "Women Religious: How Does a Nun Retire?" Paper presented to the Ninth Annual Conference of the Northeastern Gerontological Society.

_____. 1990a. "The Crisis of Legacy: Life Review Interviews with Elderly Women Religious." *Journal of Women & Aging* 2(3): 67-79.

_____. 1990b. "The Call to Vocation: Life Histories of Elderly Women Religious." *International Journal of Aging and Human Development* 31(3): 197-203.

_____. 1991. "Elder Women Religious: A Phenomenological View." Paper presented at the Gerontological Society of America 44th Annual Meeting.

Wood, C.M. 1996. "Staying Connected and Letting Go: Quality of Life for Elderly Nuns in Convent Care Centers." Unpublished doctoral dissertation, Graduate Division: Nursing, University of California, San Francisco.

THREATS TO ACADEMIC IDENTITY AND COMMITMENT FOR FACULTY OF COLOR

Robert K. Leik and Alexandra R. Goulding

ABSTRACT

Scholars are trained to be experts in their discipline and to develop disciplinary identities and commitments. Faculties and administrators expect evidence of those identities and commitments in the form of publications and professional service for
promotion and tenure. Yet faculty of color are typically disproportionately loaded
down with special committee assignments, task force requests, student demand, and
so on. The intent is certainly not malevolent. It is in the nature of "Oh, we need a
Black/Hispanic/Indian/Asian...representative. Can you help us out?" or "Finally
there is someone who can advise our Black/Hispanic/Indian/Asian...students."
Such demands serve the university's interests but have little to do with scholarly
identities and commitments. They consume time needed to establish scholarly cre-
dentials, and they undermine disciplinary identities and compete with disciplinary
commitments. In effect, the faculty member has her/his racial identity thrust upon
her/him as THE primary identity. Yet when promotion and tenure roll around,
colleagues who were so welcoming wonder why she/he wasn't more academically

Advances in Life Course Research, Volume 5, pages 143-157.
ISBN: 0-7623-0033-7

productive. There must be mechanisms for supporting the disciplinary identities and commitments of all faculty and reducing conflicting demands on their time and resources, or we will systematically destroy, for faculty of color, just that which we presume to value most.[1]

The problem of "keeping our faculties" is, in social psychological terms, one of creating a workplace which fosters identities and commitments that are in agreement with the formal and informal criteria by which faculty earn academic respect, tenure, and promotion. Our position here is that typical expectations for new faculty of color do not foster such identities and commitments. On the contrary, they undermine them. This is not to imply that academe is in the business of intentionally derailing careers via white-only schemes.[2] We believe, however, that regardless of myriad good intentions, current academic practices toward new faculty of color systematically erode the very basis on which successful academic careers must be founded. In fact, the process begins during graduate training of students of color. In the interest of focus, however, we will concentrate on the faculty problem. Our approach to defending our assertion of systematic erosion requires examining what we mean by the terms *identity* and *commitment* and their existence within ongoing *social networks*.

IDENTITY

Informally, each of us has many identities. Each identity is a collection of things about oneself having to do with how we think and feel about who we are, what we do, how well we do it, and so on. Also, each identity depends on the situation we happen to be in at any given time. Someone may feel confident and at ease among friends, hesitant but hopeful in a new academic setting, or unappreciated and resentful among critics. The collection of these situationally specific identities does not constitute a jumbled pile, but typically forms an integrated, hierarchical structure; a social self (Rosenberg 1979; Stryker 1980, 1987). The self has great influence on what we choose to do, where we do it and who we do it with. In short, a social self consists of an organized set of identities, or self references, that are interdependent, differentially salient and link the actor with properties or roles that provide social placement. The self is hierarchical in that some identities are broadly linked, hence constitute core aspects of self. Other identities are more peripheral. The more central an identity is, the more costly it is to change or lose that identity. To lose the most basic aspects of self is to lose who and what one is as a human being.

Identities are social constructions that develop in interaction with others. Furthermore, as a friend and noted social psychologist commented many years ago, "socialization goes on and on."[3] That is, as we move through life, we continually ind some activities, situations, and people rewarding, others essentially neutral, ind some to be avoided if possible. A general principal from social exchange theory is that positive outcomes in social situations increase the likelihood that we vill seek those situations out in the future; negative outcomes decrease that ikelihood. As new situations are experienced, our sense of who and what we are :ontinues to be shaped by our successes and failures.

Some aspects of one's social self are likely to remain fairly stable over the life :ourse, in part because they generate relatively consistent responses from others. External physical characteristics are convenient, if often erroneous, hangers for :ocial placement. They become "status characteristics" (Berger, Connor, and Fisek 1974) used by others to assign us to convenient categories so as to be able :o select actions toward us that are deemed appropriate; friendly, haughty, condescending, subservient, competitive, collaborative, dependent, ignoring, and so :orth. Such characteristics obviously include race and gender. In Mead's "Looking Glass Self" sense, we learn to see ourselves as others see us (Mead 1934). Fhat is, our sense of self derives from how we see ourselves reflected in others' pehaviors to us and about us. Much of who we think we are depends upon these /isible status characteristics and how others have reacted to them. We carry racial ind gender identities with us in all social situations, though we may be forced to :onsider them more important in some settings than in others.

Incidentally, it should be apparent, as is now widely recognized, that race is :ocially constructed; it depends little on genetics and biology and greatly on what others assume, based on one having been assigned a race label. As Omi and Winant state, "…our ongoing interpretation of our experience in racial terms :hapes our relations to the institutions and organizations through which we are :mbedded in social structure. Thus we expect differences in skin color, or other racially coded characteristics, to explain social differences. Temperament, sexuality, intelligence, athletic ability, aesthetic preferences, and so on are presumed :o be fixed and discernible from the palpable mark of race. Such diverse questions is our confidence and trust in others (for example, clerks or salespeople, media figures, neighbors), our sexual preferences and romantic images, our tastes in music, films, dance, or sports, and our very ways of talking, walking, eating, and dreaming become racially coded simply because we live in a society where racial iwareness is so pervasive" (Omi and Winant 1994, p. 60).

Other aspects of the self depend upon behaviors more than upon looks. Being in outstanding athlete or a brilliant scholar generates approval and reinforces our :ense of who we are regardless of what we look like. Obviously, if we are rewarded for our scholarly expertise, we will generate an identity as a scholar. Fhat identity will likely be specific to our field of study, and will be relevant primarily in settings involving other scholars, or at least others who respect scholars. Fhe grocery clerk or the auto mechanic isn't apt to care much about such an identity, and we aren't too likely to play on it when dealing with either of them. In a iniversity setting, however, that identity as scholar is supposed to be paramount.

We may be sociable or athletic or from a wealthy family, but what counts is supposed to be our scholarly work. Like any other aspect of self, to the extent that our sense of identity as a scholar is reinforced and rewarded, it will flourish and become more central to our overall life organization. To the extent that it is not rewarded, it will wane and we will likely seek reinforcements in other venues.

COMMITMENT

The more salient an identity, the more committed one becomes to those roles and relationships which evoke and reinforce that identity. Commitment, in the sense of being committed to an identity, a role or a relationship, involves four dimensions: focus, consistency, emotion, and duration (see, for example, Becker 1960; Bielby 1992; Burke and Reitzes 1991; Hoffer 1951; Kanter 1972, Leik, Owens, and Tallman 1999).

Focus means we are committed to *something*: a social protest movement, a marriage, an academic specialization. Consistency means that to the extent that we are committed to something, we act in the interest of maintaining both it and those aspects of our identity that are associated with it. Not all actions are carefully thought out, of course, and not all behaviors are internally consistent. Sometimes people do things that violate their commitments or subvert important identities. In general, though, the more committed someone is to some focus and to those aspects of self invested in that focus, the more consistently that person will act to protect and enhance the focus, the identity which depends upon it, and the broader range of situations in which that identity will be salient.

The terms, *emotion* and *duration*, are fairly obvious. We care about that to which we are committed. There are strong feelings involved. Similarly, the type of commitment we are discussing here is not for some arbitrary contractual period, but for an indefinite future. People seldom enter a profession or a marriage with the idea that it will do for a year or two, until something better comes along.

As noted earlier, repeated satisfactory exchanges in a given situation are likely to increase the importance of aspects of identity associated with that situation. Consequently, receiving social rewards such as praise, recognition, and respect generate commitments to the settings in which such rewards occur. If we are rewarded as scholars, we not only think of ourselves as scholars, we also become committed to the scholarly enterprise. Such commitments often generate "side bets" (Becker 1960), such as service to professional associations and reviewing for academic journals. Indeed, the more committed one is to a scholarly profession, the more one's scholarly identity takes precedence over other possible selves. Most exchange theories seeking to explain commitment conceptualize relationships as beginning with market economy notions in which actors are concerned for their individual well-being, and end with a focus on the well-being of the committed unit.

In sum, then, to the extent that we generate identities and commitments to a particular scholarly field, the more we are likely to do the very things which further enhance our standing in that field: publication, teaching, and service specific to the field. But those identities and commitments require consistent rewarding in the particular scholarly field. Any other situation will erode commitments and relegate the scholarly identity to a lesser place in the overall self. The process is seldom static: an upward spiral leads to increased stature in, and focus on, one's field. A downward spiral leads to disinterest and devotion of efforts elsewhere deemed more rewarding.

It is useful at this point to distinguish between commitments that are chosen and those that are thrust upon us. Becoming a sociologist or a physicist requires intentional selection of a field of study, adequate capability, a great investment of time and effort, and the right "moves" in developing a career and its concomitant rewards. Mostly, this is an active choice process. Having status characteristics such as race, gender, and age is not a matter of choice (although attempting to mask increased age is more and more common). Others acting toward or reacting to us in terms of our personal achievements is particularly rewarding because it demonstrates the effectiveness of our own efforts. On the other hand, having others treat us in terms of immutable status characteristics can be distracting or even demeaning in situations that are supposed to be governed by universal criteria. All too often, faculty of color have identities and commitments thrust upon them that are couched in terms of race rather than academic accomplishment. We hope to expand on this point as our discussion proceeds.

SOCIAL NETWORKS

There is always a social basis for identities and commitments. It is important to recognize that social processes exist in networks of actors. Wellman (1988) has suggested three general principles basic to social network conceptions of social reality. Two of those are particularly relevant here. (1) *Behavior is interpreted in terms of structural constraints on activity, rather than in terms of "inner forces."* That reemphasizes the importance of social milieu in shaping individual action. (2) *Patterned relationships among multiple others jointly affect network members' behavior*, which is to say that structure of the whole network exerts strong influences on the opportunities and constraints facing each individual member. Indeed, a great deal of experimental work demonstrates that one's placement in social networks exerts overwhelming influence on such outcomes as social power.

Two useful concepts from network theory are *connectivity* and *structural balance*. Consider a simple triad of individuals, each socially linked with the other two. If A enjoys working with B, and B dislikes working with C, either A will have to avoid working with C, will have to do so in B's absence, or will have to

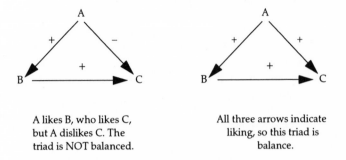

A likes B, who likes C,
but A dislikes C. The
triad is NOT balanced.

All three arrows indicate
liking, so this triad is
balance.

These conditions of balance or imbalance may not be perceived identically by all participants in the network. If, for example, C perceived the A-B and B-C links correctly, and believes that she or he is liked by A as well, then for C the network will be balanced. Any set of arrows which create a connected path in the network will be balanced if the product of the signs of those arrows is positive.

Figure 1.   Simple Balanced and Imbalanced Social Networks

avoid working with B. If all three try to work together, the network is structurally unbalanced. When existing commitments in a social structure are unbalanced, there will be a tendency to reduce or alter those commitments most in conflict with the rest of the system. Similarly, when existing commitments form incomplete cycles, there will be a tendency to establish relationships and eventual commitments that complete those cycles in a balanced manner. Figure 1 shows two simple triadic networks, one balanced and the other imbalanced.

SO WHAT DO WE DO TO FACULTY OF COLOR?

Let's consider first, what occurs in most students' graduate experience. Graduate students of color are typically so identified during the application and selection process, primarily for placement regarding potential sources of funding. Their scholarly orientation is a secondary point of interest in this process. When those students enter the department or program, they are referred to organizations and services specifically for students of color. Faculty suggestions for professional networking often include mention of the racial similarity between the student and the recommended colleague, while such recommendations to majority-group students are most often based solely upon common interest areas. Graduate students of color are sought to serve on university committees where diversity is desired, with their primary qualification being their racial designation rather than their scholarly focus. They receive requests from faculty, their departments, and institutional offices to contribute time and energy to mentor other students of their racial group, to volunteer in support of other students, and to assist the university in recruiting more students of color.

Though all of these suggestions and requests are intended to help the student become invested in the institution, the time and effort required pull the student away from his/her primary requirement: developing an academic identity and progressing as a scholar. Instead, the recognition and rewards provided are related to identifying as a member of a racial community within the institution, and working on behalf of that community. In other words, race is thrust upon the student in a context that ostensibly considers race an inappropriate criterion for success or failure. This is certainly not to say that one's race is problematic. It is to say that expectations and rewards based on race can indeed be problematic; they violate the universality which is a supposed hallmark of academe, and impose time and resource demands unrelated to the presumed goals of higher education.

What is supposed to happen in graduate school is different. We'll refer to sociological training for convenience, but one should feel free to mentally substitute any field. Unless either prior experience or work as an undergraduate has provided unusual preprofessional socialization, most students first encounter the idea of establishing a professional sociological identity as they pursue their graduate studies. Faculty and more advanced students, both by example and by mentoring, implant the idea that, on completion of graduate work, one should think of oneself as a sociologist. That implies a host of things one should do: keep abreast of current sociological work, do theoretical or empirical sociological research and publish the results, teach sociology, and participate in regional, national, and international sociological associations. As graduate training is completed and the young scholar achieves a faculty position, all those activities create and enhance a budding professional standing.

As one participates in such activities, two things normally occur. First, if the work one does is good, there will be direct rewards. People will begin to recognize you, or at least your name, in professional circles. You will receive requests for reprints, offers to participate in scholarly symposia or to write professional texts for profit, and perhaps even competing job offers. It is a simple principle behind the concepts of identity and commitment that such rewards will make you feel good about your professional work, which in turn will enhance your professional identity and your commitment to that profession. Especially as you form friendships and collegial relationships beyond the bounds of your own institution, you will find increased pleasure in the very participation that enhances your status, reinforces your scholarly identity, and strengthens your commitment. In short, you are establishing a professional network, an absolutely crucial cog in the gears of professional advancement.

It will be helpful to distinguish between a scholarly identity formed in the manner just described, from racial and university identities. Figure 2 briefly summarizes the essence of these three identities. Certainly all three of these aspects of a faculty member's total identity may be congruent and mutually

Scholarly Identity	Racial Identity	University Identity
A sense of self as a respected member of an intellectual or artistic peer group. Scholarly status is based on the quality of contributions one has made to the field.	A sense of self as a member of a socially defined status group typically assumed to have a biological basis, a distinctive heritage and a common culture.	A sense of self as a member of a local organization which serves students and local community as well as a broader intellectual and artistic audience.

Figure 2.   The Essence of Three Different Identities

reinforcing. When such is the case, the fortunate person is able to merge her/his personal passions in serving both the local and the scholarly communities. It is important to recognize, however, that there are different factors involved in each and they may not be compatible.

All of this no doubt sounds simple enough and pretty obvious. Our point, however, is that the typical expectations which greet a new faculty member who happens to be other than white systematically erode the very processes just described for developing a scholarly identity. Consider the following typical behaviors. First, there is always the question of whether one was hired because of a professional identity or a racial one. Surely we do not assume that unprofessional people are hired just because of their color. However, the message received by the new hire may well raise doubts or suspicions. Having a budget line which allows "targeted opportunity hires" for faculty of color outside normally allocated lines is a very useful tactic *for the institution*, but what message is delivered to the person hired? Also, what message might be implied to current faculty about the new hire? The problem is that color, or race, was the crucial element. The person may well be the best on the market in her/his field, but the very first bureaucratic process has a "race stamp" all over it. We certainly are not arguing for eliminating ways of augmenting the number of faculty of color. We are arguing that the process itself begins by placing race ahead of professional achievement as the principle criterion for hiring; by thrusting race upon the candidate.

So what happens when the new person arrives on campus? A most likely series of events is a warm welcome (we all would appreciate that), followed by a very large number of requests for departmental and campus service activities which, again, are predicated on color rather than professional stature. "We'd love to have you join our work force on diversity." "You will be on the following departmental committees, to assure breadth of representation." "There are so many students of (whatever) color who have been dying to have someone like you here that they can talk to about their work." The list could go on and on. See Myers (1995) regarding the pressures to be racial representatives that faculty of color encounter. We all know faculty of color who have experienced just that type of "welcome" to the academic community.

Yes, but isn't that very positive? Don't people like to feel wanted? The answers to those questions lie in the consequences of all those invitations or assignments. First, note that the requests all serve the university, not the profession. Nothing about serving on campus committees or task forces has any impact on regional, national, or international scholarly standing. In fact, those activities directly interfere with achieving scholarly standing because they take up an inordinate amount of time—time that other new scholars in the field who don't happen to be of color do not have to spend. The only network being established is a local one. It might be useful for local politics and it might make one feel needed locally, but that means we are only reinforcing local political activity, not professional accomplishment.

Consider the consequences in light of the activities that do enhance one's professional status. Keeping up with the field requires extensive time spent just reading. Doing research and publishing requires time in the field or the lab or wherever one's research should take place. In most areas research also requires time to prepare grant proposals to fund the work to be done. Attending professional meetings, especially as a presenter rather than a face in the crowd, requires a lot of time preparing. Developing one's identity in professional circles requires much activity away from campus doing things like chairing meeting sessions or holding professional office or serving on journal boards. Universities everywhere must begin to realize that *every time a new local demand is made, a broader professional need must be sacrific*ed. When those demands are inordinately placed on faculty of color, there is systematic undermining of the opportunities those faculty members need to develop their professional networks; to become noted professionals in their fields. The process may serve local campus interests, but it subverts professional equal opportunity.

CHANGES IN IDENTITIES AND COMMITMENTS

The process just outlined is the first stage of a predictable, long-term decay of professional identities and commitments in favor of racial identities and commitments. Most new faculty arrive with a strong sense of identity and commitment linked to their field as well as a racial identity. As stated before, the two are not inherently incompatible, and for some fields may be mutually reinforcing. However, every time someone serves on a special committee or task force because of her/his race, a racial identity is emphasized and a professional one is ignored. Every time one is rewarded for activities related to race, racial commitment is enhanced. In terms of the concept of *status characteristics*, mentioned earlier, the primary status characteristic for local participation becomes race. But when it comes to such honors as named chairs or Regents' Professorships (i.e., distinguished rank), status in one's scholarly field is the only relevant status characteristic. Thus we honor those who have achieved greatness in their field while

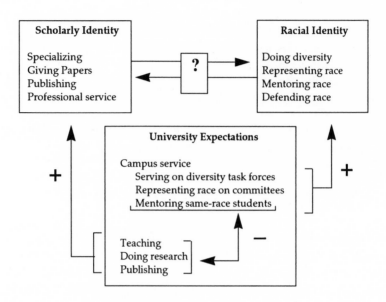

Excessive campus service negates scholarly work. If service reinforces racial identity but interferes with scholarly identity, it forces an opposition between those identities. The resulting sign between racial and scholarly (the question mark) will be negative.

Figure 3.   Structural Imbalance Created by University Expectations

making it unusually difficult for new faculty of color to accomplish what it takes to earn such honor.

Earlier we noted that structural balance in one's network relations is crucial for maintaining and enhancing that network. When local expectations and demands counter time and effort needed for professional enhancement, imbalances occur. If I spend a lot of time on this committee to improve racial attitudes *on campus*, I can't accept that invitation to be on a journal editorial board. If I have to be here for piles of meetings, I can't get to professional association meetings. In short, a local network imposes demands that contradict a professional network. The result is structural imbalance for the person caught in the situation. Figure 3 represents the identity imbalance implied by university demands curtailing scholarly achievement.

As much research demonstrates, when imbalance occurs, either of two responses is possible. First, one might just try harder to meet all demands. That, of course, is close to impossible and undoubtedly will generate early burnout, lower performance in all areas, and negative evaluations by others of one's abilities. For the problem at hand, the most likely recourse is to rescind some of the commitments so as to attain overall balance. If local commitments cannot be rescinded because of pressures from administrators or colleagues to represent one's race on committees, task forces, and so on, that leaves only the professional commitments up for grabs. At any given time, that may be a minor problem. Over sufficient time, as one or another professional linkage is cast aside, the structural support for the rest of the professional identity becomes seriously eroded. The long-term process is one of developing local, race-based identities and commitments at the expense of regional, national, and international professional identities and commitments.

There is an insidious aspect to the process we are describing. A request that a faculty member of color serve the goals of racial equality or enhance the opportunities for others of her/his race is very hard to refuse. To do so is likely to be viewed by that faculty member, as well as by her/his colleagues, as a lack of commitment to or a rejection of one's race. Regardless of one's personal desire to get involved in local, race-based activities, it is extremely difficult to say "no." The difficulty is evident in Figure 3, where campus service positively reinforces racial identity. To refuse such service can create uncomfortable imbalance in the overall identity structure. If I say no, am I really saying no to my heritage, my race, my people? Am I setting a terrible example for those who follow me? Do I really deserve to be a faculty member? The problem, then, is not just convincing young faculty of color that they should not be distracted by such requests. It is one of stopping the flood of those requests before they create such dissonance and erode the potential positive reinforcement link between one's racial and one's scholarly identity.

What happens after six years? Although the time span may vary from one institution to another, the most critical point is when "up or out" time arises. Do we promote and tenure this new scholar or say, "Sorry, your professional achievement simply does not meet our august standards." By now, our conclusion should be obvious. To the extent that we have induced a process of erosion of professional identities and commitments in favor of local service, the hopeful candidate will have little publication or professional activity in her/his vita. The candidate may have mentored dozens of students and improved student retention, but it will be commented "What a shame that she didn't pay equal attention to her professional priorities." The departmental and collegiate promotion and tenure committees will shake their heads and lament having to turn down someone who seemed like such a promising scholar a few years ago. We will not manage to keep that particular faculty member of color, or indeed many others who have tried to survive the same treadmill.

Additional complications exist when either of the following conditions occurs. When one's primary qualification for committee membership is race, it is often assumed that her/his contributions to committee deliberations will automatically be biased in favor of race and, therefore, not fully credible. Not only does such a situation reduce the individual's ability to contribute, it also reflects negatively on her/his university and professional statuses. Secondly, extensive research shows that minority members will, on the average, be accorded lower status in mixed-race, task-oriented groups when race is the primary status characteristic relevant to participation. Such need not be the case, of course. If race is not made salient to the group process (i.e., not activated in group selection or interaction), this status bias does not occur (Foschi and Takagi 1991). The implications for one's identity and related issues of self-esteem in a scholarly setting should be obvious.

SOME COMMENTS ABOUT ETHNICITY VERSUS RACE

Thus far we have been concerned with race rather than ethnicity. For many people, those terms are used interchangeably. We think it important to recognize that race, as indicated earlier, is a social status construct. People are *assigned* race labels by whatever current cultural logic distinguishes one identifiable group from another, and we know the rules of assignment have varied widely across history. Ethnicity has to do with social and cultural styles common to interacting groups. It pertains to ways of thinking, feeling, and behaving, and as such is learned and carried by each person as part of what seems "natural" and a central part of the self. Cornell and Hartmann (1998) suggest that ethnic identity is usually constructed by both selves and others, whereas racial identity is constructed by others. They also stress, as we do, that race overrides ethnicity in the way people classify others.

For some racial groups, there may be relatively little within-group variation in ethnic culture. In many respects, African Americans come closer to having a single racial culture, hence a single ethnicity, than do many other racial groups. By contrast, consider the great variety in American Indian tribal cultures, or the vast array of distinctive native African cultures, or the ethnic variety across groups lumped under the racial label "Asian." When race is the primary focus of the process that urges new faculty of color to do local service at the expense of scholarly achievement, then not only does this racialization negate the scholarly identity, it ignores or even negates the individual's true ethnicity as well.

To some extent, universities do not care about this question. To think in ethnic rather than racial terms would imply huge numbers of categories with such small numbers in many that no overall image of broad representation would emerge. Our point is that, for the institution, it is not the individual's cultural contribution that is desired. Rather, it is the ability to say "we have racial diversity." It would seem that if our visible rainbow is sufficient, we're happy.

Of course, there are programs that try to foster ethnic diversity and understanding. If our commentary about institutional interests and approaches seems too extreme, it is because we wish to make our point as clearly as possible. Fortunately, not all instances represent an opposition of scholarship versus race/ethnicity. In some academic fields, the subject of race or ethnicity or both

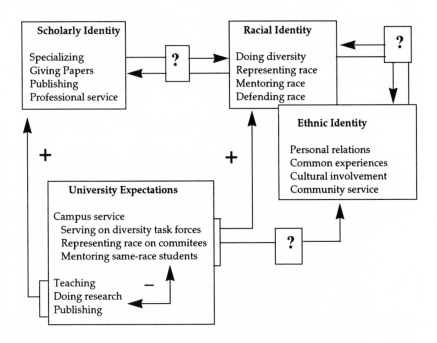

Ideally, all arrows will have positive signs. However, when university expectations emphasize racial identity at the expense of ethnic identity, the system cannot be balanced without rejecting some part of this total identity structure.

Figure 4. Adding Ethnicity to the Quandary

can be a legitimate scholarly focus, just as gender can be. Where academe fosters a mutual reinforcing of scholarly and racial or ethnic identities, the individual can merge the passions of each into a more cohesive self. Where ethnic identity is denied or swept under the carpet of race, an inherent negative relationship between racial and ethnic identity is created. Figure 4 represents that more complex effect on the individual.

Let's return briefly to the concept of commitment. If commitments are tied closely to one's identity, then rewarding behavior which evokes that identity will enhance commitment to the source of rewards. Might we conclude that rewarding participation in the local university community will enhance commitment to the university, regardless of loss in potential professional advancement? Won't that retain the faculty? When we consider the total network of relations involved, the answer is clearly "No." Inhibiting or obstructing professional rewards generates resentment toward the source of obstruction, the university. Not gaining status in one's field may result in decreased scholarly commitment, but that will not mean a corresponding increase in university commitment. Without professional standing, the faculty member would likely conclude that retention was for the university's convenience to maintain racial representation, not for her/his inherent value as a scholar. The likely result is a sense of betrayal by the university.

WHAT IS THE ANSWER?

There is no simple answer, but there are some simple principles which should guide us in seeking an answer. First, do not allow local demands to usurp professional development time. It is not uncommon to offer new faculty a reduced teaching load their first year to allow them to establish themselves. Let's not let that time get gobbled up with local business. Second, do everything to encourage professional advancement. That is, of course, what mentoring any new faculty member is supposed to be about. We cannot expect a glowing vita six or whatever years hence unless we allow it to be developed. Finally, do not allow race to become the prime, local status characteristic. That is not to negate the importance of race, but simply to act consistently on the premise that neither a faculty member's scholarly merit nor his/her obligations to the university have anything to do with race.

NOTES

1. This chapter is an expanded version of a paper presented at "Keeping our Faculties: Addressing the Recruitment and Retention of Faculty of Color in Higher Education," University of Minnesota conference, October 18-20, 1998, Radisson Hotel Metrodome, Minneapolis.

2. For a brief discussion of representation of faculty of color at all academic levels see Spalter-Roth, Levine, and Sutter 1999.

3. Personal conversation between Richard M. Emerson and Sheila A Leik. Emerson's actual comment was "Isn't it wonderful how socialization goes on and on?"

REFERENCES

Becker, H. 1960. "Notes on the Concept of Commitment." *American Journal of Sociology* 66: 32-40.
Berger, J., T.L. Conner, and M.H. Fisek. 1974. *Expectation States Theory: A Theoretical Research Program*. Cambridge, MA: Winthrop.
Bielby, D.D. 1992. "Commitment to Work and Family." Pp. 281-302 in *Annual Review of Sociology 18*, edited by J. Blake and J. Hagan. Palo Alto, CA: Annual Reviews, Inc.
Burke, P.J., and D.C. Reitzes. 1991. "An Identity Approach to Commitment." *Social Psychology Quarterly* 43: 18-29.
Cornell, S., and D. Hartmann. 1998. *Ethnicity and Race: Making Identities in a Changing World*. Thousand Oaks, CA: Pine Forge Press.

Foschi, M., and J. Takagi. 1991. "Ethnicity, Task Outcome and Assessment." Pp. 177-203 in *Advances in Group Processes, Vol. 8*, edited by E.J. Lawler, B. Markovsky, C. Ridgeway, and H.A. Walker. Greenwich, CT: JAI Press.

Hoffer, E. 1951. *The True Believer.* New York: Haper and Row.

Kanter, R.M. 1972. *Commitment and Community.* Cambridge, MA: Harvard University Press.

Leik, R.K., T.J. Owens, and I. Tallman. 1999. "Interpersonal Commitments: The Interplay of Social Networks and Individual Identities." Pp. 239-256 in *Handbook of Interpersonal Commitment and Relationship Stability*, edited by W.H. Jones and J.M. Adams. New York: Plenum.

Mead, G.H. 1934. *Mind, Self and Society.* Chicago: University of Chicago Press.

Myers, S.L. 1995. *MHEC Minority Faculty Development Project. Final Report.* Minneapolis, MN: Midwestern Higher Education Commission.

Omi, M., and H. Winant. 1994. *Racial Formation in the United States: From the 1960s to the 1990s* (2nd ed.). New York: Routledge.

Rosenberg, M. 1979. *Conceiving the Self.* New York: Basic Books.

Spalater-Roth, R., R.J.H. Levine, and A. Sutter. 1999. "The Pipeline of Faculty of Color in Sociology." *Footnotes* (American Sociological Association) 27(4): 4-5.

Stryker, S.1980. *Symbolic Interactionism: A Social Structural Version.* Palo Alto, CA: Benjamin/ Cummnings.

_____. 1987. "Identity Theory: Developments and Extensions." Pp. 89-103 in *Self and Identity: Psychosocial Perspectives*, edited by S. Stryker. New York: Wiley.

Wellman, B. 1988. "Structural Analysis: From Method and Metaphor to Theory and Substance." Pp. 19-61 in *Social Structures: A Network Approach*, edited by B. Wellman and S.D. Berkowitz. Cambridge, England: Cambridge University Press.

WHAT DOES IT MEAN TO "KNOW THYSELF" IN THE UNITED STATES AND JAPAN?

THE CULTURAL CONSTRUCTION OF THE SELF

Susan E. Cross

ABSTRACT

To "know thyself"—to develop a self-concept—is a social and cultural process. This chapter describes differences between Japanese and North American understandings of the nature of the person and the consequences of these understandings for the structure and content of the self. For many North Americans, the self is represented as independent from other people, autonomous, bounded, and composed of a relatively stable collection of attributes, abilities, wishes, and goals that transcend social contexts and highlight the person's uniqueness. For many Japanese, the self is represented as situational, context-dependent, interdependent with others, and defined by one's relationships, group memberships, and social contexts. Social processes that contribute to the Japanese construction of an interdependent self-construal are briefly reviewed. A study that examines the effects of situational variation on the self-descriptions of Americans and Japanese is described. This study revealed

Advances in Life Course Research, Volume 5, pages 159-179.
ISBN: 0-7623-0033-7

160   SUSAN E. CROSS

that situational factors had much more influence on how Japanese college women described themselves than on how American college women described themselves, reflecting the situated, or context-sensitive nature of the Japanese self-construal. The consequences of these differences in the self for self-enhancement and self-esteem are also discussed.

Visitors to Japan who have the opportunity to observe village life are sometimes struck by the openness and flexibility of the homes' designs. Walls in the traditional Japanese home are made of paper, allowing persons in one room to overhear conversations in adjoining rooms. These walls slide, so that a room that is used for one purpose at one point might be used for another purpose at another time. For example, a family may sleep in one room, and in the morning their bedding would be rolled up and stored away. The room would then become the family room where everyone eats, drinks, works, and relaxes for the remainder of the day. According to one observer, the consequence of growing up in a traditional Japanese home is that one develops a sense of oneself as part of a larger entity. "[Japanese families] regarded themselves as 'one flesh';...the *uchi* (household, home) was constituted according to a principle of indivisibility....It is impossible to live under such conditions for very long without a common household identity emerging which naturally takes precedence over individual wishes" (Morley 1985, p. 37).

This notion of the individual as indivisible from the family is also reflected in the Japanese language. The Japanese term for household or home, *uchi*, is also used to refer to oneself (i.e., as the first-person pronoun "I"). When Japanese persons refer to themselves with the term "uchi," they also are referring to their family, or the place and people to whom they belong (Morley 1985).

Ambitious visitors to Japan—those who attempt to learn the language—often struggle with this and other terms used to refer to oneself. In the Japanese language, there is no simple translation of "I," "me," or "mine." Instead, there is a wide array of terms used, depending on the situation. Kondo (1990) argues that there is no "I" that can stand alone, irrespective of the context; instead, the term used depends on the context. "The I is shaped by formality, kinship, occupation, other people's desires and usages, and myriad other 'contextual' factors" (Kondo 1990, p. 29).

What do Japanese houses and first person pronouns have in common? They reflect the core cultural beliefs about the nature of the person and the relations between persons and society. The traditional Japanese home reflects the belief that individuals are indivisible from the family; private space, such as an individual's own room, is not considered necessary because there is little about a family member that is not shared by others in the family (Morley 1985). Other family practices, such as co-sleeping and co-bathing, also reflect these values. Similarly, the use of differing terms to refer to the self, depending on one's audience and the individuals in the situation, reflects a notion of the person as situated, as embedded in social relations, and as defined by specific contexts.

This understanding of the person as part of a whole, as defined by contexts, situations, relationships, and roles is markedly different from the understanding of the person that has prevailed in the West and that has dominated most Western social psychological research. In this view, the person is believed to be an individual set against society who is an integrated, bounded, separate, and autonomous being. In this chapter, I will briefly describe how divergent views of the person in North American and Japanese society are communicated through cultural institutions (e.g., educational systems) and cultural practices and norms (e.g., childrearing, employment practices, and linguistic conventions) (Markus and Kitayama 1994; Markus, Kitayama, and Heiman 1996). These systems, norms, practices, and conventions in turn shape the self-system, which directs and organizes behavior. I will also briefly review the emerging literature that shows that East Asian understandings of the self as interdependent with others impact affective and motivational processes.

CULTURAL BELIEFS ABOUT THE PERSON ARE REFLECTED IN CUSTOMS, INSTITUTIONS, AND LANGUAGE

A culture's beliefs about the nature of the person and the relationship between the person and society are transmitted through its social, economic, and political institutions, and its everyday customs, norms, and practices (Markus and Kitayama 1994; Markus et al. 1996). Beginning in the home, parents and families begin to shape children into the types of persons valued by the society. In North American homes, children are encouraged to be independent and self-reliant, and to develop an identity that is separate from their family. Often children sleep in their own rooms from birth, and decorating one's room as one wishes is an assumed right of the adolescent. In Japan, not only do children not have their own rooms, but they often sleep with their parents or grandparents for several years. Disciplinary practices also reflect these differing views of the person; children who misbehave in Japan are threatened with the possibility of being locked out of the house and isolated from the family, in contrast to the practice of restricting a child's freedom to be away from home ("grounding") that is common in many North American households.

Cultural beliefs about the nature of the person are also communicated through the everyday practices and policies of schools. The development of good social skills and the ability to be a productive group member is key to Japanese education. Studies of preschools and kindergartens in Japan show that the training of these abilities begins very early (Lewis 1995; Tobin, Wu, & Davidson 1989). When parents in Japan and North America were asked what were the most important things for children to learn in preschool, the most striking difference was in the importance of relational skills and attitudes versus independence orientations (Tobin et al. 1989). American parents were far more likely than Japanese parents to endorse self-reliance and self-confidence as the most important to learn, whereas Japanese parents overwhelmingly endorsed learning empathy and concern for others as most important for children to learn. In fact, Japanese parents tended to believe that social skills and good character could only be taught in school. "To grow up exclusively in the bosom of a nuclear family is to risk not becoming truly Japanese, to risk being too self-centered and too dyadic rather than group-oriented in one's interpersonal relations" (Tobin et al. 1989, p. 58). This contrasts with the growing home schooling movement in the United States, which is often touted as a way to protect children's character from the corrupting influence of schools.

Preschool teachers prepare their students for a system that is based on group participation and cooperation in ways that may seem antithetical to individual development and achievement. Preschool teachers in Japan see one of their chief tasks as encouraging children to view themselves as similar to others in fundamental ways (Tobin et al. 1989). This includes an effort by teachers to speed up and encourage slower learners and at times to slow down more talented members of the class. "Teachers do not view as a disservice this holding back and slowing down of the more capable students because they believe that students benefit in the long run by developing an increased sensitivity to the needs of others and a sense of security that comes from being a member of a seemingly homogenous group" (Tobin et al. 1989, p. 25-26). In contrast, American schools tend to reinforce the uniqueness of the individual and are oriented toward students' development of unique and distinctive abilities and talents. Schools are expected to tailor the educational environment to meet individual students' needs; fostering students' sense of individual competence and giving them a chance to develop at their own pace are the expressed goals of many preschool programs (Tobin et al. 1989).

The belief that the individual is an indivisible part of a group begins in the family, is further taught in the schools, and is the foundation of Japanese adults' work life. It has often been remarked that in Japan, the individual's employer is viewed as a surrogate family. In fact, in small businesses, the company owner or manager acts *in loco parentis*—in the place of the family (Kondo 1990). For example, many small businesses recruit new employees through family ties; once hired, unmarried employees are often housed in company-owned dormitories or apartments. The owner of the company takes a parental role in many ways, such as by celebrating employees' birthdays, throwing parties for the new year, and acting as the ritual go-between when employees are married (Kondo 1990). In larger companies, employees are hired "for life" and seldom change companies. Raises and promotions are based on seniority. In contrast, in the United States, large companies tend to place greater value on the so-called "bottom line" or profit than on developing a committed work force, and large-scale layoffs of employees are common. Raises and promotions are based on merit and perceived promise; young "hot-shot" employees are very often promoted over the heads of older, more senior employees.

Finally, language reflects and reinforces cultural beliefs about the nature of the individual. The prominence of the individual is embedded in the grammatical rules of English, but in the Japanese language the individual is "submerged in the whole" (Ikegami 1991, p. 290). For example, a speaker may drop the pronoun from a sentence in Japanese, but in English pronoun use is obligatory (Kashima and Kashima 1998). The sentence "I cut my hair" in Japanese would read "Kami o katta," literally "Hair cut-past" or "Cut hair" (Ikegami 1991, p. 312). In the English version, the speaker is the most prominent component of the statement, whereas in the Japanese version, the speaker is an implicit component of the context rather than the central focus. Furthermore, one must also choose the proper verb in a sentence depending on the situation and taking into account the relationship between oneself and one's listener. Verbs and negations come at the end of the sentence, so it is possible for the speaker to state the subject and object, watch the listener's reaction, and adjust the verb or add a negation at the end to accommodate to the listener (Weisz, Rothbaum, and Blackburn 1984).

In some cases, the human element is highlighted in English to such an extent that some phrases are illogical if read literally. For example, one might encounter signs in a storefront that read "We are closed today" or "We are sold out." "Either of these sentences...would strike a Japanese speaker as odd. What is closed or what is sold out is not 'we' at all, but something like 'our store' or 'our goods' respectively" (Ikegami 1991, p. 301). Imagine how a Japanese speaker would initially react to hearing the statement "I took the bus to school today!" (Images of a school bus parked outside a classroom might come to mind.) In this and many other ways, the English language makes the speaker stand out and emphasizes personal agency or action, even when the person was not responsible for the action. (In the case of the bus, the more literally correct phrase is "The bus took me to school today.") In Japanese practice, the person is de-emphasized, to the extent that the individual is often not represented as an agent who acts, but as a single element in a larger whole that is shifting with time (Ikegami 1991). In short the grammatical structures and vocabularies of the Japanese language and the English language reinforce the cultural conceptions of the person as either a part of a particular context or as a distinctive, agentic individual.

CONSEQUENCES OF DIVERGENT VIEWS OF THE PERSON FOR THE SELF

These differing cultural practices and conventions arise from divergent representations of the person and persons' roles in social relationships. In Japan and much of Eastern Asia, the person is constituted in and through social relations and social obligations. In North America, the person is viewed as a unique individual who is believed to be separate from social roles and statuses. Because of these divergent representations of the person, individuals in Japan and North America will tend to develop very different conceptions of themselves. The Western view of the self has been described as a "bounded, unique, more or less integrated motivational and cognitive universe, a dynamic center of awareness, emotion, judgment and action organized into a distinctive whole and set against other such wholes and against a social and natural background" (Geertz 1975, p. 48). This "independent self-construal" (so named by Markus and Kitayama 1991) is assumed to be composed of a relatively stable collection of attributes, abilities, wishes, and goals that have been identified by the person as making him or her distinctive and unique and that transcend social contexts. In this characterization, feeling good about oneself derives from demonstrating one's unique characteristics and from expressing and affirming one's beliefs, values, and central abilities (Markus and Kitayama 1994). As Bellah and his colleagues observe, "We [Americans] insist...on finding our true selves independent of any cultural or social influence, being responsible to that self alone, and making its fulfillment the very meaning of our lives" (Bellah, Madsen, Sullivan, Swidler, and Tipton 1985, p. 150).

In contrast, the Japanese and East Asian concept of the person as an organic part of social relations results in a self that "is not a constant like the ego but denotes a fluid concept which changes through time and situations according to interpersonal relationships" (Hamaguchi 1985, p. 302). This "interdependent self-construal" (Markus and Kitayama 1991) is situation-specific, indeterminate, and responsive to the demands of others in a situation (Bachnik 1992; Kondo 1990; Rosenberger 1989). As the example of the use of first person pronouns described earlier suggests, to describe oneself requires consideration of a particular reference group, context, or relationship. Feeling good about oneself, given this self-structure, is based on maintaining harmony in relationships and on fulfilling one's proper role in a particular context.

An important caveat is necessary at this point: It would be wrong to assume that Japanese individuals never think of their enduring, internal personality characteristics or that North American individuals never think of themselves as interdependent with others or as part of social groups. Both independent ways of representing the self and interdependent ways of representing the self are available in both Japanese and American cultures. Cultures differ, however, in the degree to which those types of self-representations are emphasized, highlighted, and cognized, and in the degree to which they influence behavior. As Trafimow, Triandis, and Goto (1991) have shown, individuals from North American cultures may describe themselves in relatively collectivistic terms when prompted; similarly, individuals from East Asian cultures describe themselves in relatively individualistic terms under specific circumstances. The situations that cue collectivist or group-oriented self-representations for Americans are likely to be less commonly encountered and less valued than are those that cue individualistic self-representations. Likewise, for Japanese, situations that cue individualistic or de-contextualized self-representations may be encountered less commonly and may be less valued than those that cue interdependent self-representations. Thus, these two forms of self-construal represent differences in degree of elaboration, complexity, and influence of the independent or interdependent components of the self.

"KNOW THYSELF": IMPLICATIONS FOR SELF-DESCRIPTIONS

When meeting a new associate, classmate, or co-worker, Americans and Japanese may tend to divulge the same information. Americans often begin by mentioning where they are from, what they do for a living, and perhaps something about their family. Likewise, Japanese persons may begin conversations by swapping information about their employers, the school they attended, and where their families are from. Although the content of these self-descriptions is very similar, their significance is quite different. This difference is illustrated in the differing practices regarding the use of business cards in these two societies. In Japan, business cards are a necessity for social interactions, and are exchanged at the time of one's introduction to a new acquaintance. Morley (1985) describes their use this way:

> The exchange of cards at even casual meetings having nothing to do with the business interests of either party might on the surface appear to be a sophisticated and convenient modern practice, but its real significance ran much deeper. Business cards endorsed not merely the identification of a person, his name and the organization to which he belonged, but also his rank and function within it. They supplied the social context of the individual that was considered indispensable to his dealing with others. Without this information many Japanese were at a loss to know what attitude and tone they should adopt towards the other party (p. 52).

In contrast, for many Americans, business cards are used primarily in business settings; to exchange them in casual settings might be viewed as pretentious (except when they are used after one has become acquainted with a new person to encourage further communication). For many middle-class Americans, the real self or important identities are very different from one's work roles or geographic origins. To really know a person, one must get below these "superficial" statements and find out what the person believes, what she is like, her feelings about issues, and her goals (Andersen and Ross 1984). In other words, close interpersonal relationships require that the person disclose his or her unique, enduring, and distinctive characteristics. Consequently, the dictum to "know thyself" is actively pursued by American middle-class adolescents and adults; in this case, the self which must be known is assumed to be relatively stable and fairly consistent across situations.

In contrast, in Japan, knowledge about a person's roles, family, and relationships are central to understanding him or her. This is not viewed as superficial information or as prelude to real knowledge about the person; instead, these statements mark where the person belongs and therefore who the person is. For the Japanese, the adage "know thyself" means to know the self that is defined by a particular situation or relationship; one must take into consideration the context in which one is embedded when characterizing the self. As situations, roles, or contexts vary, self-representations and self-knowledge varies accordingly.

Consistent with these two views of the self-situation dialectic, studies of the self-descriptions of Americans and East Asians have shown that North American adults describe themselves with many more abstract, situation-free trait descriptions than do East Asian adults. East Asians, on the other hand, tend to include more references to social memberships and relationships in their self-descriptions than do Americans or Western Europeans. Most of these studies, however, have ignored the role of the situation in making salient particular roles, identities, and self-representations.

Recognizing this limitation of the existing cross-cultural research, Kanagawa, Cross, and Markus (in press) examined the self-descriptions of American and Japanese college-aged women in different situations. They hypothesized that in addition to global differences in the self-concept between Americans and Japanese students, common situations would influence self-descriptions. In specific, they hypothesized that American students' self-descriptions would be fairly similar across different situations (such as when alone versus when describing oneself to a professor), because American culture emphasizes the importance of abstract, stable, internal, dispositions in explaining behavior across situations. For Japanese students, however, they hypothesized that self-descriptions would tend to depend on the situation, because Japanese society views the self as situation-specific or context-dependent.

In this study, American and Japanese college women were assigned to one of four conditions. In each situation, the women responded twenty times to the question "Who are you?", which is a frequently used task to assess the self-concept (Cousins 1989; Kuhn and McPartland 1954). In the condition most comparable to previous studies of the self-concept, the women completed this task in a large group of 20-30 other students. The other situations employed in this study were settings that are commonly encountered by students—meeting with a faculty member, interacting with a peer, and being alone. Some students were seated alone with a faculty member, who posed the "Who are you?" question 20 times for them to answer. Other students were paired with a peer, who posed the question to them repeatedly. Finally, some students were placed in individual cubicles and taped instructions posed the "Who are you?" questions. In each case, the students wrote their responses on paper, and could write as much or as little as they desired.

These responses were coded into commonly used categories, such as statements referring to physical attributes, psychological traits, abilities, or attitudes;

Table 1.   Categories Used to Code Self-descriptions, with
Percentages of each Category by Culture

Categories	Examples	Japan	U.S.
Physical	I am tall. I have short hair.	13.38	4.69***
Relationships	I love my family. I am the youngest child in my family.	6.27	10.19***
Social memberships and roles	I am a student. I am a member of a tennis club.	9.00	9.73
Preferences, interests	I like to cook. I like to see movies.	16.51	15.22
Goals, aspirations	I want to be a nurse. I would like to go to Australia.	13.21	12.60
Activities	I often work out at the gym. I have a part-time job.	10.28	6.53***
Short-term activities	I bought a T-shirt today. I went to my grandfather's yesterday.	3.76	0.70***
Qualified traits	I am sometimes grouchy in the morning. I am apt to get tense in public.	1.40	4.62***
Pure psychological attributes	I am out-going. I am self-centered.	7.18	17.59***
Attitudes	I am not a racist. I am against the Japanese troops going to Cambodia.	2.03	10.38***
Abilities	I am good at math. I am not able to play any musical instruments.	2.47	3.36
Individuating self-references	My name is Michelle. I am a human being.	3.85	1.47***
Immediate situation	I am hungry now. I am in a psychology class.	6.73	1.55***

Notes: $^*p < .05.$, $^{**}p < .01.$, $^{***}p < .001.$
Source: The first example for each category was generated by an American student and the second
     example by a Japanese student. Table adapted from Kanagawa, Cross, and Markus (in press).

statements referring to one's relationships or group memberships; and statements about one's activities or the present situation. (The total number of self-descriptions generated by individual students was often more than 20 because a single response could include more than one unit of information. For example, the description "I am good at math and music" would be coded as two references to one's abilities.) The most frequently used categories (i.e., those mentioned by at least 40 percent of the participants of either group) are described in Table 1.

Americans were much more likely to describe themselves in terms of pure psychological attributes or traits (e.g., "I am kind," "I am outgoing," or "I am quiet in the morning") than were the Japanese women (see Table 1). In fact, the U.S. students used almost three times as many trait terms and attitude statements to describe themselves as did the Japanese students. This is consistent with Western beliefs that personality traits importantly direct behavior. Although the Japanese women used relatively few qualified traits or pure psychological attributes to describe themselves, they frequently described themselves in terms of their preferences ("I like cats") and goals ("I will go to the coast for vacation"). They also tended to describe themselves in behavioral terms more often than did the American students. For example, they mentioned their activities ("I play on the tennis team") and the immediate situation ("I am hungry right now") much more often than did the American students. This pattern of behavioral responses may be a function of bringing to mind images of oneself in specific situations or contexts rather than thinking of oneself in terms of abstract, context-free traits. In many East Asian cultures, personality traits very often are assumed to play a secondary role to situational factors and roles in directing behavior (see Cross and Markus 1999, for a review).

One surprising finding in these data was that the Americans students generated significantly more self-descriptions revealing something about their relationships with friends and family than did the Japanese students. One possible interpretation of this finding is that for the Japanese, the family is very private and personal, and is seldom discussed with others (Takeuchi 1995). The particular sample used in this study (i.e., college-aged women) may also be one source of this finding. When previous studies have found differences between Americans and Japanese on this dimension (e.g., Cousins 1989), they have used both men and women in their samples. Women in Western populations are more likely to think of themselves as relational or connected to others than are men, and so are more likely to describe themselves in terms of specific others (Cross and Madson 1997).

There were also differences in the overall number of self-descriptions generated by the two groups. The American women generated a greater number of self-descriptions than did the Japanese women. This is not surprising, given the American emphasis on self-knowledge and on the self as a reference for social behavior. Surprisingly, however, the Japanese participants used a greater *variety* of categories in their self-descriptions. For example, it was not unusual for an American student's self-description to be comprised largely of a list of traits and abilities ("I am generous, caring, outgoing, and good at math"). In contrast, the profiles of the Japanese women were much more likely to include a diverse array of self-descriptions, including physical descriptions, activities, social memberships, and statements about the self in the immediate situation (e.g., "I am hungry"). Again, this reflects the notion that Japanese selves are realized in specific situations, and therefore will reflect a variety of situations, in contrast to the American view of a core self that is abstracted from and transcends situations.

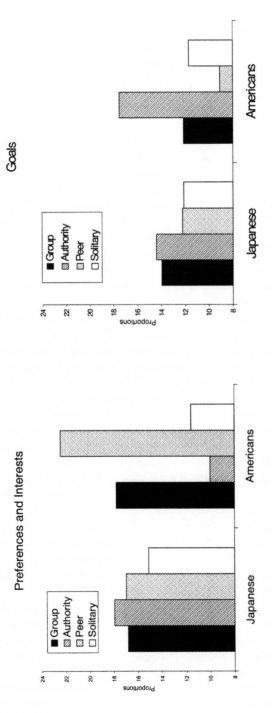

Figure 1. Comparison of Japanese and American Responses for Categories that Varied by Condition for Americans

Most importantly, the findings revealed that the Japanese students' self-descriptions were more likely to be influenced by the situation than were the American students' self-descriptions. The American students tended to describe themselves similarly in the different situations; only two categories of self-state-ments differed significantly in different conditions (see Figure 1). The most strik-ing findings in the American data was that when paired with a peer, the American students generated fewer statements overall and they were more likely than the other participants to describe themselves in terms of their preferences and inter-ests. This situation seemed to prime a "get acquainted" script for these students, and they responded as they might on the first day of class or when at a party. In becoming acquainted with a new person, it may be critical not to offend, resulting in disclosure of relatively safe information, such as one's likes and dislikes. When describing themselves in front of a professor, the American students generated the greatest number of statements about their goals and plans. It was as though the question "What do you want to do when you finish college?"—a frequently discussed issue in professors' offices—were framing their self-descriptions.

The Japanese students' self-descriptions showed more influence by the situa-tion than did the American students' self-descriptions; the frequencies of seven categories varied signficantly across conditions. These conditions affected the frequency of statements related to physical attributes, activities, pure psychologi-cal attributes, attitudes, abilities, statements about the immediate situation, and individuating self-references (e.g., I am a human being). (Figure 2 presents the proportions of the four categories with the greatest degree of change.) For the Jap-anese, the students in the peer condition also seemed to have a getting-acquainted script in mind, but this script included different content than for the Americans. When paired with a peer, the Japanese women included many more references to the immediate situation (e.g., "I am running out of answers") and fewer references to their activities or their psychological attributes than did women in the other conditions. This emphasis on the immediate situation and neglect of more reveal-ing information about personality attributes is one way to present oneself as easy-going or laid-back; among contemporary young Japanese students, it is socially undesirable to appear overly serious (Kuramitsu 1993).

In the group condition, the Japanese students generated the fewest self-descrip-tions and used fewer categories to describe themselves than did participants in the other conditions. One way to interpret this pattern is that these women had trouble thinking of themselves in specific terms, perhaps because the context did not imply specific relationships or roles. In a large group, consensual guidelines for how to be are not evident, so there may not be a well-elaborated self-representa-tion in this context, compared to the others.

In summary, the study by Kanagawa and colleagues (in press) demonstrates that the interdependent self-construal of Japanese women is indeed more situa-tion-specific than that of American students. In the United States, daily practice and social interaction encourages and affords a focus on one's stable, abstract, and

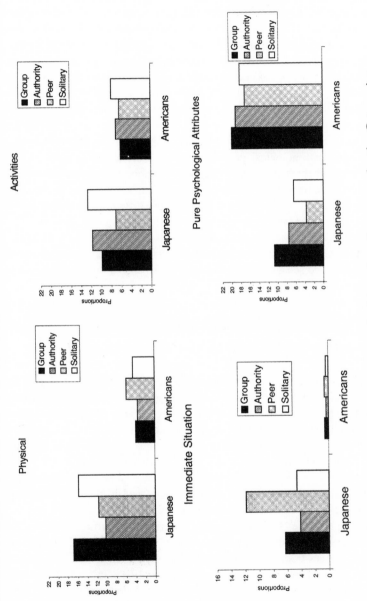

Figure 2. Comparisons of Japanese and American Responses for the Categories that Varied the Most by Conditions for Japanese Participants

internal attributes, abilities, wishes, and attitudes, and these are viewed as independent of one's social relationships, memberships, and contexts. In contrast, daily life in Japan encourages and affords attention to one's proper role in a specific situation, and one's individual attributes, dispositions, attitudes, and wishes are framed in terms of the demands of the situation. In other words, when American students consider the injunction to "know thyself," they are most likely to bring to mind a self that transcends situations and that can be characterized in terms of enduring qualities. In contrast, when Japanese students consider this injunction, the self brought to mind depends much more on the context in which they are found.

These differences in the nature and structure of the self have important implications for many psychological phenomena. Two decades of research in the West on the role of the self as the "executive function" in cognition, emotion, motivation, and behavior have assumed an independent, autonomous, Western construction of the self. If the self is structured very differently in non-Western cultures, will associated behaviors vary as well? Slowly, evidence is accumulating that indicates the answer is "yes," and sometimes the variations are surprising. In the next section, I describe new evidence that shows that the processes of self-enhancement and self-esteem are importantly dependent on the nature of the self-construal.

CONSEQUENCES OF DIVERGENT SELF-CONSTRUALS FOR SELF-ENHANCEMENT AND SELF-ESTEEM

When a Japanese speaker at a conference or symposium begins to address an audience, it is quite common to hear an opening statement of this sort: "I am very honored to have a chance to talk to you today. I am not sure that my talk is good enough for you, but I will be grateful if you are generous enough to listen to my boring talk" or "Thank you for spending your precious time coming to hear my boring talk. I appreciate your generosity." To Western ears, such modesty would seem contrived or as evidence of low self-esteem. Such is not the case in Japan. In fact, the socially skilled Japanese person has learned to present himself or herself modestly and to understate his or her accomplishments.

As this example suggests, self-esteem and esteem-related processes depend on the nature of the self-construal. At its most basic, self-esteem, or feeling good about oneself, derives from the sense that one is being a good person in one's cultural context (Heine, Lehman, Kitayama, and Markus 1999). In the Japanese cultural context, that means that one must maintain harmonious relationships, play one's proper part in a situation, and contribute to the goals of one's group. To accomplish this, one must first identify the consensual standards of excellence for the particular relationship, role, or situation, and then recognize ways that one falls short of that standard (Kitayama, Markus, Matsumoto, and Norasakkunkit

1997). Consequently Japanese individuals are vigilant for ways in which they can improve. This vigilance is part of the social skills training begun in preschool; at the end of each day children reflect on their behavior and are encouraged to think of ways they can improve the next day (Lewis 1995). The value of self-reflection and self-criticism pervades Japanese society. In the study of Japanese and American women by Kanagawa and colleagues (in press), the students' descriptions of their physical attributes, qualified traits, pure psychological attributes, and abilities were also identified as either positive, negative, or neutral. We found that the Japanese students made many more negative statements about themselves than did the American students (see Table 2). In fact, whereas the American students' self-descriptions tended to include more positive statements than negative, the Japanese student's self-descriptions were heavily weighted toward negative statements. For example, the Japanese women were much more likely than the American women to make statements such as "I have bad eyes"; "I am lazy"; or "I am not good at singing." Unexpectedly, there were no significant differences between the two groups in the proportion of negative statements categorized as "qualified traits." This category includes statements that are qualified by a situation, a condition, or a relationship, such as "I am grumpy in the morning" or "I tend to be shy around strangers." As Table 2 reveals, Americans are sometimes willing to acknowledge negative things about themselves, but only in circumscribed domains or in particular situations. Compartmentalizing negative attributes in this way protects self-esteem and permits the person to maintain a generally favorable view of herself (Showers 1992).

In addition, the proportion of negative attributes generated by the Japanese women depended on the experimental condition. We collapsed the categories and

Table 2. Percentage of Positive and Negative Descriptors

Categories	Japan	U.S.A.
Physical		
Positive	7.91%	8.85%[**]
Negative	28.03	9.83[**]
Qualified Traits		
Positive	22.81	37.50
Negative	67.02	55.34
Pure Psychological Attributes		
Positive	35.22	72.06[***]
Negative	56.75	24.61[***]
Abilities		
Positive	41.22	74.84[***]
Negative	58.78	21.49[***]

Notes: [**]$p < .01.$, [***]$p < .001$, 2-tailed.

Source: For convenience, the percentage of the statements categorized as neutral was omitted from this table. Table adapted from Kanagawa, Cross, and Markus (in press).

created a ratio of positive to negative statements. Across situations, the Americans generated more than three times more positive statements than negative statements (the average ratio score was 3.38) but the Japanese students generated more negative statements than positive statements (the average ratio score was .77). The Japanese students who interacted alone with a faculty member generated the greatest proportion of negative statements (the ratio score was .39) whereas those who completed the task alone tended to describe themselves in more positive than negative ways (the ratio score was 1.23). There was no difference across the conditions in the ratio of positive to negative statements among the American students. In short, the Japanese students were much more self-critical than the American students, especially in a situation with a higher-status person. They were least self-critical when they were removed from social interaction in the alone condition. In this condition, there was no one with whom one needed to harmonize and no standards to meet, so the person did not need to attend to negative aspects of herself. Yet it is critical to note that even when alone, the Japanese students were much more self-critical than were the American students.

Other research suggests that this self-critical stance is not associated with poor well-being, as it is in North American research (Campbell 1981; Lucas, Diener, and Suh 1996). Kitayama and colleagues (1997) found that the Japanese tendency to be self-critical was not correlated with low self-esteem. Indeed, other research has shown that private emotions are not as important for the determination of well-being or life satisfaction for East Asians as for North Americans (Suh, Diener, Oishi, and Triandis 1998). North Americans are taught to "listen to their feelings" to understand themselves; understanding an individual's private emotional states is viewed as the key to knowing the person (Andersen and Ross 1984). Much less attention is paid to internal, private emotional states among the Japanese; instead, maintaining harmony in one's important relationships is much more strongly related to well-being for East Asians than for North Americans (Kwan, Bond, and Singelis 1997).

In the North American cultural context, self-esteem is based on the cultural mandates to be unique and different from others, and to express one's own personal choices, wishes, and abilities. One way to demonstrate one's uniqueness is to demonstrate to others (and to oneself) that one is better than others in important areas. For example, the mediocre student can enhance his self-esteem by being the best athlete on the playing field. Many theories of self-esteem and self-enhancement have been based on these premises. In particular, Tesser's Self-Evaluation Maintenance theory suggests that two processes are important for self-evaluation: reflection and comparison (Tesser 1988). Reflection occurs when individuals associate themselves with high-performing friends, family, or colleagues in order to bask in their reflected glory (Cialdini, Borden, Thorne, Walker, Freeman, and Sloan 1976). For example, a college student engages in the reflection process when he brags to his classmates that his roommate was picked as the Most Valuable Player in the recent tournament.

But will the college student brag on his roommate if he had also suited up but sat on the bench, watching his roommate shine during the tournament? Probably not. In this case, the student will engage in *comparison* processes. In this case, he will compare his own poor performance with his roommate's award-winning performance, and feel badly. In short, three factors influence whether one will choose the reflection process or the comparison process: the closeness of the relationship with the other person, the importance of the domain to the individual's self-concept, and the level of the individual's performance. If one's close friend performs better than oneself in a domain that is not self-relevant, then the individual can bask and self-enhance through association with a star. In contrast, if the close friend wins an award that the person has coveted or wins acclaim that the individual desires for himself, the individual's sense of uniqueness and specialness is challenged, threatening self-esteem.

This process, however, hinges on the Western understanding of the self and self-enhancement processes. Will individuals with an interdependent self-construal behave similarly? If one views oneself in terms of close relationships, then beliefs or behaviors that potentially harm an important relationship may be avoided. Situations that make oneself appear superior to one's friend may be aversive, and other strategies that allow one to "fit in" and maintain harmony in the relationship may be preferred. If a relationship with a close friend is part of the self, then affirming that relationship may enhance the self.

This theory was tested in a study that replicated one of Tesser's early studies (Tesser and Campbell 1982). In the original study, pairs of friends were brought into the lab and asked to complete two types of judgment tasks: a social sensitivity task and an aesthetic judgment task (each task had 16 items). They were also asked to indicate how important social sensitivity and aesthetic judgment were to their views of themselves. The social sensitivity task consisted of 16 short scenarios that presented a problem in a social interaction; participants were given two possible solutions to the problem and had to choose the one they thought would be most effective. The aesthetic judgement task consisted of 16 sets of paired pictures or drawings. The participants chose the picture or drawing they viewed as most aesthetically pleasing. Working individually, the participants were shown an item with two response choices. They announced their response to each item aloud to the experimenter, who gave them immediate feedback as to whether they were correct or incorrect. (They were told they were correct on half the items.) At this point, the participants were also asked to estimate how they thought their friend would respond. Tesser and Campbell (1982) found that American students who viewed the domain as self-defining estimated that their friends would perform much more poorly on the tasks than did students who viewed the tasks as irrelevant to their own self-definition. In other words, students enhanced their own self-evaluations by derogating their friends (i.e., expecting their friends to perform more poorly than themselves) when they viewed themselves as especially competent or invested in having good aesthetic judgment or social skills.

Would individuals with an interdependent self-construal behave similarly? Cross, Liao, and Josephs (1992) hypothesized that for individuals who defined themselves as interdependent with others, derogating the friend's ability may not enhance the self. They brought thirty pairs of same gender friends from Taiwan into the lab (all were international students who had resided in the United States less than one year). In addition to measuring how important aesthetic judgment and social sensitivity were to the students, they also measured the extent to which being a good group member and other elements of the interdependent self-construal were self-descriptive. The participants completed the two judgment tasks just as Tesser and Campbell's (1982) participants did: after selecting a response and receiving feedback, they estimated their friend's response. In contrast to Tesser's findings, there was no evidence of comparison processes. In fact, the Chinese students were somewhat more positive about their friend's performance when the task was self-relevant than when it was not. The Chinese students who viewed themselves as very interdependent were also more generous toward their friends than were others, particularly after being told they had answered the question incorrectly. When told they had given the wrong answer, these highly interdependent participants tended to estimate that their friend had answered correctly. Perhaps the Chinese are more likely to engage in the reflection process, basking in the anticipated glory of their friends' successes. Presumably, disparaging the friend would not enhance the self, but would further diminish one's own positive affect or esteem. So individuals with an interdependent self-construal may enhance the self by enhancing close others.

Self-representations and self-enhancement are but two of many processes that are contingent upon the nature and structure of the self. Research shows that other self-related processes such as cognitive dissonance, self-serving biases, and intrinsic motivation are also affected by variation in the self-construal (see Cross and Markus 1999, for a review). Simply testing the generalizability of existing Western theories of behavior limits the potential of cross-cultural research, however. Much may be gained by considering concepts indigenous to other cultures in order to better understand the foundations of behavior in North America. For example, Cross and Madson (1997) suggested that many gender differences in behavior found in the West can be understood as deriving from differences in the self-construal. Women (and members of some religious and minority groups) may tend to view themselves as importantly interdependent with others; thus, the insights gleaned from cross-cultural research can suggest new ways of thinking about women's experiences in this culture. Further investigations among non-Western populations may suggest a variety of constructs useful in the development of a global theory of the person and human behavior.

CONCLUSIONS

Being a person, and constructing a self, is a social and cultural process; it requires incorporating a specific set of cultural beliefs about what it means to be human through participation in the social environments created by these beliefs. The meaning and experience of being a person is therefore completely interdependent with the beliefs, values, and meaning systems embodied in particular sociocultural environments (Fiske, Kitayama, Markus, and Nisbett 1998). Thus, where cultural meaning systems and theories of the person differ, the nature of the self and identity will also differ.

Careful scrutiny of the nature of these differences, their sources, and their consequences can provide insight into unexamined assumptions, untested theories, and unproven generalizations about psychological phenomena. It will raise many important questions and issues that are often overlooked in Western social science research. For example, in what other ways have Western assumptions about the nature of the person influenced contemporary research on the self? Does an interdependent self-construal develop in the same way as an independent self-construal? What are the developmental processes that uniquely shape the self and identity in non-Western cultures? What are the aging-related changes in the self and identity in a culture that values and respects its elders? Ultimately, investigations into these and other questions raised by cultural comparisons will open new windows of understanding into the ways that self and society are mutually constituted, and their effects on human behavior and well-being.

REFERENCES

Andersen, S.M., and L. Ross. 1984. "Self-knowledge and Social Inference: I. The impact of cognitive/ affective and behavioral data." *Journal of Personality and Social Psychology* 46: 280-293.

Bachnik, J.M. 1992. "The Two 'Faces' of Self and Society in Japan." *Ethos* 20: 3-32.

Bellah, R.N., R. Madsen, W.M. Sullivan, A. Swidler, and S.M. Tipton. 1985. *Habits of the Heart*. New York: Harper & Row.

Campbell, A. 1981. *The Sense of Well-being in America: Recent Patterns and Trends*. New York: McGraw-Hill.

Cialdini, R.B., R.J. Borden, A. Thorne, M.R. Walker, S. Freeman, and L.R. Sloan. 1976. "Basking in Reflected Glory: Three (Football) Field Studies." *Journal of Personality and Social Psychology* 57: 626-631.

Cousins, S.D. 1989. "Culture and Self-perception in Japan and the United States." *Journal of Personality and Social Psychology* 56: 124-131.

Cross, S.E., M. Liao, and R. Josephs. (1992, August). *A Cross-cultural Test of the Self-evaluation Maintenance Model*. Paper presented at the annual convention of the American Psychological Association, Washington, DC.

Cross, S.E., and L. Madson. 1997. "Models of the Self: Self-construals and Gender." *Psychological Bulletin* 122: 5-37.

Cross, S.E., and H.R. Markus. 1999. "The Cultural Constitution of Personality." Pp. 378-396 in *Hand book of Personality Theory and Research*, 2nd ed, edited by L. Pervin and O. John. New York Guilford Press.

Fiske, A.P., S. Kitayama, H.R. Markus, and R.E. Nisbett. 1998. "The Cultural Matrix of Socia Psychology." Pp. 915-981 in *Handbook of Social Psychology*, edited by D.T. Gilbert, S.T Fiske, and G. Lindzey. New York: McGraw-Hill.

Geertz, C. 1975. "On the Nature of Anthropological Understanding." *American Scientist* 63: 47-53.

Hamaguchi, E. 1985. "A Contextual Model of the Japanese: Toward a Methodological Innovation in Japan Studies." *Journal of Japanese Studies* 11, 289-321.

Heine, S.J., D.R. Lehman, H.R. Markus, and S. Kitayama. 1999. Is There a Universal Need for Posi tive Self-Regard? *Psychological Review* 106, 766-794..

Ikegami, Y. 1991. "'Do-langauge' and 'Become-language': Two Contrasting Types of Linguisitic Representation." Pp. 285-326 in *The Empire of Signs: Emiotic Essays on Japanese Culture* edited by Y. Ikegami. Philadelphia: John Benjamins Publishing Co.

Kanagawa, C., S.E. Cross, and H.R. Markus. 1998. "Who Am I: The Cultural Psychology of the Conceptual Self." *Personality and Social Psychology Bulletin*. Manuscript submitted fo publication.

Kashima, E.S., and Y. Kashima. in press. "Culture and Language: The Case of Cultural Dimension and Personal Pronoun Use." *Journal of Cross-Cultural Psychology* 29: 461-486.

Kitayama, S., H.R. Markus, H. Matsumoto, and V. Norasakkunkit. 1997. "Individual and Collective Processes in the Construction of the Self: Self-enhancement in the United States and Self-criticism in Japan." *Journal of Personality and Social Psychology* 72: 1245-1267.

Kondo, D. 1990. *Crafting Selves: Power, Gender and Discourses of Identity in a Japanese Workplace* Chicago: University of Chicago Press.

Kuhn, M.H., and T.S. McPartland. 1954. "An Empirical Investigation of Self-attitudes." *American Sociological Review* 19: 68-76.

Kuramitsu, O. 1993. "Gendai-seinen-no Jikoishiki-to Taijinkankei. [Self-consciousness of Recen Japanese Youth and Their Interpersonal Behavior]." *Gendai-no esupuri [Lesprit daujourdhui* 2: 103-113.

Kwan, V.S.Y., M. H. Bond, and T.M. Singelis. 1997. "Pancultural Explanations for Life Satisfaction Adding Relational Harmony to Self-esteem." *Journal of Personality and Social Psychology* 73: 1038-1051.

Lewis, C.C. 1995. *Educating Hearts and Minds: Reflections on Japanese Preschool and Elementary School.* New York: Cambridge University Press.

Lucas, R.E., E. Diener, and E.M. Suh. 1996. "Discriminant Validity of Subjective Well-being Measures." *Journal of Personality and Social Psychology* 71: 615-628.

Markus, H., and S. Kitayama. 1991. "Culture and the Self: Implications for Cognition, Emotion, and Motivation." *Psychological Review* 98: 224-253.

{3m}. 1994. "A Collective Fear of the Collective: Implications for Selves and Theories of Selves." *Personality and Social Psychology Bulletin* 20: 568-579.

Markus, H.R., S. Kitayama, and R.J. Heiman. 1996. "Culture and 'Basic' Psychological Principles." Pp. 857-913 in *Social Psychology: Handbook of Basic Principles*, edited by E.T Higgins and A.W. Kruglanski. New York: Guilford.

Morley, J.D. 1985. *Pictures from the Water Trade: An Englishman in Japan.* London: Andre Deutsch

Rosenberger, N.R. 1989. "Dialectic Balance in the Polar Model of Self: The Japanese Case." *Ethos* 17 88-113.

Showers, C. 1992. "Compartmentalization of Positive and Negative Self-knowledge: Keeping Bad Apples out of the Bunch." *Journal of Personality and Social Psychology* 62: 1036-1049.

Suh, E.M., E. Diener, S. Oishi, and H.C. Triandis. 1998. "The Shifting Basis of Life Satisfaction Judgments Across Cultures: Emotions Vs. Norms." *Journal of Personality and Social Psychology* 52: 881-889.

Takeuchi, Y. 1995. *Nihonjin-no soshiogurama* [The Socio-grammer of Japanese]. Tokyo: Toyokeiza-ishinposha Press.

Tesser, A. 1988. "Toward a Self-evaluation Maintenance Model of Social Behavior." Pp. 181-227 in *Advances in Experimental Social Psychology*, vol. 21, edited by L. Berkowitz. New York: Academic Press.

Tesser, A., and J. Campbell. 1982. "Self-evaluation Maintenance and the Perception of Friends and Strangers." *Journal of Personality* 50: 261-279.

Tobin, J.J., D.Y.H. Wu, and D.H. Davidson. 1989. *Preschool in Three Cultures: Japan, China, and the United States*. New Haven, CT: Yale University Press.

Trafimow, D., H.C. Triandis, and S.G. Goto. 1991. "Some Tests of the Distinction Between the Private Self and the Collective Self." *Journal of Personality and Social Psychology* 60: 649-655.

Weisz, J.R., F.M. Rothbaum, and T.C. Blackburn.1984. "Standing Out and Standing In: The Psychology of Control in America and Japan." *American Psychologist 39*: 955-969.

AGENCY IN YOUNG ADULTHOOD
INTENTIONAL SELF-CHANGE AMONG COLLEGE STUDENTS

K. Jill Kiecolt and J. Beth Mabry

ABSTRACT

Life course research assumes that development and change depend partly on individual agency, but often fails to elaborate. We posit that individuals exercise agency by pursuing self-related goals, specifically by trying to change themselves in ways that they believe will generate more favorable self-conceptions. Drawing upon sociological theories about self and identity, gender, stress and coping, and the life course, and upon psychological theories about goals, we analyze survey data on 376 college students to explore the process of self-change. More men than women pursue achievement-related goals, whereas more women than men seek to increase their self-confidence and to improve their appearance. Aspects of the extant self-conception (positive self-worth, self-deprecation, and self-efficacy) selectively influence individuals' motivations for self-change and their perceptions of their progress toward self-change. Self-deprecation is positively related to changing in order to raise one's self-esteem and to avert the danger of becoming a "feared" self, whereas self-efficacy is positively related to changing in order to increase authenticity and bring one closer to one's ideal self. Self-deprecation increases the perceived

Advances in Life Course Research, Volume 5, pages 181-205.
Copyright © 2000 by JAI Press Inc.
All rights of reproduction in any form reserved.
ISBN: 0-7623-0033-7

difficulty of self-change, whereas positive self-worth and self-efficacy increase expectations of success. Emotion-focused, cognitive strategies for self-change increase expectations of success, but emotion-focused, behavioral strategies decrease it.

How people develop and change over the life course is "socially organized and socially produced, not only by what happens in early life, but also by the effects of social structure" and social interaction (Dannefer 1984, p. 106). In addition, because individuals exercise agency (Elder and O'Rand 1995), development and change over the life course is also self-produced in important ways (Lerner and Busch-Rossnagel 1981; Wells and Stryker 1988). Of the various ways in which individuals can exercise agency, our interest in this study is in the "...[i]nvestments of effort that persons make in their own behalf (commitments) and the mobilization of resources to attain desired goals" (Clausen 1986). That is, throughout the life course, individuals set goals for themselves and try to reach them.

Such goals provide information about how people structure their lives. Researchers have studied (1) what kinds of goals individuals pursue, (2) what motivations give rise to particular goals, and (3) how these goals guide individuals' actions (Gollwitzer and Bargh 1996; Pervin 1989). Of course, individuals' goals are themselves social products. Thus, individuals' goals not only should differ by age and stage in the life course (e.g., Cantor and Langston 1989), but they also should be related to other social characteristics.

Some of individuals' goals involve changing aspects of themselves—their behavior, their ways of thinking, their feelings, or their appearance. Individuals consider the fit between their extant self and their desired self (Higgins 1996; Markus and Nurius 1986; Rosenberg 1979; Wells and Stryker 1988), and if they see a discrepancy, they may try to become more like their desired self. Thus, understanding how individuals develop and change over the life course requires investigating deliberate attempts at self-change.

Attempts at self-change may be more likely to occur at points of transition in the life course. One such point is the college years. Even before entering college, as high school seniors, students anticipate casting off undesirable identities (Karp 1998). Once in college, young adult students formulate new goals for themselves as they begin to assume adult roles. In this study we explore the kinds of self-related goals (self-changes) that college students pursue, as well as gender differences in those goals. After investigating students' motivations for self-change, we describe the strategies they use to change themselves, adapting Thoits' (1991) typology of coping responses. Our ultimate interest is to explain what influences the perceived difficulty and likelihood of successfully changing oneself. To anticipate, we find that aspects of students' extant self-concepts (positive self-worth, self-deprecation, and self-efficacy) selectively influence how students perceive and implement the process of self-change.

COLLEGE AS A TIME OF TRANSITION AND SELF-CHANGE

While not all life transitions elicit awareness of personal transformation or deliberate efforts at self-change, certain events, such as becoming a spouse or a parent, turn individuals' attention to shifts in identities and the self-concept more generally. For many middle- and upper-class youths, college is an important and expected life course transition. Leaving home affords students an opportunity to "make over" their self-concept. Karp (1998) found questions of identity central to young people anticipating the transition to college as they "plan to affirm certain of their identities, imagine creating new identities, and contemplate discovering unanticipated identities" (p. 255). Students view college as a fresh start where they can discover who they "really are." In addition, going away to college allows students to discard undesirable identities and to create aspects of self apart from biographical ties to family and community.

Moreover, students often see college as the context within which they will forge adult identities. Consequently, they are aware of the developmental tasks they face during their college years, such as making new friends, succeeding academically, and managing daily life on their own (Cantor and Langston 1989; Emmons 1989; Karp 1998). Students develop strategies for meeting these challenges and for changing themselves in desired directions. By deliberately trying to change themselves during the transitional moment that college provides, students exercise agency in attaining desired life goals for themselves.

SELF-CHANGE AS A GOAL

Sociologists assume that selves develop and change over the life course (e.g., Demo 1992) and that they exercise agency in doing so (Elder and O'Rand 1995). Nevertheless, studies of how people go about constructing selves over time and of the psychological processes involved are rare. To describe how people might construct selves over time, we use psychological research about individuals' goals. This research assumes that much behavior is goal-directed (Gollwitzer and Bargh 1996; Pervin 1989) and that in setting goals, people are motivated partly by their cognitive representations of their "possible selves"— the selves that they believe they could become (Markus and Nurius 1986). Thus this research investigates individuals' goals, as well as their motivations for attaining their goals.

Four similar, overlapping concepts appear in this literature: First, "life tasks" are "problems that people are currently working on" in a particular life stage. Young adults, for example, may try to "find intimacy" or "get married" (Cantor and Langston 1989, p. 130). Second, "personal strivings...represent what an individual is typically trying to do" (Emmons 1989, p. 92), such as "'think[ing] of the needs of others'" (p. 100). Third, "personal projects" (Little 1987) are interrelated sequences of actions intended to achieve some personal goal, such as "getting along with as many people as I can" (p. 233). Finally, attempts to solve "everyday problems" also are goal-directed. For example, deciding which parent to live with after a divorce also involves trying to maintain social relationships (Strough, Berg, and Sansone 1996).

Desired changes in the self are a subset of persons' goals. Attempts at self-change resemble life tasks (Cantor and Langston 1989), personal strivings (Emmons 1989), and personal projects (Little 1987) more than attempts to solve everyday problems, in that they are explicitly future-oriented. Like life tasks, they probably vary over the life course. Like personal strivings and personal projects, they may be ends in themselves or intermediate goals in service of long-term goals. Some changes in the self, such as "become a better student" reflect current concerns. Other changes, such as "be more outgoing," reflect more enduring concerns.

Research on young adults' goals is most pertinent to our study. Using data on college students, Emmons (1989, p. 100) has classified personal strivings into seven categories: (1) achievement (e.g., "Work toward higher athletic capabilities"); (2) affiliation ("Be friendly with others so they will like me"); (3) intimacy ("Help my friends and let them know I care"); (4) power over others ("Force men to be intimate in relationships"); (5) personal growth/health ("Develop a positive self-worth"); (6) self-presentation ("Be concerned about my physical appearance always"); and (7) autonomy ("Make decisions on my own"). Two additional themes that Emmons (1989, p. 107) has later identified are emotion management ("keep jealousy under control") and the expression of emotion ("express myself honestly").

Cantor (Cantor and Langston 1989, p. 133) has found that four fifths of college students' life tasks can be classified into six categories: "(a) getting good grades, (b) setting goals—planning for the future, (c) managing time;...(d) being on one's own away from family, (e) developing an identity, and (f) making friends." Taken together, Cantor's and Emmons' studies suggest several major themes that may appear in college students' accounts of self-change: achievement, self-presentation and appearance, changes in the self to improve social relationships, personal growth, the management and expression of emotion, and autonomy.

Although these themes undoubtedly cut across various social groups, how frequently students pursue them and how they do so may differ along the lines of social class of origin, race/ethnicity, and gender. Unfortunately, most college student samples, including this one, are fairly homogeneous along racial/ethnic and class lines. Thus, gender remains as the most likely source of variation in self-related goals and their pursuit among college students.

Gender and Type of Self-Change

We assume that goals, including attempts at self-change, are culturally pre-scribed (Benton 1993; Meyer 1986; Ryan, Sheldon, Kasser, and Deci 1996) and that people try to become the kinds of selves that they believe will be rewarded (Stryker 1980). "From birth, women and men are bombarded with cultural mes-sages about gender, with which we construct the hazy line between male and female realms of appropriate behavior" (Simonds 1992). Gender not only is inte-gral to individuals' self-concept (Rosenberg 1979), but it influences how individ-uals develop and change over the life course (e.g., Clausen 1991). We argue that one way in which men and women "do gender" (West and Zimmerman 1987) is by pursuing somewhat different "desired selves" (Rosenberg 1979) or "possible selves" (Markus and Nurius 1986). An intriguing study (Diener 1995) finds not only gender differences in the content of personal strivings, but also gender differ-ences in the resources that individuals see as important for attaining their personal strivings. Women mention speaking articulately, having good manners, and hav-ing social skills, and men mention having athletic ability, self-confidence, and influential connections. Individuals, of course, vary by the meanings of their gen-der identity, how much they have internalized gender role expectations, and how they enact gender roles. We hypothesize three ways in which intentional self-change may vary by gender.

First, we predict that more men than women will be pursuing goals involving achievement. In Western societies men are supposed to be more instrumental and achievement-oriented than women. For men, prestige comes primarily from suc-cess in achievement-oriented realms, including work, having money and material possessions (Frieze 1978; Holland and Eisenhart 1990). Of course, women pursue achievement goals as well. This is because "women are often taught to aspire up to the male realm, while also receiving the traditional line on what femininity should be" (Simonds 1992). Women, too, are expected to be able to be financially independent, as "illustrated in the declining legitimacy of 'housewife' as a full-time occupation for women" (Bumpass 1990, p. 490). Consistent with this, Lytle, Bakken, and Romig (1977) find that adolescent girls and boys do not differ on achievement-oriented identity development. Nevertheless, we expect women's efforts at self-change to be more dispersed, so that a smaller percentage of women primarily pursue achievement-related goals.

Second, we predict that more women than men will be trying to improve their appearance. Appearance provides women with "a means of achieving status, pop-ularity, opposite-sex companions, and ultimately a marriage partner more than it does for men" (Mori, Chaiken, and Pliner 1987, p. 693). Men have more opportu-nities than women to acquire status and prestige, so attractiveness is less impor-tant in order for men to succeed socially (Holland and Eisenhart 1990; Mori et al. 1987). Put differently, physical attractiveness usually is advantageous for both men and women, but unattractiveness may be more socially damaging for women

(Piliavin and LePore 1995). Men in college and adult samples rate their own attractiveness higher than women do (Harter 1997), and women have more negative body images than men (Cash and Henry 1995). Perhaps this is partly because culture prescribes that to be attractive, women must be thin (Holland and Eisenhart 1990; Mori et al. 1987). Consequently, we expect more women than men to be trying to improve their appearance and lose weight.

Third, culture prescribes that women be interpersonally sensitive, harmonious, and supportive. Women are expected to strive to maintain positive relations and urged to refrain from displays of anger and contempt (Cross and Madson 1997). Consequently, we expect more women than men to have goals involving emotion management.

THE PROCESS OF INTENTIONAL SELF-CHANGE

Individuals engaged in intentional self-change undoubtedly reflect on the process. Previous research on individuals' personal projects has tapped some of these reflections by asking individuals to rate their personal projects on various dimensions, such as visibility to others, difficulty, and anticipated outcome (Little 1987). In the present study, individuals were asked to assess their own self-change in terms of difficulty and likelihood of success. The question is, what influences these assessments? We discuss three sets of factors.

Self-Esteem and Self-Efficacy

How people feel about themselves and assess their capabilities may influence the process of intentional self-change. Two aspects of the self-concept which may be particularly important are self-esteem and self-efficacy. Both are fairly stable, and both have consequences for individuals' behavior (Gecas and Burke 1995).

Self-esteem, or sense of self-worth, is expected to be negatively related to the difficulty of changing oneself and positively related to expected success. For people with high self-esteem, succeeding at self-change (usually self-improvement) both enhances self-esteem and is consistent with their views of themselves. For people with low self-esteem, however, succeeding at self-change poses a problem because it is inconsistent with their self-views. As Swann and his associates have repeatedly demonstrated, self-consistency strivings outweigh self-enhancement processes (McNulty and Swann 1991).

What complicates matters, however, is that Owens (1993, 1994) has found that self-esteem is actually two-dimensional, consisting of positive self-worth and self-deprecation. Of the two, self-deprecation is more strongly associated with pessimism and depression. By implication, then, high self-deprecation may inhibit progress toward self-change more than low self-worth does.

Self-efficacy, one's sense of control over one's outcomes, is expected to be strongly and positively related to expectations of successfully changing oneself. First, self-efficacy is positively related to a variety of health-related behaviors, such as overcoming anxieties (reviewed by Gecas and Burke 1995, p. 48). If self-efficacy is related to actual changes in behavior, it also should be related to individuals' assessments of their eventual success in changing themselves. Second, longitudinal studies have found constructs similar to self-efficacy to be strongly and positively related to several desirable life-course outcomes. Mortimer, Finch, and Kumka (1982) have found that self-competence in senior college men is positively related to income, work autonomy, evaluation of one's career progress, employment security, marital satisfaction, and life satisfaction. Similarly, Clausen (1991) has found that individuals who as adolescents scored higher on "planful competence," including self-confidence, had more stable careers and marriages. These findings suggest that all else equal, individuals with greater self-efficacy are better able to effect desirable life course outcomes for themselves.

Motivations for Self-Change

What motivates individuals to try to change some aspect of themselves? Persons may be motivated to change themselves to attain or maintain favorable self-attitudes. Three self-attitudes which Gecas (1991) and others argue are especially important sources of motivation are self-esteem, self-efficacy, and sense of authenticity (one's sense of living up to a core self [Erickson 1995]).

Another set of factors which may motivate intentional self-change involves people's perceptions' of their "actual selves"—their current self-concept—in relation to the "possible selves" they could become (Markus and Nurius 1986). Higgins' (1996) self-discrepancy theory predicts that individuals are motivated to reduce discrepancies between their "actual self" (current identities and attributes) and an "ideal" self, whose identities or attributes they'd like to have, or between their "actual self" and an "ought" self, whose identities or attributes they feel obliged to have (Gecas and Burke 1995, p. 49; Higgins 1996; Markus and Nurius 1986). Alternatively, individuals may wish to avoid becoming a "feared" self, whose identities or attributes they are afraid of acquiring (Markus and Nurius 1986). Thus individuals may be motivated to become more like an ideal self or an ought self, or to avoid becoming a feared self.

Strategies of Self-Change

How do individuals go about changing themselves? Research on how individuals work to solve life tasks emphasizes that individuals pursue various problem-solving strategies. Cantor and Langston (1989) define such strategies as "patterns of appraisal, planning, retrospection, and effort" (p. 131). Strategies are "diverse in content, involving thoughts, feeling, and efforts, sometimes directed toward the self, and other times more focused on influencing others or on controlling the task activity itself" (Cantor and Langston 1989, p. 131). Unfortunately, conceptual schemes from research on goals are not very useful for studying strategies of self-change. For example, research on adolescents' personal projects (Little 1987) views strategies as the more "molecular" acts through which individuals complete specific projects. For example, a student who wishes to "decide what to do in the future" might "visit their campus career center." Research on college students' life tasks (Cantor and Langston 1989) separately characterizes students' strategies for accomplishing academic goals (defensive pessimism versus optimism) and social goals (e.g., social constraint, in which students let others take the lead in interaction).

What is desirable is a framework for classifying strategies which permits comparison across types of self-change. In this study we conceptualize strategies for self-change as coping responses and adapt Thoits' (1991) model of coping with stressful events. The extent to which intentional self-change occurs in response to stressors is unknown (Kiecolt 1994). Yet just as individuals must cope with the demands that stressors make on them, they must also cope with the demands and challenges that new roles and social contexts present over the life course (Cantor and Langston 1989).

Thoits (1991, p. 237) distinguishes four main types of coping responses[1] based on two dimensions. First, individuals may direct their coping efforts to "solving or adjusting to the demand itself (problem-focused coping)" and/or to lessening the emotional distress from the demand (emotion-focused coping). Second, individuals may respond behaviorally, by taking action, or cognitively, by changing the meaning of the situation. At a more concrete level, Thoits (1991) identifies 21 subtypes of coping. For example, problem-focused, behavioral coping strategies include acting, seeking advice, and leaving a situation. Problem-focused, cognitive coping strategies include reinterpreting a situation and trying not to think about it. Emotion-focused, behavioral coping strategies include exercising and expressing one's feelings. Emotion-focused, cognitive coping strategies include prayer and meditation.

Predictions as to how these four types of coping responses will influence the process of self-change are hard to make. In general, we expect most individuals to use more problem-focused than emotion-focused strategies. Individuals tend to use problem-focused strategies in response to stressors they see as controllable and emotion-focused strategies in response to uncontrollable stressors (Thoits 1995). By extension, the fact that individuals are attempting self-change indicates a belief in some degree of eventual success. Yet individuals also may use emotion-focused strategies if they experience distress in connection with their self-change. Moreover, whether problem-focused strategies or emotion-focused strategies will be more related to expected success in changing oneself is unknown. In the literature on stress, for example, researchers have not identified "the types of coping which reliably reduce distress or ill health in response to particular types of situations" (Thoits 1995, p. 61).

METHODS

The Sample

The sample consisted of 442 students at a large state university in the mid-Atlantic region of the United States. The students completed the questionnaire during class in an introductory sociology course and an upper-division communications course, respectively, during spring 1997. Students in the sociology course received $2.00 for participating in the survey, and students in the communications course received extra credit. We excluded 14 respondents who did not answer the questions on self-change, 1 who did not want to change, 2 who were not trying to change themselves, and 19 respondents whose type of change was classified as "miscellaneous" because it was vague or idiosyncratic. Missing data on some variables further reduced the sample size for analysis. The resulting sample of 376 students was 56 percent female and 83 percent white, 3 percent African-American, 2 percent Hispanic, 8 percent Asian, and 4 percent other race/ethnicity. The mean age was 19 years.

Measures

Type of Self-Change

In response to an open-ended question, students listed as many as three things that they were currently trying to change about themselves. This method had the advantage that it did not require respondents to reconstruct and possibly revise an account of their past actions (Ross 1989).[2] Respondents then designated the change that they most wanted to make. Based on these responses, we developed an initial, detailed coding scheme, which had 65 categories such as "study more," "work harder," "be more responsible," "be more considerate of others," "lose weight," and "get fit."

We then classified types of self-change into six broad categories. (1) *"Become more work- or goal-oriented"* reflected efforts to improve time management and study habits and to work harder; to cease or control the use of drugs, drinking, and smoking; and to be more responsible, spend less money, and focus on one's future occupation. (2) *"Be a better or nicer person"* involved trying to be kinder, more tactful, and more considerate in one's dealings with others, including significant others. It also involved seeking to be more open-minded toward people in general, not just one's acquaintances. (3) *"Improve appearance/physique"* entailed improving one's fitness or appearance and losing weight. (4) *"Be more confident/*

optimistic" referred to attempts to worry less about others' opinions of oneself, to have a more positive attitude about oneself, and to accept oneself. (5) *"Be more outgoing/engaged"* involved seeking to be more assertive or expressive in social situations and to take more interpersonal risks. (6) *"Manage negative emotions"* consisted of attempts to control negative feelings such as anger, hurt, jealousy, and frustration.

Expected Outcome

Two items assessed respondents' progress in changing themselves. The difficulty of changing oneself in terms of the thought and effort required was measured by an item whose responses ranged from 1 ("very easy") to 5 ("very difficult"). Perceived likelihood of success was measured by the item, "How likely are you to succeed in making this change?" The responses ranged from 1 ("not at all likely") to 4 ("very likely").

Self-Attitudes

Three types of self-attitudes may influence the process of self-change: positive self-worth, self-deprecation, and self-efficacy. Based on Owens' (1993, 1994) findings that self-esteem is better treated as a bi-dimensional construct, we created two indices of self-esteem using six items from Rosenberg's self-esteem scale. Three positively-worded items were summed to create an index of positive self-worth (alpha = 0.74), and three negatively-worded items were summed to create an index of self-deprecation (alpha = 0.72). Six items from Pearlin's mastery index were summed to created an index of self-efficacy (alpha = 0.71). (The items are shown in Appendix A1.)

Motivations for Self-Change

Respondents rated the importance of six motivations for self-change on six Likert-scaled items, from "not at all important" (coded 1) to "very important" (coded 4). (1) The item "to have more respect for myself," adapted from the Rosenberg Self-Esteem Scale, indicated the importance of *increasing self-esteem*. This item measures a desire to reduce self-deprecation more than a desire to enhance positive self-worth. (2) An item from Pearlin's Mastery Scale, "to have more control over the things that happen to me" measures the importance of *increasing self-efficacy* (Pearlin, Lieberman, Menaghan, and Mullen 1981). (3) The item "to become more like the person I genuinely am" measures the importance of *increasing one's sense of authenticity* (Erickson 1995; Turner 1976). (4) The item "to become more like the kind of person I would like to be" measured the importance of *becoming more like an ideal self* (Higgins 1996) or a desired possible self (Markus and Nurius 1986). (5) The importance of *becoming an "ought self"*

(Higgins 1996) was measured by the item, "to become more like the kind of person I ought to be." (6) The importance of *avoiding becoming a "negative possible self" or "feared self"* (Markus and Nurius 1986) was measured by the item, "to avoid becoming the kind of person I'm afraid of becoming."

Strategies of Self-Change

After asking respondents what they most wanted to change about themselves, we asked them to describe in detail what they were doing to make this change. We initially coded their responses into the 21 subtypes of coping which Thoits (1991) identified. Of those 21 subtypes, respondents to this study named 15. No respondents redefined their feelings or used drugs/alcohol, fantasy expression, waiting, desensitization, or music as strategies for self-change. In addition, we excluded four respondents whose strategy was self-acceptance. (Appendix A2 gives examples of each of the 15 strategies.) We then classified these 15 detailed strategies for self-change into four categories according to whether the effort was aimed at the problem or at one's feelings, or whether the mode of action was behavioral or cognitive (Thoits 1991, p. 242).

Sociodemographic Variables

Several sociodemographic characteristics also were ascertained. Gender was dichotomous (1 = women; 0 = men). Grade point average was coded to category midpoints: 1.75 (below 2.0), 2.25 (2.0-2.49), 2.75 (2.5-2.99), 3.25 (3.0-3.49), or 3.75 (3.5-4.0). How religious or spiritual respondents were was an item that ranged from 1 (not at all) to 4 (very). Race/ethnicity and age were initially included in the analyses, but were dropped because of lack of significance, probably due to the homogeneity of the sample.

RESULTS

We first cross-tabulated respondents' most important self-change by gender (see Table 1). Of the six types of self-change, the most prevalent was related to achievement—trying to become more work- or goal-oriented. As predicted, a higher percentage of men than women named this type of self-change as their most important. Because many respondents in this category were seeking to raise their grade point average and because men's grade point averages were lower than women's, we tested whether controlling for grade point average explained the gender difference. We performed a logistic regression in which the dependent variable was whether a respondent was trying to become more work- or goal-oriented versus all other types of self-change, with grade point average and gender as predictors (not shown). The higher the grade point average, the less likely

Table 1. Type of Self-Change, by Gender

Type of Self-Change	Men (%)	Women (%)	Total (%)
Improve work habits, be more goal-oriented	43.3	20.3	30.3
Become a better/nicer person	11.6	13.2	12.5
Improve appearance/physique	13.4	18.4	16.2
Be more outgoing/engaged	15.2	14.2	14.6
Be more confident/optimistic	8.5	25.9	18.4
Manage negative emotions	7.9	8.0	8.0
Total percent	99.9	100.0	100.0
Total number	164	212	376

Notes: Chi-square ($df = 5$) = 33.1, $p < .001$.

respondents were to be trying to become more work- or goal-oriented. Nevertheless, gender remained a significant predictor.

The second most prevalent type of self-change for the total sample was trying to become more confident. Women were more than three times more likely than men (25.9% versus 8.5%) to be endeavoring to increase their confidence. We tested whether this gender difference was due to men's slightly higher mean score on positive self-worth ($p < .05$) by performing a logistic regression, entering gender and positive self-worth as predictors of whether respondents were trying to become more confident (not shown). Only gender was significant.

As predicted, more women than men were aiming to improve their appearance. The disaggregated categories showed a gender difference in the direction predicted. Of the 22 men and 39 women who were trying to improve their appearance, 46 percent of men ($n = 10$) versus 21 percent of women ($n = 8$) were trying to get fit ("get in better shape"). In contrast, 41 percent of women ($n = 16$) but only 18 percent of men ($n = 4$) were trying to lose weight. For example, one woman said, "My appearance—I am starting to like how I look more—I'm 5'5" and at one point weighed 170—now I'm down to 145!" (The other 8 men and 15 women in this category were trying to "improve their appearance." Percentages did not differ by gender.)

Approximately 15 percent of respondents were endeavoring to be more outgoing. About 13 percent of respondents were trying to be nicer to people or to be "better persons," e.g., to be "a better son" or to be less critical and judgmental. These two types of self-change did not differ by gender.

Men and women were equally likely to be aiming to manage troublesome negative emotions. When we examined the more detailed classification of self-changes, however, we found that of the 13 men and 17 women who were trying to better manage negative emotions, women were disproportionately trying to manage feelings of anger (59% of the women compared with 39% of the men).

Although the number of cases was small, men were more evenly dispersed across various emotions (e.g., jealousy) than women were.

In results not shown, we found that type of intentional self-change was somewhat related to positive self-worth ($p < .05$) and to self-deprecation ($p < .10$). Respondents highest on positive self-worth and lowest on self-deprecation were most likely to attempt to become better or nicer persons. Respondents lowest on positive self-worth and highest on self-deprecation were most likely to be trying to increase their confidence and be more optimistic. Self-efficacy was unrelated to type of intentional self-change.

Motivations for Self-Change

Next we performed a regression analysis of respondents' self-related motivations for changing themselves (see Table 2). On average, all the reasons given were important to respondents, with means of over three on four-point scales. Becoming one's ideal self was the highest-rated reason for changing, and increasing one's sense of authenticity was the second highest-rated. Respondents rated becoming an "ought" self and avoiding becoming a feared self as the least important reasons for changing.

Overall, men and women had very similar motivations for changing. The only motivation on which they differed significantly was that increasing one's self-esteem was a more important motivation for women than for men. Students'

Table 2. Motivations to Change Oneself, Regressed on Social Characteristics and Self-Attitudes

Independent Variables	Increase Self-Esteem	Increase Self-Efficacy	Increase Sense of Authenticity	Become Ideal Self	Become Ought Self	Avoid Becoming Feared Self
Social characteristics						
Female (yes = 1)	.14**	−.03	.08	.00	.01	.06
Grade point average	−.04	−.14**	−.06	−.03	−.03	−.02
Religiosity	.09+	.05	.08	.14**	.16**	.00
Self-attitudes						
Positive self-worth	.07	.02	.03	−.07	−.06	.02
Self-deprecation	.27***	.16+	.05	.14+	.05	.14+
Self-efficacy	.04	.08	.16*	.18**	.07	.03
N	369	368	369	370	368	369
Adj. R^2	.06***	.02*	.02*	.03*	.02*	.00
Mean	3.46	3.48	3.56	3.69	3.30	3.32

Notes: +$p < .10$, *$p < .05$, **$p < .01$, ***$p < .001$, two-tailed tests.

grade point averages were only related to one motivation for self-change: the higher the grade point average, the less students were motivated by a desire to increase their self-efficacy.

With regard to self-attitudes, positive self-worth was not associated with any of the six motivations for self-change. In contrast, the higher the self-deprecation, the more students were motivated to change in order to increase their sense of self-worth and self-efficacy, to become an ideal self, to become an ought self, and to avoid becoming a feared self. Self-efficacy was related to two motivations for self-change: the higher self-efficacy, the more students were motivated to increase their sense of authenticity and to become more like their ideal self.

Religiosity also was positively related to several of the motivations for changing oneself. More religious or spiritual respondents were more motivated to become more like an ideal self and more like an ought self. Since religion provides people with both ideals and moral guidelines, both are plausible.

Strategies of Self-Change

We next computed the frequencies of respondents' strategies for changing themselves and cross-tabulated them by type of self-change (see Table 3). Respondents were most likely (71.3%) to use a problem-focused, behavioral strategy, usually some sort of direct action. In fact, direct action was the strategy most frequently used overall. Next most prevalent were problem-focused, cognitive strategies (43.1%), such as reinterpreting a situation more positively or analyzing a situation. Only 12.2 percent of respondents used emotion-focused, behavioral strategies, most commonly catharsis (expressing feelings). Finally, only 4.0 percent of respondents used emotion-focused, cognitive strategies, and all but one case involved prayer. In sum, the most common techniques were changing one's behavior to change a problem with oneself, cognitively changing one's interpretation of a situation, and behaviorally manipulating one's emotions. On average, respondents reported using 1.31 types of strategies for changing themselves.

A few differences in strategies for self-change by the type of self-change attempted are worth noting (Table 3). Nearly all respondents who were trying to become more work- or goal-oriented or improve their appearance used a problem-focused, behavioral strategy. Respondents who were trying to become more confident or optimistic or to manage negative emotions were by far the most likely to adopt a problem-focused, cognitive strategy. Respondents who wanted to become more outgoing were the most likely to adopt an emotion-focused, behavioral strategy, usually expressing their feelings more freely. (Even these respondents, however, were more likely to use a problem-focused, behavioral strategy.) Perhaps not surprisingly, respondents who wanted to be better or nicer persons were the most likely to pray for help. More frequently, however, they also used a problem-focused strategy.

Table 3. Strategies Used to Change Something about Oneself, for Total Sample and by Type of Self-Change (Percentage Mentioning Strategy)[a]

Strategy	Total Sample (N = 376)	Work-/Goal-Oriented	Better/Nicer Person	Improve Appearance/ Physique	More Outgoing/ Engaged	More Confident/ Optimistic	Manage Negative Emotions	Sig.[b]
Problem-focused, behavioral	71.3[c]	91.2	59.6	98.4	60.0	46.4	36.7	***
Direct action	69.1							
Seek support	3.5							
Leave the situation	2.4							
Problem-focused, cognitive	43.1[c]	29.8	53.2	8.2	32.7	84.1	73.3	***
Reinterpret situation	29.5							
Analyze situation	13.6							
Use thought-stopping	2.7							
Distraction	0.5							
Fantasy solution	0.5							
Emotion-focused, behavioral	12.2[c]	2.6	17.0	3.3	38.2	7.2	23.3	***
Catharsis	8.0							
Hide feelings	2.1							
Other physiological	1.9							
Exercise	0.5							
Emotion-focused, cognitive	4.0[c]	0.0	23.4	0.0	0.0	4.3	3.3	***
Pray	3.7							
Write about it	0.3							
$\bar{x}$ types of strategies	1.31	1.24	1.53	1.10	1.31	1.42	1.37	***
$\bar{x}$ specific strategies	1.38	1.30	1.64	1.13	1.38	1.52	1.50	***

Notes: +$p < .10$, * $p < .05$, ** $p < .01$, *** $p < .001$, two-tailed tests.
[a] Percentage of respondents who used a given strategy, for $N = 376$ respondents who reported a strategy.
[b] Significance of chi-square test or F test, respectively.
[c] Total percentages for specific strategies may exceed the category percentages because some respondents used more than one strategy in a category.

195

The mean number of different strategies used also differs significantly by type of self-change. Those trying to become a better or nicer person, to be more confident and optimistic, and to manage negative emotions used more strategies in trying to change themselves. Most respondents used problem-focused, behavioral strategies. Emotion-focused strategies appeared to be supplemental or secondary.

The Difficulty of Changing Oneself

We then performed a regression analysis of the perceived difficulty of changing oneself (see Table 4). The predictors were gender, religiosity, self-attitudes, moti-

Table 4. Regression Analyses of the Difficulty of
Changing Oneself and the Perceived Likelihood of Success
(Standardized Regression Coefficients)

Independent Variables	Difficulty of Changing Oneself	Perceived Likelihood of Success
Female (0,1)	.02	−.08+
Religiosity	.00	.13**
Self-attitudes		
Positive self-worth	−.03	.18**
Self-deprecation	.22**	−.02
Self-efficacy	−.08	.14*
Motivations for Changing Oneself		
Become ideal self	.10+	.05
Become ought self	.17**	.06
Avoid becoming feared self	.01	−.07
Increase self-esteem	.05	.04
Increase self-efficacy	−.08	−.01
Increase authenticity	−.01	.05
Type of Change[a]		
Better/nicer person	−.08	−.09
Improve appearance/physique	.02	.01
More outgoing/engaged	.01	.00
More confident/optimistic	.09	.03
Manage negative emotions	.12*	.02
Strategies for Changing Oneself		
Problem-focused, behavioral		.00
Problem-focused, cognitive		−.01
Emotion-focused, behavioral		−.12*
Emotion-focused, cognitive		.13*
Number of Sources of Encouragement		.10*
Difficulty of Changing		−.34***
N	368	367
Adj. R^2	.13***	.31***

Notes: +p < .10, *p < .05, **p < .01, ***p < .001, two-tailed tests.
    [a] "Be more work- or goal-oriented" is the omitted reference category.

vations for changing, and the type of change attempted. Few of the predictors were significant. The most important was self-deprecation: The more self-deprecating the respondents were, the more difficult they found self-change. In addition, the more strongly that respondents were motivated to become more like an "ought" self, a self they felt obliged to be, the more difficult self-change was. One type of self-change, managing negative emotions, was significantly more difficult than the others.

Likelihood of Success

The survey also addressed what influenced respondents' assessments of their likelihood of changing. Overall, respondents were fairly confident that they would succeed. Forty-six percent of respondents believed that they were "very likely" to succeed, and another 50 percent believed they were "somewhat likely."

The perceived likelihood of success was regressed on self-attitudes, type of change attempted, strategies for changing, number of sources of support enlisted, and the perceived difficulty of changing, with gender and religiosity controlled (see Table 4). Women were marginally less confident of success than men (p<.10). The higher the respondents' positive self-worth and sense of self-efficacy, the more confident they were that they would succeed. In contrast, self-deprecation (negative self-esteem) had no effect on the perceived likelihood of success. Perceived likelihood of success also did not differ by the type of change that respondents were attempting. Whether respondents used any of the four types of strategies for changing themselves were included in the regression analysis as dummy variables. Using a behavioral or cognitive problem-focused strategy did not influence their perceived likelihood of success. Using a behavioral, emotion-focused strategy (mostly expressing or hiding one's feelings) was associated with a lower perceived likelihood of success. Only using a cognitive, emotion-focused strategy (prayer) significantly increased the perceived likelihood of success. Also, the more religious or spiritual that respondents were, the higher their perceived likelihood of success. Similarly, previous studies have found that believing in God's love and God's participation in one's life fosters a sense of "(vicarious) efficacy" (Ellison and Sherkat 1995, p. 1258).

Earthly social support also positively influenced respondents' assessments of eventual success. The more sources of encouragement that individuals had, the higher were their assessments of success. Finally, the strongest predictor of perceived likelihood of successfully changing oneself was difficulty: The more difficult that respondents rated the self-change they were attempting, the lower their perceived likelihood of success.

DISCUSSION AND CONCLUSIONS

In this study, we investigated individuals' intentional efforts to changes themselves during a transitional moment in the life course. Our focus was on the types of self-change in which college students typically engage, their motivations and strategies for changing themselves, and influences on the perceived difficulty and likelihood of success. We found that individuals' identities and self-concepts contribute to differences in the types of self-change they attempt and in the process itself. These findings have implications for research and theory about self and identity, goals, gender, and the life course.

With respect to *self and identity*, the findings provide further evidence that individuals actively cultivate particular aspects of their self-concepts. Only three students out of more than 400 indicated no current effort or intention to change themselves. Men and women were trying to change in ways that would bolster their gender identities. Those with less positive self-attitudes sought to enhance their self-perceptions. More religious individuals were inspired to become a more ideal self, perhaps the same "ought" self they believed they should be. These young adults set goals for themselves that they believe will bring them closer to their desired selves.

Aspects of the self-concept not only play a role in motivating self-change, but seem to affect individuals' perceptions of the difficulty of the change and the likelihood of success. Those with a more positive sense of self-worth and self-efficacy sought to attain better, more ideal selves and believed themselves more likely to succeed in doing so. Self-deprecating individuals, however, sought to change themselves in ways that increase their confidence and self-respect and bring them on par with the selves they believe they should and could be. While they feel no less likely that their efforts will be successful, self-deprecating students found changing themselves more difficult, as did others striving to be the person they "ought" to be. Since greater difficulty in changing decreases the perceived likelihood that one will be successful, self-deprecation may indirectly make success less likely and thereby contribute to a consistent self-view. Nevertheless, the extent to which attempts at self-change contribute to changes or stability in the self-concept over the life course remains to be studied.

With respect to *goals*, as psychologists have noted, the goals that individuals set for themselves help guide their behavior and may result in life changes. In the short term, setting goals stimulates assessments of "the self-perceived fit between where one is and where one aspires to be" (Wells and Stryker 1988, p. 204). People are motivated by discrepancies between their desired self and their extant self. The primary differences in students' types of self-change fall along gender lines. Over 40 percent of men in the sample were trying to become more work- or goal-oriented, the most prevalent type of self-change among men. This is consistent with cultural prescriptions that men concentrate their efforts on achievement. Although the women in this sample were only half as likely as men to be trying to improve their work habits or to be more goal-oriented, this type of change was the second most prevalent indicated by women. Its prevalence may reflect newer norms which prescribe that women succeed in achievement-oriented realms as well as in traditional domestic roles (Bumpass 1990).

Becoming more confident was the most prevalent type of self-change among women, but only the fifth most prevalent among men. In keeping with evidence that women tend to think of themselves as others see them and in terms of their relationships (Cross and Madson 1997; Holland and Eisenhart 1990), these college women want to be more self-confident and worry less about what other people think of them. In addition, despite an absence of substantial differences in men's and women's self-attitudes, women were more motivated than men to change themselves in order to enhance their self-esteem and feelings of authenticity. These women may want to feel less constrained by others' expectations and evaluations of them. Nonetheless, women perceived themselves as less likely than men to accomplish their desired changes.

Other gender differences in types of self-change were less readily apparent. Men and women were equally likely to be trying to manage their emotions, the type of self-change students felt was most difficult. However, women focus more on managing anger which is consistent with gendered feeling and emotional display norms. Both men and women were trying to improve their appearance; however, men were more concerned with "getting fit" and women emphasize "losing weight." This result parallels previous findings (Franzoi 1995) that "females are taught that their body-as-object is a significant factor in how others will judge their overall value" (p. 418). In contrast, males are taught that "power and function" are more important criteria than their appearance for evaluating their body (p. 419). It remains to be seen how gender, ethnicity, and social class interact to influence goals, however. For example, compared with Anglo and Hispanic women, African-American women are more satisfied with their appearance and less concerned about losing weight (Cash and Henry 1995).

The strategies students selected to accomplish their goals reflect something of the nature of the goals themselves. Students favored problem-focused, *behavioral* strategies for the types of self-change with relatively concrete, tangible outcomes, such as becoming more work- or goal-oriented and improving one's appearance. Individuals engaged in more subjective self-change, such as becoming more confident/optimistic and managing negative emotions, tended to use problem-focused, *cognitive* strategies to change perceptions and meanings. Emotion-focused strategies were used primarily by those whose type of self-change emphasized interpersonal interaction, such as becoming more outgoing and engaged or being a better, nicer person. It may be difficult for individuals to sustain self-change efforts that requires controlling emotional displays, either through greater expression or suppression, as those using emotion-focused, *behavioral* strategies believed themselves less likely to succeed in changing. On the other hand, emotion-focused, *cognitive* strategies, such as prayer, appear to reinforce optimism about successful self-change. Regardless of the type of change, students preferred strategies that target the problem or situation rather than their feelings.

The findings also have implications for *gender*. Attempts at self-change are one more way in which men and women "do gender" (West and Zimmerman 1987). To the extent that self-related goals and motivations are gendered, men and women will develop and change differently over the life course. Understanding how cultural meanings of gender are internalized and become goals requires explaining how individuals actively and selectively enact these meanings in constructing selves. To the extent that men and women develop and change differently over the life course, they reproduce gendered social structures. The gender differences in respondents' goals probably reflect corresponding differences in their present and future adult roles.

Psychological research on how goals relate to personality and development has just begun to investigate gender differences in the goals that individuals set for themselves (Strough et al. 1996). Our findings indicate that more research is warranted. In particular, psychological research on goals recognizes that individuals pursue numerous goals simultaneously (Cantor and Langston 1989; Emmons 1989; Little 1987). How men and women juggle their various self-related goals will add to our understanding of how men and women construct their life courses.

With respect to the *life course*, many of the students' self-related goals reflect common early-adulthood themes of achievement and instrumentality in anticipation of assuming adult roles of career and family (Wells and Stryker 1988). The goals of the students in this sample indicate greater efforts at self-control, whether concerning work habits, self-confidence, physical appearance, or emotions. In seeking greater self-control, these students in transition from adolescence to adulthood may be shedding behaviors and characteristics that are liabilities in adulthood as they acquire attributes that will better serve them in their future.

In addition to goals involving self-control, a substantial and similar percentage of men and women are trying to be more outgoing. For example, one man was trying to be a "friendlier person—meeting more people and going up to people I don't know and meet them." Since the mean age for this sample is 19, this finding may reflect the requirements of the life course transition into college wherein individuals must forge new social networks and identities within them. Similarly, Cantor has found making friends ranks high in importance among college students' goals (Cantor and Langston 1989). The pursuit of new relationships among first-year university students is a predictable response to separation from previous networks, reduced interaction with family and childhood friends, and new opportunities for friendship which "almost require restructuring of the self" (Wells and Stryker 1988, p. 213). In adapting to a new social environment, students' intentional choices about their identities and interaction contexts have reciprocal effects. As Dannefer points out, "...the social context is itself constantly being reconstituted through human activity" (1996, p 150).

These findings augment research which suggests that individuals are committed to developing identities that they believe will generate positive information about themselves (Schwalbe and Staples 1991). "Successful identity performances generate positive affect (e.g., self-esteem or pride in self, respect or liking in others); inadequate performances produce negative emotions (e.g., embarrassment or shame in self, disappointment or anger in others)" (Thoits 1989, p. 332). In addition, people foster aspects of themselves that are likely to serve them as they move throughout the life course. The self "includes anticipations of future events and outcomes which provide motivational as well as referential structure for present activity" (Wells and Stryker 1988, p. 222). Attempts at self-change are one way that people intentionally influence their development over the life course. Whether self-change brings the rewards that people anticipate or whether some changes bring higher self-evaluations than others remains to be studied.

Appendix A1.   Self-Concept Indicators

Indicators		Questionnaire Items[a]
Positive Self-Worth	P	I feel that I am a per son of worth, or at least on an equal plane with others.
	P	I feel that I have a number of good qualities.
	P	I take a positive attitude toward myself.
Self-Deprecation	N	All in all, I'm inclined to feel like a failure.
	N	I feel I do not have much to be proud of.
	N	I wish I could have more respect for myself.
Self-Efficacy	N	There is really no way I can solve some of the problems I have.
	N	Sometimes I feel that I'm being pushed around in life.
	P	What happens in the future mostly depends on me.
	N	I have little control over the things that happen to me.
	P	I can do just about anything I really set my mind to.
	N	There is little I can do to change many of the important things in my life.

Notes: [a] Items prefixed with "P" denote positively-worded items, and those prefixed with "N" denote negatively-worded items. Possible responses are: 1 = agree, 2 = tend to agree, 3 = tend to disagree, and 4 = disagree.

Appendix B2. Examples of Strategies Used to Change Something about Oneself

Strategy	Type of Self-Change	Example
Problem-focused, Behavioral		
Direct action	Improve appearance/physique	"exercising 3-4 times a week"
Seek support	Better/nicer person	"having others keep me accountable"
Leave the situation	More work-/goal-oriented	"staying away from people that drink"
Problem-focused, Cognitive		
Reinterpret situation	More outgoing/engaged	"not care what people think of me as much"
Analyze situation	More work-/goal-oriented	"trying to prioritize what needs to be done first"
Use thought-stopping	More confident/optimistic	"don't get down on myself about stupid things"
Accept the situation		
Distraction	Manage negative emotions	"I count when I get mad"
Fantasy solution	Improve appearance/physique	"I would like to be more model-like"
Emotion-focused, Behavioral		
Catharsis	Better/nicer person	"showing that I care about the people that I am in charge of"
Hide feelings	Manage negative emotions	"not yelling all the time"
Other physiological	More confident/optimistic	"try to relax more"
Exercise	Manage negative emotions	"I am trying to relieve my tension or anger through my dance or exercise"
Emotion-focused, Cognitive		
Pray	Better/nicer person	"praying more"
Write about it	Better/nicer person	"I write mean things in my journal about [people instead of gossiping about them]"

ACKNOWLEDGMENTS

Our thanks to Christine White for her assistance with coding and to Rachel Parker-Gwin, Dale Wimberley, JoAnn Emmel, and Richard D. Gandour for helpful comments and suggestions on earlier drafts.

NOTES

1. Thoits (1991) elaborates the four types of coping response into seven by dividing behavioral and cognitive emotion-focused strategies according to whether the target is physiology, expressive gestures, or the emotional label. (Of course, one can't change an emotional label behaviorally.) Since so few respondents in this study use emotion-focused responses, however, we use the four-fold typology, which does not subdivide emotion-focused strategies.

2. These results are consistent with previous research (e.g., Little 1987) which finds that nearly all individuals have ongoing personal projects.

REFERENCES

Benton, J.S. 1993. "Self and Society in Popular Social Criticism 1920-1980." *Symbolic Interaction* 16: 145-170.

Bumpass, L.L. 1990. "What's Happening to the Family? Interactions between Demographic and Institutional Change." *Demography* 27: 483-498.

Cantor, N., and C.A. Langston. 1989. "Ups and Downs of Life Tasks in a Life Transition." Pp. 127-167 in *Goal Concepts in Personality and Social Psychology*, edited by L.A. Pervin. Hillsdale, NJ: Erlbaum.

Cash, T.F., and P.E. Henry. 1995. "Women's Body Images: The Results of a National Survey in the U.S.A." *Sex Roles* 33: 19-28.

Clausen, J. 1986. *The Life Course: A Sociological Perspective.* Englewood Cliffs, NJ: Prentice-Hall.

_____. 1991. "Early Adult Choices and the Life Course." *American Journal of Sociology* 96: 805-842.

Cross, S.E. and L. Madson. 1997. "Models of the Self: Self-Construals and Gender." *Psychological Bulletin* 122: 5-37.

Dannefer, D. 1984. "Adult Development and Social Theory: A Paradigmatic Reappraisal." *American Sociological Review* 49: 100-116.

_____. 1996. "Commentary." *Human Development* 29: 150-152.

Demo, D. 1992. "The Self-Concept over Time: Research Issues and Directions." *Annual Review of Sociology* 18: 303-326.

Diener, E. 1995. "Resources, Personal Strivings, and Subjective Well-Being: A Nomothetic and Idiographic Approach." *Journal of Personality and Social Psychology* 68: 926-935.

Elder, G., and A. O'Rand. 1995. "Adults Lives in a Changing Society." Pp. 452-475 in *Sociological Perspectives on Social Psychology*, edited by K.S. Cook, G.A. Fine, and J.S. House. Boston: Allyn and Bacon.

Ellison, C.G., and D.E. Sherkat. 1995. "Is Sociology the Core Discipline for the Scientific Study of Religion?" *Social Forces* 73: 1255-1266.

Emmons, R.A. 1989. "The Personal Striving Approach to Personality." Pp. 87-125 in *Goal Concepts in Personality and Social Psychology*, edited by L.A. Pervin. Hillsdale, NJ: Erlbaum.

Erickson, R. 1995. "The Importance of Authenticity for Self and Society." *Symbolic Interaction* 18: 121-144.

Franzoi, S.L. 1995. "The Body-as-Object versus the Body-as-Process: Gender Differences and Gender Considerations." *Sex Roles* 33: 417-437.

Frieze, I.K. 1978. "Achievement and Non-achievement in Women." Pp. 234-254 in *Women and Sex Roles: A Social Psychological Perspective*, edited by I.K. Frieze, J.E. Parsons, P.B. Johnson, D.N. Ruble, and G.L. Zellman. New York: W.W. Norton.

Gecas, V. 1991. "The Self-Concept as a Basis for a Theory of Motivation." Pp. 171-87 in *The Self-Society Dynamic*, edited by J.A. Howard and P. Callero. Cambridge, UK: Cambridge University Press.

Gecas, V., and P.J. Burke. 1995. "Self and Identity." Pp. 41-67 in *Sociological Perspectives in Social Psychology*, edited by K.S. Cook, G.A. Fine, and J.S. House. Boston: Allyn and Bacon.

Gollwitzer, P.M., and J.A. Bargh, (Eds.). 1996. *The Psychology of Action: Linking Cognition and Motivation to Behavior*. New York: Guilford Press.

Harter, S. 1997. "The Personal Self in Social Context: Barriers to Authenticity." Pp. 81-105 in *Self and Identity: Fundamental Issues*, edited by R.D. Ashmore and L. Jussim. New York: Oxford University Press.

Higgins, E.T. 1996. "Ideals, Oughts, and Regulatory Focus: Affect and Motivation from Distinct Pains and Pleasures." Pp. 91-114 in *The Psychology of Action: Linking Cognition and Motivation to Behavior*, edited by P.M. Gollwitzer and J.A. Bargh. New York: Guilford Press.

Holland, D.C., and M.A. Eisenhart. 1990. *Educated in Romance: Women, Achievement, and College Culture*. Chicago: University of Chicago Press.

Karp, D. 1998. "Leaving Home for College: Expectations for Selective Reconstruction of Self." *Symbolic Interaction* 21: 253-276.

Kiecolt, K.J. 1994. "Stress and the Decision to Change Oneself: A Theoretical Model." *Social Psychology Quarterly* 57: 49-63.

Lerner, R.M., and N.A. Busch-Rossnagel. 1981. "Individuals as Producers of Their Development: Conceptual and Empirical Bases." Pp. 1-36 in *Individuals as Producers of Their Development: A Life-span Perspective*, edited by R.M. Lerner and N.A. Busch-Rossnagel. New York: Academic Press.

Little, B.R. 1987. "Personal Projects and Fuzzy Selves: Aspects of Self-Identity in Adolescence." Pp. 230-245 in *Self and Identity: Perspectives across the Life Span*, edited by T. Honess and K. Yardley. London: Routledge and Kegan Paul.

Lytle, L.J., L. Bakken, and C. Romig. 1997. "Adolescent Female Identity Development." *Sex Roles* 37: 175-185.

Markus, H., and P. Nurius. 1986. "Possible Selves." *American Psychologist* 41: 954-969.

McNulty, S.E., and W.B. Swann, Jr. 1991. "Psychotherapy, Self-Concept Change, and Self-Verification." Pp. 213-237 in *The Relational Self: Theoretical Convergences in Psychoanalysis and Social Psychology*. New York: Guildford Press.

Meyer, J. 1986. "The Self and the Life Course: Institutionalization and Its Effects." Pp. 242-260 in *Human Development and the Life Course: Multidisciplinary Perspectives*, edited by A.B. Sorenson, F.E. Weinert, and L.R. Sherrod. Hillsdale, NJ: Erlbaum.

Mori, D., S. Chaiken, and P. Pliner. 1987. "Eating Lightly and the Self-Presentation of Femininity." *Journal of Personality and Social Psychology* 53: 693-702.

Mortimer, J.T., M.D. Finch, and D. Kumka. 1982. "Persistence and Change in Development: The Multidimensional Self-Concept." Pp. 263-313 *in Life-Span Development and Behavior*, vol. 4, edited by P.D. Baltes and O.G. Brim, Jr. New York: Academic Press.

Owens, T.J. 1993. "Accentuate the Positive—and the Negative: Rethinking the Use of Self-Esteem, Self-Deprecation, and Self-Confidence." *Social Psychology Quarterly* 56: 288-299.

_____. 1994. "Two Dimensions of Self-Esteem: Reciprocal Effects of Positive Self-Worth and Self-Deprecation on Adolescent Problems." *American Sociological Review* 59: 391-407.

Pearlin, L.I., M.A. Lieberman, E.G. Menaghan, and J.T. Mullen. 1981. "The Stress Process." *Journal of Health and Social Behavior* 22: 337-356.

Pervin, L.A. (Ed.). 1989. *Goal Concepts in Personality and Social Psychology*. Hillsdale, NJ: Erlbaum.

Piliavin, J.A., and P.C. LePore. 1995. "Biology and Social Psychology." Pp. 9-41 in *Sociological Perspectives in Social Psychology*, edited by K.S. Cook, G.A. Fine, and J.S. House. Boston: Allyn and Bacon.

Rosenberg, M. 1979. *Conceiving the Self.* New York: Basic Books.

Ross, M. 1989. "The Relation of Implicit Theories to the Construction of Personal Histories." *Psychological Review* 96: 341-357.

Ryan, R.M., K.M. Sheldon, T. Kasser, and E.L. Deci. 1996. "All Goals Are Not Created Equal: An Organismic Perspective on the Nature of Goals and Their Regulation." Pp. 7-26 in *The Psychology of Action: Linking Cognition and Motivation to Behavior*, edited by P.M. Gollwitzer and J.A. Bargh. New York: Guilford Press.

Schwalbe, M.L., and C.L. Staples. 1991. "Gender Differences in Sources of Self-Esteem." *Social Psychology Quarterly* 54: 158-168.

Simonds, W. 1992. *Women and Self-Help Culture: Reading between the Lines*. New Brunswick, NJ: Rutgers University Press.

Strough, J, C.A. Berg, and C. Sansone. 1996. "Goals for Solving Everyday Problems across the Life Span: Age and Gender Differences in the Salience of Interpersonal Concerns." *Developmental Psychology* 32: 1106-1115.

Stryker, S. 1980. *Symbolic Interactionism: A Social Structural Version*. Menlo Park, CA: Benjamin/ Cummings Publishing Co.

Thoits, P.A. 1989. "Sociology of Emotions." *Annual Review of Sociology* 15: 317-342.

_____. 1991. "Patterns in Coping with Controllable and Uncontrollable Events." Pp. 235-258 in *Life-Span Developmental Psychology: Perspectives on Stress and Coping*, edited by E.M. Cummings, A.L. Greene, and K. Karraker. Hillsdale, NJ: Lawrence Erlbaum.

_____. 1995. "Social Support Processes: Where Are We? What Next?" *Journal of Health and Social Behavior* (extra issue): 53-79.

Turner, R.H. 1976. "The Real Self: From Institution to Impulse." *American Journal of Sociology* 81: 989-1016.

Wells, L.E., and S. Stryker. 1988. "A Stability and Change in Self over the Life Course." Pp. 192-224 in *Life Span Development and Behavior*, vol. 8, edited by P.B. Baltes, D.L. Featherman, and R.M. Lerner. Hillsdale, NJ: Lawrence Erlbaum Associates.

West, C., and D. Zimmerman. 1987. "Doing Gender." *Gender and Society* 1: 125-151.

ACCOMPLISHMENT AND DISCOURAGEMENT AT SCHOOL
AN INTERNATIONAL COMPARISON OF DEVELOPMENTAL TRENDS

John Modell

ABSTRACT

As children advance from primary to secondary school in both the United States and England, they become less rosy in their evaluations of their own excellence in mathematics and science. Their self-evaluations become more closely attuned to their actual, measured, achievement in those subjects, but also to their schoolmates' measured, and fancied, achievements. The attunement to their own and their schoolmates' achievements, however, is different: children evaluate their accomplishments higher when they are measurably higher, but they evaluated their accomplishments lower when their classmates' scores are higher.

Children in the United States are more rosy in their self-evaluations than children in England, and they are also more responsive to their own scores in their self-evaluations, by comparison with English children. English children, by contrast, are more

Advances in Life Course Research, Volume 5, pages 207-231.

prone to think less well of their own accomplishments when their classmates made excellent scores, than were American children.

These common subjective tendencies, and the differences between the two countries in the way that they are produced, conditions the way that the passage through schools serves to differentiate emerging generations.

This paper rests on secondary analysis of two recent comparative studies of educational achievement.

ACCOMPLISHMENT AND DISCOURAGEMENT

Children rarely succeed well at school when they anticipate that they will fail. Instead, they withhold the effort necessary to learn and avoid the risks of public embarrassment that are inevitable components of school-learning (Nicholls 1989; Stipek 1988). This powerful observation is no secret to teachers—in the example that follows, a teacher in an American second-grade class early in the fall term.

> Those who volunteer to display their work include some like Peter, who is robustly confident of his competence. He is more able than most at reading, writing, and speaking. He seems to know this and relishes telling his story to the class. Tim is also falling over himself to communicate his experience, but he is no Peter. He is relatively incompetent at reading and writing. For now, however, the question of his competence does not occur to him....[The teacher's] mission is to allay these fears, to help the children come to terms with the fact that everyone can't be above average, and, above all, to help keep them looking up, focused on the tasks ahead, discussing where they are going rather than their standing in the class, the state, or the nation (Nicholls and Hazzard 1993, pp. 29-30).

Thus, Kaplan, Peck, and Kaplan (1994, p. 171) conclude from a sophisticated longitudinal analysis of a large sample of American junior high students begun in 1971 that "school failure is motivated behavior. One may view school failure as an adaptation to previous self-devaluing experiences within a school context, whereby students forestall further experiences of self-rejection by withdrawing effort and questioning the validity of evaluative standards based on school achievement."

We might even say that school failure is a *career*, one often intricately integrated with the occupational career that follows school, indeed, in some ways, anticipating it (Hargreaves 1967; Mac an Ghaill 1994; Willis 1977; and in the American setting, Ogbu, 1974; and see Turner 1960). We might also say, naively, that schools ought to do everything they can, like the American second-grade teacher in the example above, to help students avoid discouragement. Or, from a more critical stance, we might ask wherein schoolchildren's discouragement at school may function to maintain a system of societal inequality in which schools participate.

Turner (1960) provided the classic ideal-typicalization of the differences ?tween United States and English formal education, 40 years ago when the dif- ?rences were more clear-cut than now, before England's schools "American- ?ed" considerably in several well-publicized steps. In the United States, Turner ?gued, a constantly ongoing "contest" determined which children would in the ?d be considered educational winners and which losers, with minimal institu- ?nal formalization of stages of the contest, in order that (in conjunction with .merican ideology about equality of opportunity) last week's losers be kept moti- ?ted in order that they may become this week's winners. By contrast, English ?hools exemplified the "sponsorship" inherent in a highly class-stratified, hierar- ?ical society, in which some inherent quality like "excellence" was supposed to ?vealed definitively and at a rather early point by evaluation processes at school, ?ter which schools were so organized as to discourage efforts to seek enhanced ?hievement, so that the now-motivated excellent be free to pursue their excel- ?nce with minimal distraction by competition with their revealed inferiors—a ?stem, one might add, quite congruent with the thoroughgoing commitment of ?nglish primary and middle schools to "social promotion."

The life course implications of even so basic a distinction have been challenged ? recent years by Kerckhoff (1990), who has shown that even when English men ?ave left formal education early and without positive distinction, they have ?ecome quite adept at bettering their occupational careers by attending skills-ori- ?nted adult education courses—often at night, while holding down a day job— ?d in this setting substantially modifying the career trajectory that the classic ?urner—or Willis—formulation would have predicted for them. More recently ?t, Kerckhoff (1993) has shown that somewhat analogous adult courses have ?egun to play a role in American working-class career formation, too. But if ?nglish and American schools have become less different, they are different nev- ?theless in the way that distinction and academic accomplishment are related in ?e years of middle childhood.

The organization of formal education presumes it to be desirable that children's ?nse of competence be linked at least to some degree to conventionally-defined ?hievements in the sphere in question, so that children may gain a sense of what ?spects of academic skill need to be improved (Michaels 1977; Terwilliger 1977). ?chools serve, even when benevolently, even when organized in terms of an ?ngoing "contest," to assort and certify children, and this process rests upon chil- ?en discovering and honing their own particular strengths and interests, and ?ing so in relation to the formal evaluations with which they are presented by the ?stitution in which they find themselves. In order to convey an ongoing account ?f current levels of academic achievement, specific to particular subjects, Ameri- ?n schools in the early grades and increasingly frequently thereafter provide chil- ?en weekly or even more often with marks on their homework and in-class tests, ?d with report-card grades of which an ideal is usually said to be an objective ?count of achievement to date, in which teacher's hopes and fears for children

are meant, at most, to be presented as separate characteristics (MacIver 199
Stiggins, Frisbie, and Griswold 1989). And from a very early age, schoolchildr
are aware of others' grades, as of others' evaluations by teachers, and they are r
shy to amplify these distinctions (Blumenfeld, Pintrich, Meece, and Wess
1982; Entwisle, Alexander, Pallas, and Cadigan 1987; Marsh 1990). If Engli
schools at one time were less filled with frequent examinations than were Ame
can schools, even their reflected evaluations of teacher's assessments of childr
has long been a centerpiece of what, for children, goes on in school (Cullingfo
1991; Pollard 1996). And in the matter of testing, English state schools have be
converging on the American model here as in other realms, the most recent co
tribution to convergence in the role of classroom examination being produced
the onset of the National Curriculum in the present decade.

Children learn from teachers and textbooks that they should be able to do t
work they are given, and to do it in so many minutes, and with an acceptat
degree of effort, and they should score at a certain level on classroom tests; a
parents and others out of school look both at children's scores and at their stru
gles to learn (to derive a sense of how good they are at subjects), interveni
intentionally or incidentally as they do so. But this is not all: as Nicholls, and o
ers, argue, one of the big things that goes on between the ages being examin
here that may mediate the connection between self-concept and test scores
social comparison. "In the class as a whole, since only one child can be 'best'
any given activity, all others experience some loss of prestige. And children
not spare each other's feelings—it is crystal clear who is chosen last to play or
eat lunch with (Entwisle and Alexander 1989, p. 32).

Children's academic self-concepts unfold developmentally, resting as they d
upon schools' increasingly intensive efforts to rate students and to convey the
ratings and their bases to the students, but, also, upon children's increasing cogi
tive capacity for social comparison. Such a capacity may begin to show up
early as the third year, but flourishes more fully only as children grow up.
Nicholls' (1989) formulation, American children at about seven years of a
begin to evaluate the difficulty of tasks according to how well peers perfor
them, and loosely to associate innate ability with their accomplishment; whi
children at about 11 entirely distinguish effort from ability so that only the ea
with which tasks are accomplished, relative to peers, marks the "smart" child.
rather touching recent English study, thus, found that the two thirds to three qua
ters of 7-year-old children who said that they were "better than others" in ma
had dropped by age 11 to 23 percent in mathematics and 49 percent in readin
Between the same ages, the group scoring the highest on the relevant standardiz
test shifted from those who rated themselves "the same" as others to that no
small fraction who asserted their superiority (Blatchford 1992).

Although social comparison is a universal aspect of the formation of self-co
cept, the way children evaluate themselves in academic terms is surely variab
across cultures, depending, for instance, upon the theories of learning underpinni

the organization of school-learning (Stevenson and Stigler 1992), and upon the extent to which they understand academic excellence to be distinct from moral excellence [Goldenberg and Gallimore 1996). The formation of self-concept is also quite contingent upon various organizational features of the situation in which a child finds him- or herself, including teachers' pedagogies, the processes by which schools allocate children to different instructional settings, and the way both teachers and schools evaluate and remark children's evolving academic skills (Eccles 1993; Rosenbaum 1976). And it may also be contingent upon the actual and expressed competence of his or her peers, if children are inspired, or overawed, by what their peers do or say.

DATA AND METHODS

How peers affect children's academic self-concept, seen developmentally and comparatively across two societies, is the focus of the present paper. The paper will proceed from an examination of American and English (and Welsh) schoolchildren's expressed estimate of their excellence in two key school subjects, in the relationship of their self-concept in these subjects to children's measured achievement, in its relationship of this connection to the peer setting in which the students find themselves. The school subjects examined are mathematics and science—I will treat them not so much in their distinctiveness from one another as in their tendency to show like patterns—as measured in two different 1990s international comparative studies. I will first examine developmental trends and differences in levels between England and the United States, finally asking whether there are any observable national differences in developmental patterns. In like fashion, I will then investigate ways in which children's school milieu may have affected their academic self-concept, in the way that this develops, and in differences between England and the United States in these regards. Commonalties in patterns between the countries will, hypothetically, begin to propose developmental regularities; differences will point us, speculatively, to differences in the educational establishments of the two countries that might make growing up in the two societies different. To keep the argument clear, my account will be decidedly spare, not distinguishing, for example, even between girls and boys.

I have earlier analyzed an international comparative study of children's school achievement (the International Assessment of Educational Progress—the IAEP—to be described shortly) with some attention to average favorability of academic self-concept in nine societies, including England and the United States (Modell 1993). I found that children in three societies whose typical standardized test scores were notably higher than those in both England an in the United States nevertheless expressed less positive academic self-concepts: this was so in France, Hungary, and Korea. But there was no simple inverse relationship of average scholarship and average self-concept, for Quebec's students were both very successful on the standardized tests and extremely self-confident in their expression of their individual excellence. There was also no clear match of closeness of individual-level self-concept and own test scores to either mean test score or mean self-concept. Each of these three dimensions is distinct from the other two, with a variety of society-level determinants that even the present close-up study of just two societies can only begin to hint at. Even in two societies as alike as England and the United States, the course of children through school to adulthood—and the normative and emotional promptings that carry them along these courses—differs subtly but significantly.

The data I present in this paper rests on two early-1990s nationally-representative international comparative tests of school achievement, the IAEP, and the Third International Study of Math and Science, the TIMSS. The IAEP was conducted in 1991, collecting data on samples of 9-year-olds and 13-year olds from 94 primary schools in England and 117 primary schools in the United States, and 90 middle schools in England and 109 middle schools in the United States. A total of 2,137 primary-school children and 1,819 middle-school children were sampled in England, with about half of those in each school being tested about mathematics, and the other half in science. The corresponding numbers of sampled children in the United States was 2,953 and 2,811. TIMMS, conducted in 1995, sampled whole classrooms from the pair of grades in which the most 9-year-old and 13-year-old English children were enrolled, and the pair of grades in which the most 9-year-old and 13-year-old English children were enrolled. In England, 134 primary schools and 127 middle schools were involved, totaling 6,182 and 3,579 children, each of whom was tested and questioned about *both* mathematics and science. American children, treated the same way, numbered 11,115 in 189 primary schools and 10,973 in 183 middle schools.[1]

The academic self-concept questions as administered by IAEP and by TIMSS, too, differ in a way of which we will wish to be aware. The IAEP testees were posed one of two items, according to whether they had been administered the math test or the science test: "I am good at mathematics," or "I am good in science." The primary-school children could choose among three answers: "Agree," "Undecided," or "Disagree," while middle-school children had their choices enriched by "Strongly agree" and "Strongly disagree."[2] The children who responded to TIMSS answered both a mathematics test and a science test, and were posed both propositions: "I usually do well in mathematics" and "I usually do well in science." They had a four-answer array to choose from: "Strongly agree," "Agree," "Disagree," and "Strongly disagree." For our purposes, I don't believe that the scoring difference matters at all. But the questions have a real difference in their face meaning: while TIMSS children were asked only to assess their typical degree of *success at school*, the phrasing of the IAEP essentialized the dimension: there was (literally) some kind of *inherent* goodness-in-math (or science) claimed by those students who assented to the question posed to them.

SOME BASES OF POSITIVE CONCEPTS OF CHILDREN'S ACADEMIC SELVES

For the moment, let us examine overall age trends in the academic self-concept variable, comparing children in primary school to children in middle school, and England to the United States. For their substantive relevance, Table 1 also presents the scores of the standardized tests in math and science that the children took, and that were the fundamental raison d'etre of the IAEP and TIMSS studies.

I have added boldface to Table 1 to draw attention to the "better" score for both the self-concept item and for the test score. (Self-concept scores that are better are lower, because the coding proceeded upward from agreement with the positively-phrased sentence offered them for their assent, toward rejection of that happy assertion.) What is clear is that, on average, it is the American children who more than the English children say that they think well of themselves in math and in science, very much so in primary school and rather much so in secondary school. Expressed confidence in math excellence surely declines developmentally in both cultures, while confidence in science seems to grow in England, while declining in the United States.

The superior American show of confidence was accomplished despite the fact that English scores—certainly in math, certainly in the older age-group—on the whole exceed those of the American children, if only slightly. There is no consistent sign of society-to-society difference in the amount of variance in the self-concept variable, nor in the test variable. American children on the average, regardless of age or subject, say and not improbably feel that their (objectively modest) achievements point to their "doing" better or "being" better in mathematics and in science than English children. (The objective modesty of American children's achievements, of course, rests on comparisons that tests like the IAEP and TIMSS are designed to make, and to which children are not likely to be privy.)

Table 1. Mean Values of Subject-Based Academic Self-concept in Math and in Science, in Primary and Middle School, for English and American Schoolchildren, IAEP and TIMSS tests

	IAEP				TIMSS			
	Self Concept		Test Score		Self Concept		Test Score	
	England	U.S.	England	U.S.	England	U.S.	England	U.S.
Math, primary school	1.64	**1.37**	**13.5**	10.5	1.77	**1.64**	15.9	**18.1**
Math, middle school	1.66	**1.52**	**16.7**	9.9	1.82	**1.80**	**20.4**	20.2
Science, primary school	1.71	**1.55**	15.8	**17.0**	1.99	**1.71**	18.3	**19.0**
Science, middle school	1.58	**1.51**	**26.7**	25.4	1.90	**1.81**	**22.1**	21.4

Table 2. Simple Correlations between Academic Self-Concept
and Score on Corresponding Standardized Test

	IAEP		TIMSS	
	England	*U.S.*	*England*	*U.S.*
Math, primary school	.173***	.243***	.064***	.165***
Math, middle school	.225***	.355***	.208***	.313***
Science, primary school	.122**	.226***	.023*	.139***
Science, middle school	.248***	.287***	.199***	.270***

Notes: *p <.05, **p <.01, ***p <.001.

An easy hypothesis to explain the interesting national disjunction of objective achievement and subjective evaluation would propose that American children are less "realistic" than English children, and that, consequently, the child-to-child correlation between achievement (as indexed by test score) and academic self-concept ought to be higher in England than in the United States. But the opposite is the case, as detailed in Table 2, which offers the simple Pearsonian correlations between children's claimed academic self-concepts and the scores that they have achieved on the corresponding IAEP or TIMSS test.

In *every* instance, the American children's self-estimations more closely track those of their standardized-test scores than do the English children's. In each case, too, there is a quite pronounced developmental intensification of the relationship: children are probably becoming more decided in their academic self-concepts, clearer about them from term to term; and they are probably basing their self-concepts on increasingly clear accounts of how well they ordinarily do when tested on the subject in question, as teachers both test them more specifically and communicate their results more unequivocally. Felson and Reed (1986b) report exactly this kind of a tightening-up of the connection between school grades and test scores (but with one anomaly) and children's academic self-concept, and, they believe, for essentially the same reason.

Indeed, many aspects of children's school lives (as measured by these studies and others like them) come together between primary school and middle school, as an important aspect of children's development—this is a central point in a larger study that I am currently carrying out.[3] But this crystallization is not a false sense of growing coherence based on the heedlessness with which younger children answer the questionnaires, in comparison to their elders. Thus, the correlation (on TIMSS, where children took both math and science tests) between self-concept in math and in science heightened from .338 to .426 in England and from .322 to .410 in the United States, notably less dramatic than the developmental increases in correlation of self-concept and score reflected in Table 2.

(There is also an interesting "study effect": the IAEP has considerably stronger correlations than does TIMSS among the primary-school students, but only slightly stronger correlations among the middle-school students. Here, the exact wording of the self-concept questions perhaps deserves notice: the IAEP children were asked whether they *are* good in the subject in question, while the TIMSS children were asked whether they *do* well in the subject in question. Younger children are considerably less likely than older ones to be closely attuned to the school's grading ("do well"); but many of them perhaps already have quite well-formed senses—presumably based on something other than a precise account of grades—of how good they "are" in given subjects.)

A closely related way of representing the way test-score achievement and academic self-concept are connected is to look at the modeled estimate of how many points in academic self-concept are gained per added point in test score: that is, to look at the metric coefficient of the linear regression model that best explains self-concept. Because the IAEP and TIMSS self-concept scores have different numbers of categories, as do their standardized test scores[4], we cannot compare the metric coefficients across tests. But they serve very well to offer meaningful comparisons of the impact upon self-concept of different values within given tests, to which my analysis will shortly turn. Table 3, in any case, offers metric regression coefficients derived from the same relationships that yielded the Pearsonian correlation coefficients shown in Table 2.

The absolute values of these numbers are small because there are few steps in the self-concept scales and relatively many in the standardized-test scores, and, of course, because the proportion of the self-concept explained by the test score alone is relatively low (only 12.5% in the case of the strongest relationship in the table, that of American middle-school children's score on the math test to those children's self-concept as mathematicians on the TIMSS test.) For this reason, in subsequent tables I will present the coefficients for the standardized tests multiplied by one hundred, denoting, thus, how many 1/100th steps higher in self-concept one will be if one's test score is one point above the average.

Table 3. Metric Coefficients of Academic Self-Concept on Own Score on Corresponding Standardized Test

	IAEP		TIMSS	
	England	U.S.	England	U.S.
Math, primary school	.173***	.243***	.064***	.165***
Math, middle school	.225***	.355***	.208***	.313***
Science, primary school	.122**	.226***	.023*	.139***
Science, middle school	.248***	.287***	.199***	.270***

Notes: *p < .05, **p < .01, ***p < .001.

As presented, we see that the added self-confidence supplied to American children by getting a better test-score grade (that is, associated with having to perform in this way on this particular test at this particular moment) varied a bit, but might be said roughly to be "twice" that gained by English children, on average, the differences being somewhat more pronounced in science than in math on the primary-school level and the other way around at the middle-school level. The findings differ in slight detail from IAEP to TIMSS, but are substantially congruent. We must entertain the possibility here that English children's knowledge of their academic achievement and their understanding of the relevance of that achievement to self-concept doesn't differ from American children's knowledge and belief, but that, instead, some characteristic of English schools weakens this connection, relative to American children's schools.

THE "BIG FISH, SMALL POND" EFFECT

Children calibrate their performances by those of their classmates. Herbert Marsh has analyzed what he calls the "big fish, small pond" effect in a number of data sets in Australia and the United States, including children at several different levels in school, seeking to perfect a model of the process by which schoolchildren develop and maintain academic self-concepts, although he has shown little interest in the *developmental* process by which it emerges (as distinct from the chronological process, which does interest him). Marsh finds, quite generally, that children among high-scoring classmates don't evaluate their academic abilities or accomplishments as favorably as they might if their classmates weren't so good at academic subjects. Equally, of course, children doing better work than the poor showing that most of their classmates accomplish would consider themselves quite good students. Among American high school students, Marsh showed, "equally able students attending higher-ability high schools were likely to select less demanding coursework and to have lower academic self-concepts, lower GPAs, lower educational aspirations, and lower occupational aspirations, in both their sophomore and senior years of high school (Marsh 1991, p. 470; and see Alwin and Otto 1977). And these disadvantages continued to cumulate, affecting even (if only slightly) college attendance. Marsh, who alone among mainstream educationists seems intrigued by the "small pond" effect, has also elaborated a similarly reasoned critique of gifted-and-talented programs, for these can be shown (here, in Australian primary-school data) to have depressed their participants' academic self-concept, relative to that of children of equally high measured achievement who attended regular classes (Marsh, Chessor, Craven, and Roche 1995). To Marsh, that this highly perverse finding should emerge in a program that seeks as a matter of policy to segregate academically gifted children in order to enhance their learning is relevant perhaps to all versions of homogeneous instructional grouping. And it may, more profoundly, be only an ironic exacerbation of a more general paradox of formal schooling, as contrasted to modes of instruction—like apprenticeship—that are tied to particular, immediate applications rather than to general remote ones mediated by schools' certification of "human capital investment."

If the "small pond" effect were far stronger in primary school than in middle school, it could explain why primary-school children's academic self-concepts are less well articulated to their test scores: younger children look around at their classmates, and, in effect, get distracted from how well they actually perform in academic subjects. Marsh (1987, p. 282) predicts just this, for "in elementary schools, these young students may have no standard of comparison except for the performance of their classmates and may not even know how the average ability level of their classmates compares with a broader frame of reference." Marsh goes on explicitly to propose testing this hypothesis, but, so far as I have seen, has not yet done so[5]. We shall shortly examine this hypothesis in our data.

Differences in the strength of the "small pond" effect in England and the United States, likewise, might explain in part why children's scores and self-concepts are less firmly linked in England than they in the United States. We will shortly test for the possibility that the "small pond" effect is one such difference.

Table 4 presents metric regression coefficients of academic self-concept, in math and in science, for primary- and middle-school children, in England and in the United States, that include among explanatory variables not only children's *own* score on the relevant test, but also that of all their other tested classmates or schoolmates[6]. We are interested here in the *direction* of the relationship, which we anticipate will run contrariwise to the individual effect, so that children who achieved a given standardized-test score in less academically good schools have higher self-concept, and vice versa, and in the *magnitude* of the effect, relative both to the individual-level effect and between societies (at the same level of school on the same study). The coefficient reflects the number of hundredths of a point improvement of subject-specific academic self-concept, on average, an individual (at the mean) might have if his or her own test score in that subject were raised by one point, or if his or her class- or schoolmates' average score were raised by one point, net of one another.

The findings are very striking indeed. Even as children become more attuned to their own (measured) subject-specific achievement in evaluating themselves, they simultaneously become more attuned to their peers' achievements: developmentally, school becomes a more sharply demarked place of awaress of the academic, and this has cross-cutting effects on individuals. The "small pond" effect works more vigorously upon the middle-school children, in both societies, awareness of peers' achievements apparently enlarging right along with awareness of one's own achievements. In contrast to the findings when only the individual-level connection between scores and self-concept are being considered, it is in England rather than in the United States that peer scores are highly influential. The

Table 4.   Metric Coefficients (x 100) of Academic Self-Concept on
Own Score and Peers' Average Score on
Corresponding Standardized Test

		IAEP		TIMSS	
		England	*U.S.*	*England*	*U.S.*
Math, primary school	Own	0.70***	0.70***	0.76***	1.38***
	Peers	−0.50**	−0.21*	−2.06***	−1.06***
Math, middle school	Own	1.02***	1.43***	1.70***	2.67***
	Peers	−0.64***	−0.95***	−1.90***	−1.33***
Science, primary school	Own	0.57***	0.94***	0.29**	1.11***
	Peers	−0.42	−0.10	−0.87**	−0.47**
Science, middle school	Own	1.06***	1.29***	1.71***	2.12***
	Peers	−0.68**	−0.21	−2.20***	−0.67***

Notes: *p <.05, **p <.01, ***p <.001.

developmental strengthening of the peer effect, however, is roughly equally strong in England and the United States.

Overall, the impact of each individual's own score on his self-concept is strengthened, relative to that found in Table 3. For instance, in Table 3 a one-point-higher math score on the primary-school IAEP test for English children was associated, overall, with an 0.0052 point more positive self-concept as a math student, somewhat less than the 0.0066 point "gain" in math self-concept for the American children at the same school level. But when we examine Table 4, where the average math score of the child's tested classmates is taken into simultaneous consideration, the English children who score a point higher in math have an 0.0070 point gain in self-concept (0.70 *hundredths* of a point gain), and this means that the gain in math self-concept from individual score improvement was now just about the same as that for the American primary-school children, when their peers' scores were taken into consideration. But, although taking the "small pond" effect into consideration in this fashion moves English children's own score closer to American children's in its contribution to academic self-concept, it does not efface all the national difference.

The impact of own achievements upon American children's academic self-concept, like upon that of the English children, had, then, been to a degree masked by the "small pond" effect. But that masking was a good deal stronger among the English children. In both societies—and to fairly well the same extent—children with higher test scores tended to go to school where other children also tested high.[7] And so, on average, children who scored well and therefore tended to view their own math abilities positively, also had classmates whose tested abilities, in effect, awed them enough that they backed down to a degree from their positive self-evaluation. The awe relative to the individual self-calibration was considerably stronger in England than in the United States, even though the correlation of individual scores to classmates' scores was no stronger in England than in the United States. This pattern is quite robust: in every instance, comparison of Table 4 with Table 3 indicates that taking peer scores into consideration increased the measured relevance of English children's individual scores to their academic self-concept more than it did for the comparable American children.

Despite this systematic difference in the impact of peer context on children's self-concept, American children continued to show stronger connections between how well they scored on the test, and how positively they rated themselves as mathematicians or scientists. At the same time, there was a corresponding quite-general stronger impact of UK children's peers' scores on their own stated self-evaluations, often a great deal stronger than in the United States.[8] Peer-average scores, of course, were not so variable as were individual scores, but it is nevertheless striking that a point difference in peers' scores sometimes had more measured impact on English children's academic self-concept than did a one-point difference in their own scores—and, of course, in the opposite direction. This means that, for instance, an English primary-school child (taking TIMSS) who, like his school peers, scored a point higher than the English average on the math test probably would have a somewhat *lower* estimation of how well he or she did in math than did the average English child. But the American child who did just the same—a bit better than the national average but no better than his or her schoolmates, would generally have a somewhat *more favorable* self-concept.[9]

DIFFERENCES BETWEEN ENGLISH AND AMERICAN SCHOOLS

So strong are some of the English peer scores in their negative relationship to academic self-concept (negative *overall* in TIMSS, although not in IAEP) that one has to suspect that the "small pond" effect is not *all* that is going on. Indeed, as the top line in each section of Table 5 will show, *on a school-to-school level*, for the most part English schools where children, on average, score higher in the TIMSS study, have pupils who on average expresses a *less favorable* academic self-concepts. It is as though children not only were comparing their own performances unfavorably with those of their nearby peers in these higher-scoring schools and rating their own performance down on account of the size of the pond they saw about them, but also as though the English schools where children score well somehow encourage their charges to be modest in evaluating their accomplishments. This pattern, clear in TIMSS, however, is present in only one of the four cases in IAEP, and this one case is not statistically significant.[10]

JOHN MODELL

Table 5. *School-level* Correlations (Student-Weighted) of
Mean Academic Self-Concept and Mean Test Score, and
Partial Correlation of Mean Academic Self-Concept to
Mean Test Score and Mean Books in Students' Homes

	IAEP		TIMSS	
	England	U.S.	England	U.S.
Primary				
Mean math score, simple	.27	.32*	−.38***	.14
Mean math score, partial	.09	.30*	−.18*	.12
Books/home mean score, partial	.11	−.09	−.25**	−.01
Middle				
Mean math score, simple	.63**	.16	−.11	.41***
Mean math score, partial	.65**	.29*	.12	.13
Books/home mean score, partial	−.35	−.24	−.27**	.20**
Primary				
Mean science score, simple	−.33	.36*	−.07	.19*
Mean science score, partial	−.26	.03	.10	−.16*
Books/home mean score, partial	.01	.31*	−.20*	.39***
Middle				
Mean science score, simple	.13	.32*	−.17	.26***
Mean science score, partial	−.44*	.31*	.17	.12
Books/home mean score, partial	.59**	−.10	−.35***	.06

Notes: *p <.05, **p <.01, ***p <.001.

The *simple* correlations in Table 5 show wherein English schools do not bear
the generally substantial tendency for positive covariation on the school-to-school
level that one would expect from the individual-level correlation of higher scores
with more favorable self-concept—certainly in comparison with the American
schools. But it is in the bottom two lines that the particularly interesting findings
appear: these show the *partial* correlation coefficients that emerge when we
examine school-average self-concept simultaneously with school-average test
scores and school-average numbers of books in the home as estimated by students, who were presented with a small set of ordinal categories. Books in the
home is an indirect indicator of family socioeconomic status, commonly used in
international surveys of schoolchildren, obviously a very imperfect measure but
reflecting something open to ready observation by child respondents and asked
about without much likelihood of causing offense. Commonly (again, in TIMSS,
but not in IAEP) English schools look more like American ones in the connection
there between high scores and favorable self-concepts, when the socioeconomic
level of the school is taken statistically into account. And when we look at the bottom line (in TIMSS) we see that English children in higher-socioeconomic status
schools may even undergo some instruction or socialization that leads them to be
especially modest about their sense of "doing well" in academic subjects, even

when they in fact do well—and this explains in part why English children in high-achieving schools seem so modest in assigning to themselves an academic self-concept.

This by no means explains away the whole "small pond" effect in England, even in TIMSS; and the rather contrariwise findings in IAEP do not lead us to great security about what TIMSS suggests. I include the whole matter because it reminds us to be quite cautious about verbalizations of such complex inner states as academic self-concept: some part of what we observe may be rules, connected perhaps with social class, perhaps with being well-integrated into the school milieu, perhaps about making public (even to a stranger on a paper-and-pencil test) one's sense of excellence, or deficiency, in school subjects. Whatever the process, it happens in England far more vigorously than in the United States, although in both countries it seems to lack a developmental component.

There are two different ways in which the higher socioeconomic level characteristic of some English schools might end up weakening student claims of academic self-concept relative to those of students in schools whose clientele on aveage came from a lower socioeconomic level. The schools where children in attendance had more bookish parents might simply have had lower average claims of "doing well" in academic subjects, while as in other schools the higher-achieving children there felt they "did better" than those who had had lower scores. Or, on the other hand, schools attended by children who had parents of higher socioeconomic status might have differed from other schools in that children there who had higher academic achievement did *not* say that they "did better" in the subject in question than less-accomplished children there.

TIMSS has a large enough sample within schools, and enough schools, that we can get some empirical purchase on this question: we examine (in the spirit but not employing the full technique of hierarchical linear modeling) the slopes and intercepts *within* each school (with adequate numbers of children) of academic self-concept on measured achievement. The findings are striking. In TIMSS, English children attending socioeconomically favored schools, at both the primary-school and at the middle-school level, had higher intercepts of within-school correlations of children's math and science self-concepts and their corresponding test scores. This is not surprising: it means that children who attended English schools where pupils were socioeconomically favored had, thereby, somewhat more favorable views of themselves "at" mathematics and science. But, surprisingly, the English children also had different (expressed) relations of academic self-concept to test score according to the socioeconomic level of the school! Children from more socioeconomically favored schools were more likely to evaluate themselves up or down on the basis of their own objective academic achievement than were children from less favored schools. That is, higher-status English (but not American) schools suppressed objectively unwarranted favorable or unfavorable self-concepts, but not warranted ones. Both primary-school children and middle-school children in England reflected these surprising patterns. They were statistically significant, and highly intriguing for those interested in the ways that social class and the day-to-day operations of teaching and learning go on.[11]

PEER CONTEXT: ASSERTION OR PERFORMANCE

From what I have so far presented, the mechanism by which children's self-deprecatory comparisons occur have not been specified: children might evaluate themselves *directly,* for instance less favorably than otherwise because they are actually aware of how good other children's performances are, and evaluate their own achievement relative to some sense of a distribution of their several peers' achievements; or they might evaluate themselves *indirectly,* gauging their own performances by the general sense that their classmates give out about how good or bad they are as students in the subject at hand—for as we have seen, self-concept and achievement *are* positively related. And as Felson and Reed (1986a, p. 104) hypothesized, "comparison effects and normative effects may suppress each other. The performance of the reference group is likely to have a negative effect on an individual's self-appraisals while the self-appraisals of the reference group members, which correlate positively with their performances, are likely to have a positive effect."

So we must ask whether children compare themselves to their classmates' *achievements* or, instead (or, in addition) to their *expressed views* of themselves. The critical question for us is whether (and to what extent) the negative impact of peers' mean test scores upon individuals' academic self-concept is lessened or heightened when peers' self-concepts are included in the regression, whether classmates' expressed confidence (merited or not) affects children's understandings of those classmates' academic excellence. If the coefficients on peer scores are weakened when we add in peer self-concept, this means that at least part of the "small pond" effect works through the big talk of peers. If, on the other hand, the coefficients on peer scores are enhanced, this means that children are actually emboldened by the claims of their peers, to some extent overcoming a pronounced tendency toward modest self-appraisal in the face of academically-excellent peers.

The answer as given in Table 6 is unequivocal: the impact of big talk on peers' self-concept is positive. Where peers cheer themselves readily, so also they cheer one another. This is so in primary and in middle school, and in England and the United States. Quite commonly, these relationships are statistically highly significant. (Unlike the test-score coefficients, which are multiplied by 100, the peer image coefficients are unitary: the IAEP entry for primary-school English children says that for each one scale step higher their peers scored, children on average rated themselves 0.36 scale steps higher, net of their own measured

Table 6.   Metric Coefficients of Academic Self-Concept on Own Score, Peers' Average Score, and Peers' Average Academic Self-Concept on Corresponding Standardized Test

	IAEP		TIMSS	
	England	*U.S.*	*England*	*U.S.*
Math, primary school				
Own score	.71***	.71***	.77***	1.38***
Peer score	−.58***	−.30*	−1.77**	−1.20***
Peer self-concept	.36***	.16	.24***	.36***
Math, middle school				
Own score	1.04***	1.43***	1.72***	2.69***
Peer score	−.84***	−.99***	−1.85***	−2.25***
Peer self-concept	.48***	.08***	.36***	.68***
Science, primary school				
Own score	.59***	.94***	.30**	1.10***
Peer score	−.50***	−.23***	−.59***	−.88***
Peer self-concept	.31***	.16***	.52***	.58***
Science, middle school				
Own score	1.08	1.29***	1.75***	2.14***
Peer score	−.82***	−.74**	−1.99***	−1.71***
Peer self-concept	.35***	.49***	.50***	.73***

Notes: *p < .05, **p < .01, ***p < .001.

achievement and that of their peers.) So, children (say they) value themselves most when their schoolmates do, too.

The impact of the peer self-concept score was slightly more prominent in the United States than in England—somewhat like the impact of own scores, then, and somewhat unlike their peers' scores. Just as the English children's "small pond" effect seems to be made the more potent in its expression by some kind of a cultural preference for modesty or modest self-expression—a preference complexly related to social class—so the American's children "small pond" effect is mitigated by a common bravado, presumably spontaneously appearing.

Neither in England nor in the United States does adding the peers' self-concept score have any impact on the measured relationship of children's own test score to their self-concept (as a comparison of Table 6 with Table 4 will reveal). But it does have an effect on the negative relationship of the peers' test score to children's self concept...but in the United States only. Here, adding the peer self-concept often *sharpens* the way peers' measured achievement affects self-concept. The impact of peer self-concepts on children's expressed view of their own excellence in these academic subjects more often than not strengthened between

Table 7.   Percentage of Variance in Individual Academic Self-Concept
Explained by Own Standardized Score, and
Percentage Added by Including Average Peer Test Score
and by Including Average Peer Self-Concept

	IAEP		TIMSS	
	England	U.S.	England	U.S.
Math, primary school				
Individual	3.0	5.9	0.4	2.7
Add per score	0.8	0.2	1.2	0.4
Add peer self-concept	2.0	0.3	0.2	0.5
Math, middle school				
Individual	5.1	12.6	2.4	0.7
Add per score	1.4	0.1	2.4	2.4
Add peer self-concept	3.9	5.1	0.7	1.9
Science, primary school				
Individual	1.5	5.1	0.1	1.9
Add per score	0.3	0.0	0.2	0.1
Add peer self-concept	1.5	0.3	1.4	1.6
Science, middle school				
Individual	6.1	8.3	4.0	7.3
Add per score	1.2	0.1	2.5	0.2
Add peer self-concept	1.5	3.2	1.7	3.9

Notes: $^*p < .05,$ $^{**}p < .01,$ $^{***}p < .001.$

primary school and middle school—but not to the extent that the impact of both
children's own scores and those of their peers affected it. Children, it would seem,
became more sensitive as they grew up to how well their peers thought of themselves as students, and calibrated their own expressions of self-confidence accordingly, but this was not as true as for their own awareness of their own achievement
(positive) and that of their peers (negative).

The final table (Table 7) that I will present allows one a simple and intuitive
sense of how much difference this all makes. The first line, for each panel, presents the percentage of the all child-to-child variance in self-concept that is
explained by children's own achievement. The second line is the *added* variance
explained when one includes school-peers' average standardized-test scores in the
regression. Rarely does the proportion of variance added by this move approach
that already explained by the individual's own test score; but when it does, it is in
England, not in the United States. The "small pond" matters far more there, that
is. And when, in the last line of each section of the table, we examine the added

variance explained by including peers' expressed academic self-image in the model, we see a complex story where subject matters a great deal. Here, what we can say is that self-concept of peers matters more in science than it does in mathematics, and that, in science, peers' self-concept on the whole matters considerably more to the explanation of own self-concept than does average peer performance on the test itself[12].

SUMMARY AND INTERPRETATION

We may usefully review our findings concisely. We have found that several of our key phenomena progressed *developmentally*, strengthening between primary and middle school.

- Children came to view themselves as somewhat less excellent mathematicians as they passed from primary to middle school, but this pattern was not present for science—for the latter subject was quite vague in the minds of the younger children, and became more readily recognized by middle school.
- Children's subject-specific self-concepts became more closely attuned to their own test scores. Although children's peers' scores more readily affected their expressed self-concepts in middle school than in primary school test score influence on self-concept increased even when peers' average test scores are controlled, and even when both peers' average test scores and their expressed self-concepts are controlled.
- Children's subject-specific academic self-concepts became more closely articulated to peers' average test scores as children passed from primary to middle school, when their own test scores are controlled, and also when their own scores and their peers' self-concept are controlled.
- Children's subject-specific academic self-concepts became somewhat more closely articulated to peers' self-concepts as children passed from primary to middle school, when their own test scores are controlled, and also when their own scores and their peers' average test scores are controlled.

That is, academic self-concept emerges between primary and middle school in both of these societies as an entity that is distinctly more articulated to what is going on in school—not only how the child him- or herself is faring at the academic subjects in question, but how the child's peers are faring, and how they see themselves faring. There is, that is, a complex academic climate at the school that includes not only each child's success at carrying out the academic tasks assigned to him or her, but also how the school's overall academic success rates in comparison to national averages, and the tenor with which the scholars view these performances.

These patterns, in general, were present in both England and in the United States. There were, in addition, telling differences in emphasis between the two societies.

- American children expressed more favorable self-concepts.
- The correlation between self-concept and standardized test score was stronger in the United States than in England. This extended to the school level: schools in which the average test score was high had, on average, higher expressed self-concepts in the United States; but this was not always true in England.
- But the negative correlation between children's self-concept and the measured achievement of their peers was stronger in England than in the United States. When pupils' average socioeconomic level is controlled for, average self-concept in English but not in American schools became less a product of the "small pond" effect.
- Many of the developmental phenomena were more markedly present in the United States than in England, but mainly in mathematics, and not in science. The characteristic English pattern of more prominent "small pond" effects, on the other hand, suggests that this pattern is one that *develops* more prominently there, too, regardless of subject.

Let us recall the argument for why the "small pond" effect is said to matter, and is presumed to be unfortunate: this point of view recalls the developmental tendency for children to abandon the kind of pride and related courage to continue with emotionally risky engagements with learning tough academic subjects that could be derived from comparing oneself today with oneself yesterday, and discerning growing mastery. Rather, children increasingly tend to compare themselves to external standards—whether these external yardsticks be teachers' often conventionalized sense of what children ought to be doing at a given age or grade, or parents' sometimes sentiment-laden hopes, dreams, and fears, or (our subject here) what other children similarly situated are visibly accomplishing. Since mediocrity is statistically the median level of measured achievement, but since universal achievement is the declared goal of most schools in contemporary democratic societies, it is not surprising that children's growing awareness of the world around them is met with contradictory responses—a growing tension within their development between different standards that they are tempted to apply to understand where they stand in the major life-course enterprise that is formal education.

We cannot study most of these standards directly here, but we do see three— own achievement, peers' achievement, and peers' self-concept—and we see that individual self-concept becomes increasingly connected with *each* of these as children grow up. One would anticipate a growing tension around the issue of academic self-concept—and, indeed, this fits with the life-course perspective, since children's orientation to school (be it favorable or hostile) becomes more pronounced as they grow older, as they seek to resolve (among other matters) tensions over self-evaluation, to assume a public identity vis a vis school and school-learning.

Self-conscious tension may be unusual, but the data we have examined suggest that this process differs in degree between English children and American children. English children, we see, are on the whole less likely to profess highly positive self-concepts, and that their self-concepts are tied less closely than American children's to their own measured achievement and also to their school peers' expressions of self-concept. What English children *do* gauge their self concepts by is the achievement of their school peers: they are quicker to rate themselves up or down according to their peers' *achievements*, even as they discount more than do American children their peers' expressed self-concepts. Why might this be so?

We have seen that in England these peer-related patterns are partly a function of the socioeconomic composition of the school—that the English "small pond" effect is brought about in two ways: children attending socioeconomically favored schools evaluate themselves less favorably, while at the same time, they are more responsive to their own tested achievement.

The "small pond," overall, is associated with English children's (expressed) less favorable self-concepts as students of mathematics and science, and associated with (especially in schools attended largely by children from economically less-favored families) reduced correlations in England between own academic achievement and self-concept. Does this make a difference to children's ambition at school? This is hard to measure in the data at hand, but let us create a crude measure of academic ambition composed of a TIMSS question about whether children "think it is important for you to do well in mathematics at school?" and its science equivalent (each dichotomous for primary-school children, but each offering children four choices in middle school). Virtually identical correlations (net of own achievement, as measured by the standardized math and science tests, which was far less closely correlated) appear (at significant levels) in both England and in the United States, a relationship that, like many of the phenomena examined in this paper, grows more pronounced as children grow up.[13] English schools, furthermore, seem to vary more one from the other than do American schools in how affirmative or rejective the students are of the importance or desirability of academic endeavor, and the different way that the "small ponds" in the two societies may be connected with this outcome.

Ethnographic evidence speaks to a greater strength of school-based cliques and climates in England by comparison with the United States, an obduracy of ties partly because these are so closely integrated with the more apparent integration of schools in England to the society's system of inequality than in the United States (Corrigan 1979; Eder and Kinney 1995; Mac an Ghaill 1994). If this is so, we can return—highly speculatively, to be sure—to Ralph Turner's old schema, which I introduced toward the beginning of this paper. English children, it would seem, exist in a school-world in which the local is highly important, both objectively and in what they make of it. This is so in the United States, too, of course, but less so. American children are in a constantly renewed contest for position—which includes remarked academic achievement although it does not include this alone. By comparison, English children are marked by where they are. The quest of the American children is connected fairly closely to what their own measured accomplishments are, and they are highly optimistic, a feeling they can share with classmates without getting greatly put off by their peers' accomplishments. English children accomplish as much or more than American children, but in most settings their expression of those accomplishments is much influenced by the "kind" of school they know they are at.

So frog ponds, contra Marsh, are distinguished not just by their size but by their rules. And these, we may suggest, are tied to the deepest structures of sentiment that underlie critical aspects of societies' respective social orders.

NOTES

1.   Both studies stratified their samples by categories of schools. I have in all instances produced tabulations based on the weighted value of students and schools provided in the data sets.

2.   For Table 1 only, I have collapsed the two positive and the two negative values in the IAEP middle-school samples to make the values essentially directly comparable to the primary-school IAEP sample.

3.   The project, "Schooling and School-Learning in Children's Lives" has been supported by the W.T. Grant Foundation and the Spencer Foundation.

4.   From here on, I employ the Rasch-normalized test scores for the TIMSS study, where each country's scores are normed around a mean of 150 with a standard deviation of 10.

5.   Intriguingly, neither Marsh (1987) nor Bachman and O'Malley (1986), in their debate (see also Marsh and Parker 1984), as they each discussed the smaller coefficients attaching to the small pond effect in their United States high school sample (the excellently adapted late 1960s longitudinal study from High School and Beyond) than to the Marsh-Parker Australian 6th-grade study, speculated that there might be national differences in the strength of the effect, focusing instead on possible age effects and sample effects.

6.   In the IAEP, the other children were other children at the same chronological age of whatever grade in the same school; in TIMSS, they were other children of whatever chronological age in the same two grades in the same school. In either case, I constructed for each student in the sample the average test score for all *other* tested children in the same school, excluding the child him- or herself: hence, it is a "peer average," not a "school average."

7.   In all but one outlying case, the correlation (averaged across all children) between their own test score and that of their class- or schoolmates on the same test was between 0.32 and 0.56, with a slight tendency for the figures to be higher among the middle-school children than those in the primary school, but with no consistent national differences, nor differences as to subject (or TIMSS as compared with IAEP). The outlier was a correlation of 0.73 between English middle-school children's math score and that of their classmates on the IAEP test.

8.   Blatchford (1992) reports that English children at age 11, who were far more reluctant than were 7-year-old counterparts to claim that they were "better than others" in math or reading, were *more reluctant yet* to claim superiority to their *classmates* in those subjects: 11 percent as compared with 23 percent in math, 20 percent as compared with 49 percent in reading. (Comparable data were not obtained from the 7-year-olds.) In my text, I have not emphasized differences in subject matter

(which are visible, although math and science are more "alike" as school subjects than are the math and reading that Blatchford discussed). The point bears discussion here, because it gives a clue about the process of forming academic self-concept: a major difference between math and science is the exceptional clarity of excellence (and the corresponding comfort in assessment technology) in the former as compared with the latter. Ability in mathematics, children and teachers believe, is pronouncedly variable among children, substantially innate, and readily discernible; science, as a subject and as a talent, is (like reading) far more diffuse and situation-specific, far harder to ascertain. The visible measurements of mathematical achievement that the school carries out, thus, carry a great deal of weight with students: they know their own math abilities and that of their peers, in a way that they do not believe that they know, with science.

    9.   Had the same children taken IAEP, on the other hand, neither would have had been less likely to say that they "are" good at mathematics.

    10.   The IAEP tests at a given school were split about evenly between those administered in mathematics and in science, and, together with sometimes small numbers of interviews at some schools, relatively many schools fell below my somewhat arbitrary minimum of 15 cases in a given subject for inclusion in correlations of school-level attributes.

    11.   Metric coefficients reflecting the impact of school-average books-in-the-home on the within-school slope of children's academic self-concept on relevant test score.

	England	*U.S.*
Math		
Primary school	.0076*	−.004
Middle school	.0060*	−.0050*
Science		
Primary school	.0074*	−.0013
Middle school	.0102***	−.0017

Notes: * $p < .05$,
      *** $p < .001$.

    12.   Felson and Reed (1986a), employing 1970 data on white U.S. high school sophomores and juniors, found just the same relationship. Upon self-appraisals of what they call *"performance,"* resting on a question about "how satisfied are you with the way you're actually doing in school," the average grade and the average self-appraisal of peers from the same track at the same school had about the same impact, net of own grades, test scores, and own and peers' socioeconomic status. But upon self-appraisals of what the authors call *"ability"* ("how do you rate yourself in school ability compared with those in your grade in school?") peers' average self-appraisal was considerably the more potent.

    13.   The partial correlation between the index of children's professed commitment to formal education and subject-specific academic self concept, holding constant the relevant test score was 0.09 for math in primary school in both England and the United States, rising in each to 0.23 in middle school. For science, the like figures were 0.19 for England and 0.10 for the United States. These rose 0.29 and 0.28, respectively.

REFERENCES

Alwin, D.F., and L.B. Otto. 1977. "High School Context Effects on Aspirations." *Sociology of Education* 50: 259-273.

Bachman, J.G., and P.M. O'Malley. 1986. "Self-Concepts, Self-Esteem, and Educational Experiences: The Frog Pond Revisited (Again)." *Journal of Personality and Social Psychology* 50: 35-46.

Blatchford, P. 1992. "Academic Self Assessment at 7 and 11 Years: Its Accuracy and Association with Ethnic Group and Sex." *British Journal of Educational Psychology* 62: 35-44.

Blumenfeld, P.C., P.R. Pintrich, J. Meece, and K. Wessels. 1982. "The Formation and Role of Self Perceptions of Ability in Elementary Classrooms." *The Elementary School Journal* 82: 401-420.

Corrigan, P. 1979. *Schooling the Smash Street Kids*. London: Verso.

Cullingford, C. 1991. *The Inner World of the School*. London: Casell.

Eccles, J. 1993. "School and Family Effects on the Ontogeny of Children's Interests, Self-Perceptions, and Activity Choices." Pp. 145-208 in *Nebraska Symposium on Motivation: Vol. 40, Developmental Perspectives on Motivation*, edited by J.E. Jacobs. Lincoln: University of Nebraska Press.

Eder, D., and D.A. Kinney. 1995. "The Effect of Middle School Extracurricular Activities on Adolescents' Popularity and Peer Status." *Youth and Society* 26: 298-324.

Entwisle, D.R. and K.L. Alexander. 1989. "Early Schooling as a 'Critical Period' Phenomenon." *Research in the Sociology of Education and Socialization* 8: 27-55.

Entwisle, D.R., K.L. Alexander, A.M. Pallas, and D. Cadigan. 1987. "The Emergent Academic Self-Image of First Graders: Its Response to Social Structure." *Child Development* 58: 1190-1206.

Felson, R.B., and M. Reed. 1986a. "Reference Groups and Self-Appraisals of Academic Ability and Performance." *Social Psychology Quarterly* 49: 105-109.

_____. 1986b. "The Effect of Parents on the Self-Appraisals of Children." *Social Psychology Quarterly* 49: 302-308.

Goldenberg, C., and R. Gallimore. 1996. "Immigrant Latino Parents' Values and Beliefs." In *Advances in Motivation and Achievement*. Greenwich, CT: JAI Press.

Hargreaves, D.H. 1967. *Social Relations in a Secondary School*. London: Routledge & K. Paul.

Kaplan, D.S., B.M. Peck, and H.B. Kaplan. 1994. "Structural Relations Model of Self-Rejection, Disposition to Deviance, and Academic Failure." *Journal of Educational Research* 87: 166-173.

Kerckhoff, A.C. 1990. *Getting Started: Transition to Adulthood in Great Britain*. Boulder, CO: Westview Press.

_____. 1993. *Diverging Pathways: Social Structure and Career Deflection*. New York : Cambridge University Press.

Mac an Ghaill, M. 1994. *The Making of Men: Masculinities, Sexualities and Schooling*. Buckingham, Philadelphia: Open University Press.

MacIver, D.J. 1990. *A National Description of Report Card Entries in the Middle Grades*. (Report No. 9.) Baltimore, MD: The Johns Hopkins University, Center for Research on Effective Schooling for Disadvantaged Students.

Marsh, H.R. 1990. "Causal Ordering of Academic Self-Concept and Academic Achievement: A Multiwave, Longitudinal Panel Analysis." *Journal of Educational Psychology* 82: 646-656.

Marsh, H.W. 1987. "The Big-Fish-Little-Pond Effect on Academic Self-Concept." *Journal of Educational Psychology* 79: 280-295.

_____. 1991. "Failure of High-Ability High Schools to Deliver Academic Benefits Commensurate with Their Students' Ability Levels." *American Educational Research Journal* 28: 445-480.

Marsh, H.W., D. Chessor, R. Craven, and L. Roche. 1995. "The Effects of Gifted and Talented Programs on Academic Self-Concept: The Big Fish Strikes Again." *American Educational Research Journal* 32: 285-319.

Marsh, H.W. and J. Parker. 1984. "Determinants of Student Self-Concept: Is it Better to be a Relatively Large Fish in a 'Small Pond' Even if You Don't Learn to Swim as Well?" *Journal of Personality and Social Psychology* 47: 213-231.

Michaels, J.W. 1977. "Classroom Reward Structures and Academic Performance." *Review of Educational Research* 47: 87-98.

Modell, J. 1993. *Desire to Learn. A Comparative View of Schooling in Children's Lives*. Princeton, NJ: Educational Testing Service.

Nicholls, J.G. 1989. *The Competitive Ethos and Democratic Education*. Cambridge, MA: Harvard University Press.

Nicholls, J.G., and S.P. Hazzard. 1993. *Education as Adventure. Lessons from Second Graders*. New York: Teachers College Press.

Ogbu, J.U. 1974. *The Next Generation; an Ethnography of Education in an Urban Neighborhood*. New York: Academic Press.

Pollard, A. 1996. *The Social World of Children's Learning*. London: Cassell.

Rosenbaum, J.E.. 1976. *Making Inequality*. New York: Wiley.

Stevenson, H.W. and J.W. Stigler. 1992. *The Learning Gap: Why Our Schools Are Failing and What We Learn from Japanese and Chinese Education*. New York: Simon & Schuster.

Stiggins, R.J., D.A. Frisbie, and P.A. Griswold. 1989. "Inside High School Grading Practices: Building a Research Agenda." *Educational Measurement: Issues and Practice* 8: 5-14.

Stipek, DJ. 1988. *Motivation to Learn: From Theory to Practice*. Englewood Cliffs, NJ: Prentice-Hall.

Terwilliger, J.S. 1977 "Assigning Grades—Philosophical Issues and Practical Recommendations." *Journal of Research and Development in Education* 10: 21-39.

Willis, P.E. 1977. *Learning to Labour: How Working Class Kids Get Working Class Jobs*. Farnborough, England: Saxon House.

DATE DUE

DEMCO 38-297